Becoming a Teacher of Writing in Elementary Classrooms

This book transforms the traditional focus of writing workshop to the more expansive and dynamic *writer's studio*. It sweeps the reader into an interactive experience that focuses on every aspect of real teaching in real classrooms at three different grade levels. It strongly supports teacher empowerment and joyful learning. It strongly communicates that becoming a teacher of writing is a dynamic, ongoing process. It is filled with authentic, practical recommendations for teaching and assessing that enable all students to achieve writing success.

—Michael Shaw, St. Thomas Aquinas College, USA

Becoming a Teacher of Writing in Elementary Classrooms nurtures teachers' identities as writers, connects to the realities of writing instruction in real and diverse classrooms, and encourages critical and creative thinking. This text is about writing instruction as a journey teachers and students embark on together. The focus is on learning how to teach writing through specific teaching and learning structures found in the Writing Studio: mini-lessons; teacher and peer conferencing; guided writing; and sharing, celebrating, and broadcasting writing.

Part I is an introduction to writing pedagogy, illustrating who elementary writers are, what writing can do for them, and how environment and routines can be established to support elementary writers. *Part II* is about assessments that provide authentic data for instructional decision making. In *Part III*, the Writing Studio goes *live*. This is a "nuts-and-bolts" section with examples and illustrations of the teaching and learning structures present in the Writing Studio. *Part IV* sweeps the view to wide angle with a look at writing curriculum for the year and a synthesis of the Writing Studio in action.

Pedagogical features include teaching structures and strategies, "Problematizing Practice" classroom scenarios, assessment resources, and a Companion Website. Because a teacher who views him or herself as a writer is best positioned to implement the Writing Studio, a parallel text, *Becoming-Writer*, gives readers space to consider who they are as a writer, their personal process as a writer, and who they might become as a writer.

Donna Kalmbach Phillips is Professor of Education, Pacific University, USA.

Mindy Legard Larson is Associate Professor of Education and Elementary Education Coordinator, Linfield College, USA.

Becoming a Teacher of Writing in Elementary Classrooms

DONNA KALMBACH PHILLIPS

MINDY LEGARD LARSON

Routledge
Taylor & Francis Group

NEW YORK AND LONDON

First published 2015
by Routledge
711 Third Avenue, New York, NY 10017

and by Routledge
2 Park Square, Milton Park, Abingdon, Oxon OX14 4RN

Routledge is an imprint of the Taylor & Francis Group, an informa business

© 2015 Taylor & Francis

The right of Donna Kalmbach Phillips and Mindy Legard Larson to be identified as authors of this work has been asserted by them in accordance with sections 77 and 78 of the Copyright, Designs and Patents Act 1988.

Library of Congress Cataloging in Publication Data

Phillips, Donna Kalmbach.
Becoming a teacher of writing in elementary classrooms : by Donna Kalmbach Phillips & Mindy
    Legard Larson.
       pages cm
    Includes bibliographical references and index.
1. Language arts (Elementary)   2. English language—Composition and exercises—Study and teaching
(Elementary)   3. Report writing—Study and teaching (Elementary)   I. Larson, Mindy Legard.
II. Title.
    LB1576.P5756 2015
    372.62'3—dc23
    2014032828

ISBN: 978-0-415-74317-4 (hbk)
ISBN: 978-0-415-74320-4 (pbk)
ISBN: 978-1-315-81381-3 (ebk)

Typeset in Minion
by Apex CoVantage, LLC

Printed and bound in the United States of America by Publishers Graphics,
LLC on sustainably sourced paper.

for Margaret

Contents

Preface

Learning to teach—like teaching itself—is always the process of becoming; a time of formation and transformation, a scrutiny into what one is doing, and who one can become.

—Deborah Britzman

You are becoming a teacher of writing. How does the title sit with you? What is your first response?

a. Great! How do I get started?
b. I didn't sign up for this (I don't really like writing).
c. I am a writer—teaching writing will be a treat.
d. While I am not terrified or dreading the title, I am not totally convinced I know how to do this.
e. None of the above fit. Here's my response:

However you responded, we believe this book will be useful to you. We don't think it is quite like any other book on learning to teach writing, so we'll take a few pages to introduce some concepts and the organizational scheme for the book. Let's start with a look at the word *becoming*. We are using *becoming* as it is described by two French philosophers, Deleuze and Guattari (1980/1987). The idea is that one never "arrives," that *becoming* as a state of constant change is a way of being in relation with other humans and nonhumans: students, desks, pencils, standards, the clock, administrators, intercom, parents—all that makes up a classroom, teaching, and learning. In other words, as teachers of writing, we never "arrive," we refute "expert-status," and we are always *in progress*. Each moment unfolding in an elementary classroom has multiple possibilities, layered with past, present, and future; everything is adapting, changing, resisting, affirming—*becoming*. We love this concept—we find this hopeful as teachers.

Although this book is specifically designed for those pursuing teaching licensure, it may also be useful to those who have teaching experience but are seeking alternatives for teaching writing or need inspiration. Depending on who and where you are in *becoming* a teacher of writing, you may choose to read this book sequentially, or you may choose to spend time on particular sections that are most relevant to you. Part I serves as an introduction to writing pedagogy, illustrating who elementary writers are, what writing can do for them, and how environment and routines can be established to support elementary writers. Part II focuses on assessments that provide authentic data for instructional decision making. In Part III, the Writing Studio goes *live*. This is a "nuts-and-bolts" section with examples and illustrations of the teaching and learning structures present in the Writing Studio. Finally, Part IV sweeps the view to wide angle with a look at writing curriculum for the year and a synthesis of the Writing Studio in action.

In summation, *Becoming a Teacher of Writing in Elementary Classrooms* addresses writing as a way to teach diverse elementary writers about the power of writing and what writing can do for them. However, this book is not a recipe book. Know that when we write about specific learning structures or processes that between and around each sentence is a space where anything can and does happen during the unpredictable act of teaching—these are the spaces of possibility. We know each classroom is a unique context, each group of writers is at different places in *becoming*-writers—a recipe will never do for the Writing Studio.

Why "Writing Studio"?

We write this book on a foundation of writing research that informed our work as public school teachers and continues to inform our work as teacher educators (Graves, 1983; Murray, 1985). In the 1980s and early 1990s, an important body of work used this research to champion a writing pedagogy known as the "writing workshop" (e.g. Atwell, 1987; Calkins, 1994; Fletcher, 1993; Graves & Hansen, 1986). As public school teachers in the height of writing workshop pedagogy, we immersed ourselves in these texts. But along the following years of writing instruction, it seems to us the name "writing workshop," and the pedagogy associated with it, has often been blurred, mischaracterized, scripted, and hijacked. Maybe it is time for the term to be retired, re-imagined, and re-vitalized. In our attempt to honor the work that has so influenced us and in the spirit of re-claiming and re-envisioning, we morph "workshop" into "studio."

Becoming a Teacher of Writing as Studio

Our hope is this book will act as a kind of studio, a place of learning and experimenting in and with community, as you are becoming a teacher of writing. Interact with this book: question, listen, argue, agree, synthesize in and around it. Don't try to interpret the text—see how you react to it. Ask, "How does this work?" "What new thoughts does it make possible to think?" (Massumi, 1992, p. 8). See where these questions take you. There are particular structures within the book to encourage this interaction.

When you see this icon , we suggest you take time to think, write, or talk about the questions or ideas presented. Sometimes, you will see this icon denoting the *Becoming a Teacher of Writing in Elementary Classrooms* companion website where you will find resources such as student writing samples, lesson plans, bibliographies, and videos. These resources can be found at www.routledge.com/cw/phillips.

At other times, you will see this practice icon . As the title suggests, these are places to pause reading and complete a related practice activity. "Studio" denotes working and learning in the company of others. We encourage you to use the thinking and practice breaks in the text to talk with your colleagues. Bring your combined experiences to this text as you imagine a future as an elementary teacher.

Becoming: Possibilities and Opportunities

This book focuses on learning how to teach writing through specific teaching and learning structures found in the Writing Studio: mini-lessons, teacher and peer conferencing, guided writing, and sharing, celebrating, and broadcasting writing. These teaching and learning structures are fluid, moving with the needs of each writer and his or her processes. In this way, they represent possibilities and opportunities. Writers fill the boxes and shells of mini-lessons; conferences, guided writing, and sharing, celebrating, and broadcasting, breathing life into them, adapting them, even as these same writers engage and expand their writing practices, process, and craft. A teacher who views him or herself as a writer is best positioned to implement the Writing Studio as possibilities and opportunity so part of this book provides space for you to consider who you are as a writer, your personal process as a writer, and who you might become as a writer.

Becoming-Writer

Becoming a teacher of writing is to *become*-writer. Therefore, there is a parallel text, *Becoming-Writer*, to be completed simultaneously with the reading of each part of *Becoming a Teacher of Writing in Elementary Classrooms*. The concept is this: as you are reading *Becoming a Teacher of Writing in Elementary Classrooms*, you will also be writing your own personal narrative—you will be both reader and writer. Connect the two experiences: What do you learn as writer that you want to remember as a teacher of writing? What are you reading about teaching writing that names what you are doing as a writer? The combined texts position you as reader, writer, and teacher of writing; we argue these are not separate roles but are entangled literate identities necessary to an elementary teacher. The *Becoming-Writer* sections, like the main text, *Becoming a Teacher of Writing in Elementary Classrooms*, are richer if shared in the community of colleagues—talk, read, write your way through both texts, and see where they take you.

Problematizing Practice

Teaching and learning with elementary writers is all about problematizing: critically and creatively deconstructing moments in the classroom. The act of problematizing is recognizing teaching and learning is not a script, but an endless moment of possibilities. Each chapter concludes with a section titled *Problematizing Practice*. After all, this is teaching at the end of any day. We settle in for a drive or ride home, sit down in our favorite chair, go for a run, or text a friend—we think through those moments, the waves that have hit us, and those waves still coming our way and problematize to find multiple possibilities for reacting differently.

The goal of the Problematizing Practice scenarios is to practice critical and creative thinking in regards to teaching writing. The goal is *not* to come up with *the* answer to the scenario or to make judgments but to practice questioning, seeking additional information, and imagining possibilities. All the Problematizing Practice scenarios are based upon real scenarios from elementary classrooms.

Introducing the Teachers in *Becoming a Teacher of Writing*

Ms. J and her teaching insights are sprinkled throughout this book. Who is Ms. J? She is a composite of us, the authors of this book, and of teachers with whom we have taught and learned. She is informed by hundreds of writers, our own teaching of writing, a host of mentor teachers, distant colleagues, and the shelves of books we have read and will read. Ms. J is *us*—all of us—and perhaps even you, the reader of this book. And she is always already *becoming-teacher* of writing. Throughout this book, we write her into existence—that is just one of the wonders of writing. In doing so, we explore the joys, the problematic, and the strategy of teaching writing in the elementary grades.

Ms. J speaks to the fact that we are not writing this book in a vacuum but in the company of many: Kindergarten teachers Ms. Coy and Ms. Furgison; Grade 3 teacher Ms. Lomas; Grades 4 and 5 teacher Ms. Hill; Grade 5 teacher Ms. Widmer, along with Ms. Gray, Ms. Tengs, Ms. Harley, and Ms. Ziemer; and other teachers who have chosen not to have their names used in this book. Additionally, there are teachers, besides Ms. J, who represent composites of teachers with whom we have learned. We also write this book in the company of children, some whose names are used, most whose names are pseudonyms, all of who have taught us greatly about *becoming-writer* and writing. We thank them for joining us here and providing the many rich illustrations woven throughout the text of *Becoming a Teacher of Writing in Elementary Classrooms*.

The Invitation

The beauty of reading is that every person reading this text will make his or her meaning of it and take it to places we as authors cannot imagine (Rosenblatt, 2013). However you answered the opening questions in this preface is where you begin this meaning making. Interacting with this text is not about interpreting what we, the authors of this text, have written and then attempting to follow *our* plan for teaching writing. It could never be that simple. Rather, may this text act as evocation, as you apply it in your own Writing Studios. We will write a conclusion to this text, but how it continues is your story, lived out in your context, your *becoming-teacher* of writing.

References

Atwell, N. (1987). *In the middle: Writing, reading, and learning with adolescents.* Portsmouth, NH: Boynton/Cook Publishers.

Britzman, D. (2003). *Practice makes practice: A critical study of learning to teach.* Albany: State University of New York Press.

Calkins, L. (1994). *The art of teaching writing.* Portsmouth, NH: Heinemann.

Fletcher, R. (1993). *What a writer needs.* Portsmouth, NH: Heinemann.

Graves, D. (1983). *Writing: Teachers and children at work.* Portsmouth, NH: Heinemann.

Graves, D., & Hansen, J. (1986). *The writing and reading process: A new approach to literacy.* Portsmouth, NH: Heinemann.

Massumi, B. (1992). *A user's guide to capitalism and schizophrenia: Deviations from Deleuze and Guattari.* Cambridge, MA: MIT Press.

Murray, D. (1985). *A writer teaches writing.* Boston, MA: Houghton Mifflin.

Rosenblatt, L. M. (2013). The transactional theory of reading and writing. In D. E. Alvermann, N. J. Unrau, & R. B. Ruddell (Eds.), *Theoretical models and processes of reading* (6th ed., pp. 923–956). Newark, DE: International Reading Association.

Preface to Instructors

We pitch our teaching into an abyss between self and self, self and other. And yet something, and hopefully not a repetitive echo, but an inquisitive, ironic echo—a difference that makes a difference—returns.

—Elizabeth Ellsworth

As teacher educators, writers, and teachers of writing, we facilitate learning as mentors and experienced teachers and we learn with teacher candidates as students of the world. The intent of this textbook is not to script teacher candidates, but to provide a fluid framework for developing nuanced teachers of writing, adaptable for all elementary children in all contexts.

Data Sets

We include data sets from kindergarten, Grade 3, and Grade 5 throughout *Becoming a Teacher of Writing in Elementary Classrooms*. We encourage instructors to supplement with data sets from schools in their unique context and from additional grades.

Further Contextualization

Most teacher candidates are placed in schools, experiencing some type of field experience during their teacher education program. Using the examples in *Becoming a Teacher of Writing in Elementary Classrooms*, teacher candidates can contextualize learning by completing sample assessment data collection at their own practicum sites, practicing data analysis, and planning for instruction based upon their own assessment data.

The Companion Website

The companion website (www.routledge.com/cw/phillips) includes videos in the Instructor Tab. These videos include images of teachers and children at work in the Writing Studio. These are real teachers and children—complexity in action. They are not provided for evaluation, but for evocation.

Problematizing Practice

The goal of Problematizing Practice is to encourage nuanced and deep conversation about some of the challenges found in the Writing Studio. Problematizing Practice sections may require guidance from the instructor. Discussion will be enhanced through contextualization and any additional readings or resources you as the teacher educator find necessary for teacher candidates in your context.

Writing with Readers of *Becoming a Teacher of Writing in Elementary Classrooms*

Becoming a Teacher of Writing in Elementary Classrooms assumes inherent to becoming a teacher of writing, is to be a writer (Atwell, 1998; Calkins, 1994; Graves, 1983). We encourage instructors to write with teacher candidates, adapting the *becoming-writer* sections as needed to suit your context. The goal is for teacher candidates to experience the Writing Studio and the sense of community writing cultivates, as they are reading and learning how to teach through the Writing Studio.

We understand as writers, teachers of writing, and teacher educators that writing creates possibilities and leads us and others to places we could not imagine; we embrace that our teaching is likewise a practice of complexities and unknowns, which does not cease at the end of any given course. Therefore, the intent of *Becoming a Teacher of Writing in Elementary Classrooms* cannot be to produce a repetitive echo of ourselves in our teacher candidates. Rather as the Ellsworth (1997) quote so beautifully states at the opening of this preface, our goal is an echo that makes a difference, an echo ringing with diversity of all who will become teachers of writing, of the capable writing voices of children, of the power of writing and what writing can do for us all.

References

Atwell, N. (1998). *In the middle: New understandings about writing, reading and learning* (2nd ed.). Portsmouth, NH: Heinemann.

Calkins, L. (1994). *The art of teaching writing.* Portsmouth, NH: Heinemann.

Ellsworth, E. A. (1997). *Teaching positions: Difference, pedagogy, and the power of address.* New York, NY: Teachers College Press.

Graves, D. (1983). *Writing: Teachers and children at work.* Portsmouth, NH: Heinemann.

part I
Introduction to Writing Instruction

Our duty is to deal with children as if they were the ambassadors of a higher culture, and not the other way around, not like we want to educate them, but we want to learn from them.

—Guillermo del Toro

Figure PartI.1 Eva, Grade 4 Writer and Author

There is no perfect time to write. There's only now.

—Barbara Kingsolver

Why Do People Write?

- Marta writes lists—she is the queen of lists, and we all love them! She makes lists of possible projects, things to do, books to buy for the library where she works, and items needed by her college daughter. Marta *writes to organize life.*
- Tim publishes books using online sites with his children's photos and copies of their schoolwork and gives these as gifts. Grandparents love these, but he also does this for his children. Tim *writes as legacy.*
- Elena's written arguments to the city convinced them to allow an exception in city code so she could build her garage. Elena *writes as an act of citizenry.*
- Mindy recently wrote multiple letters to state legislators voicing opposition to educational legislation she felt would be harmful to children. Mindy *writes as advocacy.*
- Gen writes funny, cryptic would-be bumper stickers (among many other more important things!), but we love these because they make us laugh. Gen *writes to make a statement.*
- Michael draws and writes graphic novels, sci-fi/fantasy, crazy, wild stories of creatures, aliens, and humans colliding! Michael *writes to entertain.*
- Donna's dad died after a long struggle with Parkinson's disease. She writes to work through the grief. Donna *writes to make sense of life.*
- We all e-mail, text, Tweet, Facebook—we *write to stay connected.*

None of us writes as practice for a standardized test, to meet a standard, to please a teacher, or for a grade. "We write to taste life twice, in the moment and in retrospection" (Nin, 1974, p. 149).

- *Why do you write?* Make a list of all the reasons you write and have written during given periods of your life. List what you may consider the mundane through the profound. Alternatively, it might be interesting for you to construct a writing timeline for yourself from childhood to adult. Mark the time when you learned to write; note places in the timeline when writing may have been a struggle, a delight, or more meaningful than other times. Note the reasons for writing throughout your life.

Having considered why you write and/or constructing a writing timeline for yourself, respond to these questions to learn more about you as a writer:

- *Do you remember how you learned to write?*
- *Can you recall a time when writing was particularly meaningful or rewarding?*
- *Can you recall a time when you hated the very thought of writing?*
- *What makes writing difficult or easy?*
- *What kind of environment is a good writing environment for you (and how does the writing task influence this description)?*

Read the responses from the preceding questions. Synthesize your responses in a few sentences. Based on these responses,

- *Who are you as a writer?*
- *What changes would you like to see in yourself as a writer?*
- *What do you feel you need to learn most about being a writer?*
- *What might this mean for you as a teacher of writing?*

Respond to the following report (Horner, 2010) synthesizing the influence of writers in schools working with children. The report concludes that

> The first priority is for **teachers to be writers** themselves. Only in this way do they learn empathy with their pupils, which enables them to give more space to pupils when they are writing and respond more appropriately to their work. They are also then able to model writing 'live' rather than repeat what has been rehearsed. (p. 30)

Being a writer and a teacher of writing allows us to examine "the relationship between our own writing practices and our classroom practice" resulting in "more authentic tasks which offer a higher than usual degree of congruence with writing in the real world" (Cremin, 2012, p. 134).

Are you ready to be *this* writer and teacher of writing?

An Invitation

How long has it been since you wrote more than an e-mail, a list of things to do, a Facebook update, a Tweet, or a required assignment? How long has it been since you wrote for yourself, "for fun"? Perhaps some of you write journals or diaries, or even write to publish, but most often, we find it has been a long time since teacher candidates we work with have been given time and space to . . . just write.

So here is an invitation: take time to write while you are reading *Becoming a Teacher of Writing in Elementary Classrooms*. Connect the two experiences: What do you learn as a writer that you want to remember as a teacher of writing? What are you reading about teaching writing that names what you are doing as a writer? Take the time to discover, rediscover, affirm, and grow your writer identity.

Becoming-Writer is a parallel text of the main text, *Becoming a Teacher of Writing in Elementary Classrooms*. Each *Becoming-Writer* section is strategically placed prior to each new part in the main text. The intent is this: as you read the main text, you will be writing your own personal narrative as guided by the *Becoming-Writer* sections. During this time, Donna will be writing along with you; Mindy will be Donna's peer for conferencing, giving her feedback along the way.

We suggest the following procedure writing and reading your way through the entire book:

1. Read and complete the writing invitations of the *Becoming-Writer* sections.
2. Continue reading the main text, *Becoming a Teacher of Writing in Elementary Classrooms*.
3. Take strategic reading breaks, and then return to your writing: play and experiment with what you are writing.

By doing this you will be prepared for each new *Becoming-Writer* section, and by the end of *Becoming a Teacher of Writing in Elementary Classrooms*, you will have a completed personal narrative or memoir to celebrate and broadcast to others.

Some might say we are guiding you through *the* process of writing in these *Becoming-Writer* sections. However, writing is always already more than a single process. It is context dependent, open-ended, influenced by emotion, personal and cultural history, and even the choice of a writing tool; when we use the term *writing process* we consider it to be plural. So, explore writing, not as a student, not as an assignment, but to see what writing can do for you. With each writing pause along the way, there will be opportunities for you to reflect on yourself as a writer and your process as a writer. There are opportunities to share your writing process and your draft writing with others. Analyze similarities and differences; consider what this means to you as a teacher of writing. Writing instruction comes alive when implemented by a teacher who sees himself or herself as a writer and as a member of a community of writers, listening and learning to one another.

By writing while reading this text, you will become a member of a Writing Studio and form a unique community of writers with your colleagues. The term *studio* has long been associated with the work of artists' gathered in a workroom, studying and experimenting with various art forms under the tutelage of a mentor. *Studio* is derived from Latin, *stadium*, meaning to study with eagerness or zeal. This is an apt term for the kind of teaching and learning illustrated and explored in *Becoming a Teacher of Writing in Elementary Classrooms*: elementary writers exploring writing as an art form, learning what writing can do for them, experimenting with a variety of genres, while learning practices, processes, and craft from their teacher, who is their writing mentor. It is also a fitting term for your experience as writer in these *Becoming-Writer* sections, as you write with your colleagues and your instructor. Your Writing Studio experience will be unique—notice and name this experience, care for the processes of writing and of becoming, practice listening to yourself and others. Study with zeal.

Becoming a teacher of writing is *becoming-writer*—see how both evolve throughout the experience of being writer of your own text even as you are reader of *this* text!

Let's Get Started Writing

Writing a personal narrative is a good way to reconnect with what writing can do for you. It is also a good place for elementary writers to start since the topics are close to home. So let's get started with what every writer experiences: the blank page and the need to find an idea one cares enough about to commit time and effort to write!

No need to look outside yourself to find a writing topic; start by looking near you. Below are four strategies for finding a personal narrative idea. Explore them all. Begin with the one that resonates immediately. Already have an idea for a personal narrative? Skip down to "Talk About It."

Finding an Idea: Strategy 1

Here is a strategy adapted from Donald Graves (1994):

- Remember back to yesterday. Make a list of the details of your day.
- Return to the list and "read the world," *your* world, by jotting down questions and comments about your list of activities.
- Reread your list and your questions. Choose something from your list and write for 15 minutes. Set a timer. Write fast. Try not to be literary. Don't be concerned about "product."
- Do it again: choose another item from your list and write for another 15 minutes.
- Yes—try it again (and again) until you are relaxed with your writing.

Modeling: An Excerpt From Donna's List

5:50 a.m. Wake up at beach. Pull myself out of bed into cold. Head for coffee shop. Why didn't I bring my work? Have book I am reading but I don't have time to just read.

Question: Why do I always feel the need to bring work when I am supposed to be getting away for a short break? Why do I work on a reward system?

8:10 a.m. It was a good book! Four dogs, three friends, one spouse, all crowded in the beach trailer, making breakfast together. Sun is out. Life is good.

Pacific City has lots of memories. I am not sure what memory I would write about. Would need to explore. I could write a book review for, Mink River: A Novel, *by Brian Doyle (2010). Great read; great reward.*

Finding an Idea: Strategy 2

Do you Facebook, Instagram, or Tweet? If yes, pull up your latest posts. Alternatively, check the pictures on your phone, or pull out a photo album, or check out photos you have hanging in your hallway or sitting on your desk or nightstand. Choose any one post or photograph. Start writing rapidly, filling in the details, the memories, the moment of the post or photograph. Conversely, write a bulleted list or sketch your memory.

Modeling: An Excerpt From Donna's Writing

Smiling Buddhist monk, Thailand. Absolutely infectious smile. I can still feel that smile, almost as intensely as the moment. Even though we were sitting in the shade, it was hot and humid but the sun was all in this monk's smile. Oh, and his laughter! I swear I could feel the laughter in my body, like a surge of goodness. . . . Too bad John was sure he was just trying for another paying recruit. Maybe I could be a recruit? Can I imagine myself submitting to such discipline for a week, a month? (Maybe not!) He told us this story of his wandering for five years all over the world and called our friend, "Superman." . . .

Finding an Idea: Strategy 3

Take some blank paper (large is good) and draw a quick sketch of a neighborhood where you lived as a child. It may be a map of an apartment or a ranch, of an urban house or a cabin, any place you have lived where you know there are memories hiding.

Once you have the map sketched, create a key for your map:

1. Laughter and good fun
2. Scary!
3. Accidents
4. Warm and cozy
5. Painful

Label all the places on your map that correspond to the key. With a "1" mark all the places, for example, that represent "laughter and good fun." Maybe you won't have any Item 1—that is okay. Maybe you'd like to add something to the key—that is okay! Add away!

Modeling: Donna's Neighborhood Map

See Figure PartIBW.1, "Donna's Neighborhood Map."

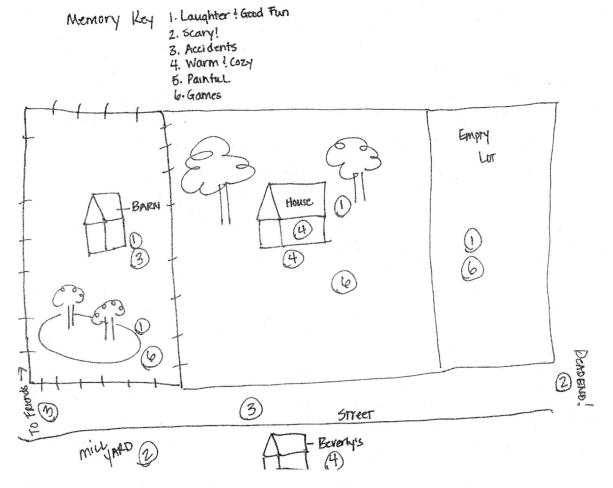

Figure PartIBW.1 Donna's Neighborhood Map

Finding an Idea: Strategy 4

Here's one more topic-finding strategy we will borrow and adapt from Georgia Heard (1998) and Nancie Atwell (2002) called "heart mapping." Draw a map of your heart. Ask yourself, "What has stayed in your heart? What memories, moments, people, animals, objects, places, books, fears, scars, friends, siblings, parents, grandparents, teachers, other people, journeys, secrets, dreams, crushes, relationships, comforts, learning experiences? What's at the center? The edges? *What's in your heart?*" (Atwell, 2002, p. 13). Spend some time with this map—don't rush it. Fill in your heart with as much detail as you can.

Modeling: Donna's Heart Map

See Figure PartIBW.2, "Donna's Heart Map."

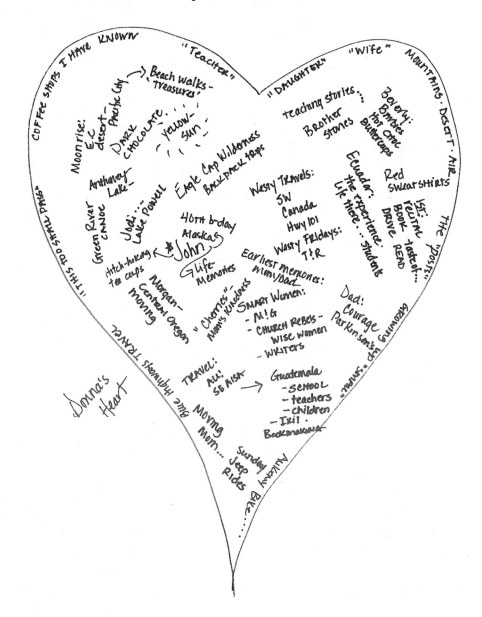

Figure PartIBW.2 Donna's Heart Map

Talk About It

Talk is a critical component to writing. So—take any one or two or three of your ideas for writing, a question from your day, a possible story behind a photograph, an item from your neighborhood map, or memory that has stayed in your heart, and *talk the story*. Tell the story, the event, or wonder aloud your questions to a friend. Meet face-to-face, do a Google Hangout or another such tool, phone or even have a live chat, but talk about your writing idea before spending time drafting that idea.

Modeling: Mindy and Donna Talk via Live Chat

D: Hey, Mindy . . . I am thinking I might write about the only pet John and I ever had. I discovered this topic doing the heart map. What do you think?

M: I wonder why you only had one pet?

D: We only had one pet because after Morgan, it is too painful to think about having another pet. We are not responsible enough. We had to give him up. I am ashamed or maybe just guilty about the whole thing.

M: Pets are like children. Ashamed? Guilty? Pretty strong words. Why?

D: We were young. Other people our age were having babies. We had a dog. Loved the thing like crazy. He ruled our world. . . . When we made the decision to leave the county and move to a city apartment, John argued it would be criminal and unethical to take Morgan and make him stay in a studio apartment ten hours a day while we were at work. So we decided to give him up.

M: BTW: remember I am terrified of dogs (all about that Doberman Pinscher that chased me when I was young). . . . So why do you think this memory of leaving Morgan is still so strong today? Sounds like you were responsible.

D: Responsible???? No one would adopt him. Friends said they would take him to the pound. Do you know what happens to dogs at the pound if no one adopts them? It was awful. . . .

[The conversation continues . . . Donna telling the story, expressing emotions. Mindy empathizing, asking questions . . .]

M: So maybe this story is more about how life changes vs. abandoning Morgan . . . Maybe it is about a sense of losing control of life, or all of the above. Maybe you'd better start writing . . .

Your Writing Goal: Start Writing

Now that you've talked your story, told a friend about your idea, find a place conducive to writing or sketching your personal narrative idea. Either way, get the supplies you need (Coffee? Music? Favorite pen? Or . . .?) and allow yourself time . . . to write.

Just get started. Get those words down—fast. Give yourself 30 minutes and see where you are in the writing. Give yourself a break; stretch—give it another go if you can.

And sometimes, "just getting started" is easier said then done. Consider two pieces of advice from Anne Lamott (1994) that we love: First, remember all you need to do is write down as much as you can see through a one-inch picture frame (you are not writing a novel). Just describe that one funny line (not everything leading up to it), that moment of panic (get to the gasping part quick!), or find that lovely beach and describe the warm sand. Second, embrace the idea of "shitty first drafts." As Lamott writes, "all good writers write them" (Lamott, 1994, p. 21).

Try not to stop and reread much and try really hard not to start revising or editing—the idea is to draft quickly and decide later if you want to keep the draft and do the work of revision. If you are using a word processor or a tablet, you may consider turning off the auto correct so annoying squiggly green and red lines under misspelled words and incorrect grammar do not distract you.

Just get it down: *draft*.

The word implies a beginning, something temporary to be developed later, a first attempt. If you get stuck—walk away and come at it again. Begin more than one draft and settle later on the one you most like. Oh—and you don't need to "finish" the draft. If everything comes to a screamin' halt—try another topic. See where that one goes.

Happy writing! When you have completed drafting, continue with this section.

Metacognition Practice

When you have completed drafting, rethink this writing experience and consider the following questions:

- How easy or hard was it for you to find a topic to write about? What did or didn't help you in this process?
- What makes the topic(s) you've chosen most interesting to you?
- How important was it for you to talk with a friend about your writing topic?
- Describe the process of drafting.
- What do you learn about yourself as a writer as you think back through the process of finding a topic and drafting?

Donna Practices Metacognition

I found it easy to pump out four pages of a rambling story about leaving our home in Central Oregon, which is why we also gave up this little half-beagle that was the love of our life. It was cathartic to write the words, own the story. The writing makes me wonder just how much leaving Morgan behind has influenced me in other ways. I suppose that is what makes the topic interesting to me. The topic is personal, close to my heart, still tender—and it has been 30 years. Go figure! Talking with Mindy is how I discovered the bigness of the story, all that leaving Morgan behind symbolizes (or might symbolize).

Writing is cathartic for me. Maybe it is because I am more introverted, so when I write all those thoughts and emotions they can just spread out and then I feel like I can walk into the world, having checked "that" off the list. The problem for me as a writer will be going back and trying to make something of the piece, trying to give the writing focus, be satisfied with it. That will take some perseverance!

References

Atwell, N. (2002). *Lessons that change writers*. Portsmouth, NH: Firsthand.

Cremin, T.M. (2012). *Writing voices: Creating communities of writers*. London: Routledge.

del Toro, G. (Writer), & Navarro, G. (Director). (2007). *Pan's labyrinth* [Motion Picture]. United States of America.

Doyle, B. (2010). *Mink river: A novel*. Corvallis, OR: Oregon State University Press.

Graves, D. (1994). *A fresh look at writing*. Portsmouth, NH: Heinemann.

Heard, G. (1998). *Awakening the heart: Exploring poetry in elementary and middle school*. Portsmouth, NH: Heinemann.

Horner, S. (2010). *Magic dust that lasts: Writers in schools—sustain the momentum*. London: Arts Council England.

Lamott, A. (1994). *Bird by bird: Some instructions on writing and life*. New York, NY: Random House.

Nin, A. (1974). *The diary of Anaïs Nin, Vol. 5: 1947–1955* (Ed. G. Stuhlmann) Orlando, FL: Harcourt Brace Jovanovich.

Thomas, C. (1994). 100 tips from bestselling writers. *Writer's Digest, 74*(8), 24.

Chapter One
The Student of Writing – The Teacher of Writing

It is the middle of August. Ms. J opens the classroom door finding boxes of supplies, crates of books, planning notebooks, and desks and chairs all stacked and corralled into the middle of the classroom for summer cleaning and painting. The whiteboard is draped with posters from last year's final writing celebration; empty bulletin boards beckon; a lone Star Wars figure is the welcoming committee from an empty child's cubby. Ms. J savors this moment. She loves every new beginning: the do-over, the re-invention of herself as a teacher with each new school year. Soon this classroom will be filled with children and their lives, their community and families, their play, dreams, disappointments, and events local and global that will alter the course of her well-intentioned plans. "It is time," she says to no one in particular. Time to begin the living narrative that will emerge as the biography of the yet unknown children and the teacher of Room 23.

Who are the elementary writers who will join Ms. J this coming school year? While composites and rubrics are developed to define kindergarten through Grade 5 writers, individual writers with their own life context do not always fit into tidy categories. Research informs us that writing is a socially situated act, mediated by culture, class, and gender expectations (Bakhtin, 1986; Davies, 2003b; Dyson, 2013; Heath, 1983; Meyer, 2010; Solsken, 1993; Street, 1995). Writing is an embodied and material act (Barad, 2007; Lenz Taguchi, 2010; Phillips & Larson, 2013).

Samuel, Joseph, and Jakinda hurry to the sandbox during playtime.

"What are you making?" the teacher asks.

"We are digging for pipes," announces Samuel.

"Yep, the pipe is broken," says Joseph.

"Oh, no!" cries Jakinda. "Watch out, it is going to be a gusher!"

The day before Mark the Plumber came with his plunger, pipes, and illustrations of basic plumbing to visit Samuel, Jack, and Jakinda's classroom. Today, they play "plumber," and not surprisingly, during the Writing Studio, they all have variations of fantastic plumber stories. Writing is a result of the social interactions of our lives. This is why so many teachers' good intentions and generic writing prompts fail to motivate—it is not the stuff of writers' lives, and in writing, we write to make meaning and further our relationships with others.

"Socially situated" (Gee, 2001) refers to how children are influenced by culture, class, and gender expectations of the community. How does the writer's home and community value writing? What kind of writing is valued? Does the child see writing as a necessary part of daily life? Such home and community values influence children's motivation, engagement, and vision of what writing can do for them.

Researchers have found trends illustrating how boys and girls are socially constructed and the influence this has on their writing (Anderson, 2002; Fletcher, 2006; Guzzetti, Young, Gritsavage, Fyfe, & Hardenbrook, 2002; Newkirk, 2000). Boys, for example, may tend to write adventure stories with more violent themes, stories outside of their own experience. Girls may tend to write more passive stories of affection and social relationship to entertain themselves and others. Despite this gendered description, other research reports that through writing, girls challenge gender boundaries. This research suggests that writing can be a way to explore alternative identities (Davies, 2003a; Dyson, 1997; Marsh, 1998; McAuliffe, 1994).

Researchers also find that writing is relational, it is a social act (Davidson, 2007; Dyson, 2003; Fisher, Jones, Larkin, & Myhill, 2010). Despite popular conceptions of writing as an isolated act, talk is a critical component from finding an idea to broadcasting one's work as an author. Collaboration, friendships, and community are fostered through writing.

The four Grade 5 boys beg their teacher, "Please, we need time to work on our story!" They gather around a table and plunge into the action.

"Let's write this fight scene!"

"Yeah—I think he draws out this sword and it is like glowing blue and . . ."

"Maybe he doesn't draw it out right away, you know, he hesitates . . ."

"That's what gets him!"

"He hesitates and this guy from behind . . ."

"No, not a guy—it is a reincarnated monster!"

Furthermore, writing is embodied and material (Barad, 2007; Lenz Taguchi, 2010; Phillips & Larson, 2013). Introduce a new technology, for example, and the substance of the writing may drop as the technology is learned. If an unknown substitute teacher is present, children are less likely to share personal stories. Children change their view of the tasks of writing based on different aspects of the environment (Hartse, Woodward, & Burke, 1984; Olson & Sulzby, 1991).

Elias squirms in his chair that is too big for him, balancing on one folded leg and then the other. His fingers clinch a pencil that is awkward in his hand. If his elbow could rest easy on the table, it would make a difference. It doesn't help that his classmate occasionally shoves his table against Elias' causing the pencil to jump out of control. Elias is supposed to write a full page. And he wants to write a full page—he wants to write about being a basketball player. Not just any basketball player, but one that dunks and swivels and wins every time—except he doesn't know all the English words, doesn't know all the Spanish words, either. Yet, Elias writes with the help of his teacher and his table-mates. When Elias finishes that page, he has a new standing with his peers (they didn't think he could write at all); he has written himself an identity (star basketball player), and it has been a material and relational effort of paper, pencil, desk, peer, teacher, community norms, and expectations.

Writing is *thinking*; therefore, it involves cognitive processing. What kind of processing is involved in writing is dependent on the purpose and audience for writing. Writing a note or a text requires immediate thought and a quick response. Desiring to write a few perfect lines to someone on a sympathy card takes considerably more time and consideration. Writing research reports evolves over time as the writer's knowledge of the subject area grows. Writing is often described as a process of finding an idea that is important to the writer and that fulfills the purpose of the writing; drafting the writing (which may involve single or multiple revisions); editing for spelling, punctuation, and grammar after content revisions are completed; and publishing the writing to the intended audience. Too often this processing is described as "*the* writing process," as if *all* writing requires the same process from each writer, each and every time. Writing is rarely so linear; the writer loops back and between and around, even while moving forward to publication; this looping process reflects thinking, the revision of thoughts and the process of meaning making. Writing is not only a cognitive process but includes emotional processing and physical work. Writing cannot always be summoned as "on demand"—it requires time and the time required is dependent upon purpose and audience (Calkins, 1994; Elbow, 1981; Fu, 2009; Graves, 1983; Harwayne, 2001; Murray, 1985).

Miley comes home from school expressing her concerns about writing in her fourth-grade class. In her classroom, writing instruction followed this pattern: Day 1/Draft; Day 2/Revise; Day 3/Edit; Day 4/Write a final draft. Miley is also a reader and a fan of author Katherine Patterson. She has read about Patterson as an author, and so she questions, "If real authors take time to write about their stories and sometimes don't even know how the story will end, why do I have to finish a story in four days?"

Who is the elementary writer? He or she is socially constructed by community expectations, culture, class, gender, and the material world in which he or she dwells. This writer is the author of his or her life, writing him- or herself an always, already changing identity.

How Do Writers Develop Across Grade Levels?

A culmination of research (Calkins, 1994; Goodman, 1988; Ray & Glover, 2008; Rowe, 2008) illustrates how elementary writers can move far beyond traditional expectations for writing (e.g., learning the basics of spelling, punctuation, and mechanics) if in a supportive environment for writing and taking writing risks. Creating such an environment includes being mindful of how writers develop.

There are those that hold to a strict learning trajectory of writing development often displayed in rubrics; these rubrics are useful in developing curriculum and expectations. They are also dangerous. Such developmental charts often focus on a narrow aspect of writing or researchers across the field of writing development are not always reporting on the same aspects of literacy development (Rowe, 2003). Patterns of development can be distinguished between the kindergarten and the Grade 5 writer, but the discerning teacher of writing understands how culture, class, gender, community values, expectations, and the material (nonhuman elements of the classroom) influence the interpretation of such patterns.

Kindergartners as Writers

Elbow (2004) notes that young children are positioned to write:

> They can read only the words they have learned to read or sound out—a fairly small lexicon. But they are beautifully positioned for writing: They can *write* all the words they can *say*. Even younger children who don't know the alphabet can write if they have seen other people write: They just scribble, scribble, scribble—but with meaning and they can 'read' their writing back to you. (p. 9)

Young writers participate in interactive and shared writing; they use everything they know to approximate their own writing, eager to tell others the stories of their lives.

Kindergartners are learning what writing can do for them. They communicate meaning through drawings and then draw with labels, spelling, as Goodman (1988) suggests, according to how they hear the words, most likely according to consonant sounds at the beginning and end of words. They use approximation to make short books telling a story that has a beginning, a middle, and an end. Kindergarteners begin to understand the relationship between print, letters, words, and sentences, showing an awareness of left-to-right directionality, the need for spaces between words, the function of text structures like where a title is placed on the page; they begin to notice author and illustrator's craft. Simple sentences develop with subject–verb agreement and these grow throughout the school year, as kindergarteners understand the role of capitalization and punctuation. Kindergarteners develop the ability to hold a pencil and position the page and to locate letters on a keyboard. They willingly explore genres through the books they read and write. They begin to draw and write for specific audiences and purposes, and they develop an ability and a motivation to add details to their drawings for their audiences. Talk, play, art, storytelling, and immersion in reading all kinds of texts are critical elements necessary to the development of young writers. Perhaps more than any other grade level, children in kindergarten develop writing abilities and writing identities in stunning and wide-ranging ways (see Pinnell & Fountas, 2011).

Take a break and read an example of writing authored by Maddie, a kindergartner in Appendix A. Maddie is an eager kindergartener. She has access to rich literacy experiences at home and in the world. Read her personal narrative about one of her favorite Christmas memories with her brother. How does Maddie's writing compare with the description above of kindergarten writing?

Travel to the companion website and listen to Ms. Coy, a kindergarten teacher, talk about young writers' development throughout their kindergarten year.

Grade 3 Writers

Grade 3 writers are lively storytellers! They understand the concept of genre and can organize text in interesting and different ways, even providing support for informational text and additional details for narratives. They have a growing awareness of author's purpose based on audience. As writers, they begin to develop voice, that human capacity to express a writer's perspective through word choice, text style, organization, and conventions. Grade 3 writers begin to use appropriate verb tense and a range of complete and compound sentences in developing their voice. Grade 3 writers typically are able to use capital letters for all kinds of appropriate purposes, and the punctuation discoveries (!)

they make (!!) can be a delightful expression (!!!) of their growing identities as authors (!!!!). Grade 3 writers can spell 300 or more high-frequency words and develop additional spelling abilities as they read and write frequently. They can use knowledge of syllables and patterns of language to approximate more advanced spelling. Grade 3 writers are able to stay with writing tasks for 60 minutes a day. They generate ideas, explore revisions, gain confidence as writers, and expand their vocabulary and use of expression through social interaction. Motor skills are developing so that handwriting is easier, and they can begin experimenting with cursive. Using word processing to plan, revise, edit, and publish their work, along with various applications, is exciting for these writers as their keyboard skills continue to develop. Grade 3 writers in a safe environment rich in reading and writing grow their writing identities, coming to see more and more the power of writing and what it can do for them (see Pinnell & Fountas, 2011).

 Take a reading break and find the example of writing authored by Morgan, a Grade 3 writer in Appendix B. Morgan's teacher read *Airmail to the Moon* (Birdseye, 1989) about a girl, Ora Mae Cotton, who accuses family members of stealing her recently lost tooth only to realize her tooth was in her pocket all along. Morgan was inspired by *Airmail to the Moon* to write her own story of a time she had lost something, her story "Lost." Compare Morgan's writing to the description above.

Let's pause and consider for a moment writing development for English learners. English learners cannot be placed into a single category or writing development stage. For example, some students are considered Long-Term English Language Learners. They may have attended U.S. schools since kindergarten. Because it takes 1 to 3 years for English learners to develop basic communicative language proficiency and 5 to 7 or more years to develop academic language proficiency (Cummins, 1981; Thomas & Collier, 1997), Long-Term English Language Learners often struggle with writing in English even if their conversational English is adequate. Other children arrive from home countries with limited extensive formal schooling, bringing with them varied writing proficiencies in their native language or languages. In such instances in which a child struggles in writing in his or her first language, it is more difficult to learn to write in English (Freeman & Freeman, 2009). Cultural differences matter as well, particularly for newly arrived immigrants who are learning mainstream U.S. culture along with academics and English. Fu (2009), in her researching and teaching with English learners, identifies four stages of English learners' writing development: (1) children begin writing in their first language; this is followed by (2) "code-switching"—or a child mixing first and second languages in his or her writing—which is followed by (3) inter-language writing, in which a student uses English words but in the first language's syntax; and (4) finally, the use of standard English.

 Carolina is an English language learner and a Grade 3 classmate of Morgan. Carolina, like Morgan, was inspired to write her own "Lost" story after their teacher read *Airmail to the Moon* (Birdseye, 1989). Find Carolina's writing in Appendix C. Compare her writing with both the description of Grade 3 writers and Fu's (2009) stages of English learner's writing development.

Grade 5 Writers

By Grade 5, most writers have been immersed in a wide range of texts, from narrative, informational, opinion, and poetic, and have a more defined vision of what writing can do and be. Main ideas are clearly communicated through relevant supports and details that are interesting and accurate. Grade 5 writers have a more developed sense of audience and of writing for a specific purpose. A Grade 5 writer is a relational writer—often writing to entertain and engage peers. For this reason, he or she writes with a more unique voice, experimenting with various author's craft such as dialogue. Writers at this grade level are developing a sense of text layout; enjoying graphic representations, or how they can arrange pictures with text while word processing; or working with a tablet application. They enjoy experimenting with titles and subtitles, underlining, and italics. They have developed grammar skills, writing in appropriate sentences, and learning to vary sentences to convey a message. Grade 5 writers are learning some of the more inconsistent or difficult usage of parts of speech (e.g., indefinite and relative pronouns). Grade 5 writers work to master the more specialized use of capitalization, such as those used for headings, and begin to view punctuation as a way to effectively communicate with readers. They include in their set of writing conventions such things as ellipses, dashes, colons, and semicolons. Grade 5 writers in a supportive environment are ready to work through writing processes in more sophisticated ways as they explore multiple genres and continue to grow their identities as writers (see Pinnell & Fountas, 2011).

 Take a reading break and find an example of writing authored by Nickolas, a Grade 5 writer in Appendix D. Nickolas's teacher was in the middle of an integrated reading and writing unit about "Theme." His teacher modeled identifying the theme of picture books and YouTube videos by thinking aloud for the class and guiding them in discussions about theme. Then, the Grade 5 writers created their own comics demonstrating a self-selected theme. Read Nickolas's comic centered on the theme of "trustworthiness." Compare Nickolas's writing to the earlier description of Grade 5 writers.

Next, compare all four writing samples. How would you describe the developmental differences across these samples? Create your own categories of development and name them. How does this inform you as a teacher of writing?

Learning to write is a beautiful human act. At any age, we have stories to tell, opinions to share, information we want others to know, poetry to sing. "We are cups, constantly and quietly being filled. The trick is knowing how to tip ourselves over and let the beautiful stuff out" (Bradbury, 1990, p. 112). Elementary writers are developing a sense of what writing can do and be, of who they are as writers, as they develop practices, processes, and craft of writing. Our role as teachers of writing is to support this development, to facilitate that tipping over of the elementary writer's life so the "beautiful stuff" can come out and be shared with the world.

Who Is the Teacher of Writing, and What Is His or Her Role in the Writing Studio?

Each teacher of writing brings his or her unique voice to the Writing Studio. Effective teachers of writing have a depth of knowledge about writing practices, processes, and craft. As writers, they know what writing can do for them. While their style varies, they also share in some common beliefs about who elementary writers are and the possibilities writing holds for them. These beliefs become the dynamic force filling the structures and strategies of the Writing Studio. Johnston's (2010, 2012) work analyzes the dynamic belief systems of effective teachers. Such teachers do not resort to quick judgments like "He is just an active boy and writing doesn't suit him." Rather, a dynamic belief system avoids generalities and creates a classroom environment empathetic to children who are growing up and will sometimes make poor decisions. Such decisions do not become life markers determining the future but opportunities for forgiveness and learning. In this dynamic classroom, risks can be taken; writers embrace writing challenges as opportunities to learn. They are not plagued by a worry of "failure." It is understood that all learning involves struggle so struggle is sought after, valued, documented, and celebrated. Writing is not an isolated act; collaboration is celebrated and encouraged. Such belief systems fill the Writing Studio as a place of possibility for each elementary writer.

Acting on such a belief system, the teacher of writing assumes multiple roles—he or she is forever an evolutionist. Nancie Atwell (1998) writes,

> I've become an evolutionist. The curriculum unfolds as my kids and I learn together and as I teach them what I see they need to learn next. . .Learning with students, collaborating with them as a writer and reader who both wonders and knows about writing and reading, has made me a better teacher to them than I dreamed possible. (p. 3)

Teachers of writing live the life of a writer, observing and wondering the world noting the moments storying our lives, and we share these wonders and observations with the writers in our classroom. Mr. Mackie, a Grade 5 teacher, demonstrates writing as a writer, modeling strategies for finding ideas, revision, editing, and broadcasting writing in all genres. As the mentor in the Writing Studio, he prompts, nudges, and directs as necessary to move writers to new writing places. Mr. Mackie also sees himself as a facilitator. He listens and observes carefully, noting that Marcos voraciously reads about spiders but hasn't once attempted to write about them. That Alannah struggles to start a piece but then, once she finds her "zone," can hardly leave it. He knows that Gabby is a pleaser and wants to "do it right" and that Rajesh, who can make everyone in the class laugh, just needs to figure out how to write down his entertaining jokes.

Mr. Mackie knows his writers through his talk with them and the assessment data he gathers; he adapts instruction and learns with and from them. Mr. Mackie is very much a Teacher with a capital T (Atwell, 1998), the one who plans, assesses, delivers instruction, and organizes the Writing Studio. His goal is to provide his elementary writers time and opportunity to develop writing practices, processes, and craft. He is cheerleader: "Kara, I know writing is hard for you, but yesterday you wrote five sentences! Five sentences! How did you do it yesterday? Can you do it the same way today?" He is critic: "I am wondering about your design. When I look at your webpage, all I see is this large picture. I am not sure what the page is about without reading way down here." And he is collaborator: "Let's write one together! What do you say? How about a six-word memoir about our field trip to the water shed!" Mr. Mackie is all of these things for one reason: his goal is for the elementary writers in his classroom to become independent, empowered writers and global citizens.

 Head to the companion website to watch interviews with four elementary teachers discussing their roles as teachers of writing. How do these videos further inform you about becoming a teacher of writing?

Community and the Writing Studio

Ultimately, writers inspire and drive the Writing Studio. There are many distractions: standards, testing, pullout services, meetings, mandates, and a classroom day filled with so many disciplines and tasks, to name a few. These are all important, but it is all too easy to have such things blur the focus of the Writing Studio. We find that as teachers of writing, when we are feeling overwhelmed with the workload and all the many important things to do, it is time to pull in close and listen to writers. Time to refocus on what inspires: creating the sentence that makes someone laugh; the poem that captures the birthday surprise; the essay that changes a mind, writing for meaning and to make sense of the world.

Problematizing Practice

The goals of Problematizing Practice are to deconstruct assumptions and beliefs and to consider multiple responses and implications of teaching decisions. It is best to do this in the company of colleagues and your instructor:

1. Read the scenario.
2. Quickly write down assumptions about the scenario. *Study your assumptions.*
3. Discuss and problematize assumptions with others and your instructor.
4. Discuss and write possible responses to the scenario.
5. Discuss the possible consequences (intended and unintended) of each response.

In discussing these scenarios, also apply Johnston's (2012) dynamic-learning frame (described earlier) for added analysis.

Scenarios

- Children in the Writing Studio report that another boy is cheating; the writer appears to be copying poems from an anthology. The writer loves to be in the center of everything. He does not like to write and, by his own account, is not very good at it.
- A kindergartner accidently spills paint on the cover of another child's book she has just completed writing. Both children are in tears!

References

Anderson, D.D. (2002). Casting and recasting gender: Children constituting social identities through literacy practices. *Research in the Teaching of English, 36*(3), 391–428.

Atwell, N. (1998). *In the middle: New understandings about writing, reading and learning* (2nd ed.). Portsmouth, NH: Heinemann.

Bakhtin, M. (1986). *Speech genres and other late essays* (Trans. V.W. McGee). Austin, TX: University of Texas Press.

Barad, K. (2007). *Meeting the universe halfway: Quantum physics and the entanglement of matter and meaning.* Durham, NC: Duke University Press.

Birdseye, T. (1989). *Airmail to the moon.* New York, NY: Holiday House.

Bradbury, R. (1990). *Zen in the art of writing.* Santa Barbara, CA: Joshua Odell Editions.

Calkins, L. (1994). *The art of teaching writing.* Portsmouth, NH: Heinemann.

Cummins, J. (1981). The role of primary language development in preventing educational success for language minority students. In *Schooling and language minority students: A theoretical framework* (pp. 3–49). Los Angeles: California State University Evaluation, Dissemination and Assessment Center.

Davidson, C. (2007). Independent writing in current approaches to writing instruction: What have we overlooked? *English Teaching: Practice and Critique, 6*(1), 11–24.

Davies, B. (2003a). *Frogs and snails and feminist tales: Preschool children and gender.* Cresskill, NJ: Hampton.

Davies, B. (2003b). *Shards of glass: Children reading and writing beyond gendered identities.* Cresskill, NJ: Hampton Press.

Dyson, A. H. (1997). *Writing superheros: Contemporary childhood, popular culture, and classroom literacy.* New York, NY: Teachers College Press.

Dyson, A. H. (2003). *The brothers and sisters learn to write: Popular literacies in childhood and school culture.* New York, NY: Teachers College Press.

Dyson, A. H. (2013). *Rewriting the basics: Literacy learning in children's cultures.* New York, NY: Teachers College Press.

Elbow, P. (1981). *Writing with power: Techniques for mastering the writing process.* New York, NY: Oxford University Press.

Elbow, P. (2004). Writing first. *Educational leadership, 62*(2), 8–13.

Fisher, R., Jones, S. J., Larkin, S., & Myhill, D. (2010). *Using talk to support writing.* Los Angeles, CA: Sage.

Fletcher, R. (2006). *Boy writers: Reclaiming their voices.* Markham, Ontario, Canada: Pembroke.

Freeman, D., & Freeman, Y. (2009). The California reading initiative: A formula for failure for bilingual students? *Language Arts, 76*(3), 241–248.

Fu, D. (2009). *Writing between langauges: How English language learners make the transition to fluency, grades 4–12.* Portsmouth, NH: Heineman.

Gee, J. P. (2001). Reading as situated language: A sociocognitive approach. *Journal of Adolescent and Adult Literacy, 44*(8), 714–725.

Goodman, Y. (1988). The development of initial literacy. In E. R. Kintgren, B. M. Kroll, & M. Rose (Eds.), *Perspectives on literacy* (pp. 312–330). Carbondale, IL: Southern Illinois University Press.

Graves, D. (1983). *Writing: Teachers and children at work.* Portsmouth, NH: Heinemann.

Guzzetti, B., Young, J., Gritsavage, M., Fyfe, L., & Hardenbrook, M. (2002). *Reading, writing and talking gender in literacy learning.* Newark, DE: International Reading Association.

Hartse, J., Woodward, V., & Burke, C. (1984). *Language stories and learning lessons.* Portsmouth, NH: Heinemann.

Harwayne, S. (2001). *Writing through childhood: Rethinking process and product.* Portsmouth, NH: Heinemann.

Heath, S. B. (1983). *Ways with words: Language, life and work in communities and classrooms.* Cambridge: Cambridge University Press.

Johnston, P. H. (2010, December). *Discursive frames in literacy learning and agentive networks of development.* Paper presented at the Annual Meeting of the National Reading Conference/Literacy Research Association, Fort Worth, TX.

Johnston, P. H. (2012). *Opening minds using language to change lives.* Portland, ME: Stenhouse.

Lenz Taguchi, H. (2010). *Going beyond the theory/practice divide in early childhood education: Introducing an intra-active pedagogy.* New York, NY: Routledge.

Marsh, J. (1998). Gender and writing in the infant school: Writing for a gender-specific audience. *English Education, 32*(1), 10–18.

McAuliffe, S. (1994). Toward understanding one another: Second graders' use of gendered langauge and story styles. *The Reading Teacher, 47*(4), 302–310.

Meyer, R. (2010). *Official and unofficial counterportraits of 'at risk' students: Writing spaces in hard times.* New York, NY: Routledge.

Murray, D. (1985). *A writer teaches writing* (2nd ed.). Boston, MA: Houghton Mifflin.

Newkirk, T. (2000). Misreading masculinity: Speculations on the great gender gap in writing. *Language Arts, 77*(4), 294–300.

Olson, K., & Sulzby, E. (1991). The computer as a social/physical environment in emergent literacy. In J. Zutell, S. McCormick, L. Caton, & P. O'Keefe (Eds.), *Learner factors/teacher factors: Issues in literacy research and instruction* (pp. 111–118). Chicago, IL: National Reading Conference.

Phillips, D. K., & Larson, M. L. (2013). The teacher-student writing conference reimaged: Entangled becoming-writingconferencing. *Gender & Education, 25*(6), 722–737.

Pinnell, G., & Fountas, I. C. (2011). *The continuum of literacy learning, grades PreK-8: A guide to teaching* (2nd ed.). Portsmouth, NH: Heinemann.

Ray, K. W., & Glover, M. (2008). *Already ready: Nuturing writers in preschool and kindergarten*. Portsmouth, NH: Heinemann.

Rowe, D. W. (2003). The nature of young children's authoring. In N. Hall, J. Larson, & J. Marsh (Eds.), *Handbook of early childhood literacy* (pp. 258–270). Thousand Oaks, CA: Sage.

Rowe, D. W. (2008). Development of writing abilities in children. In C. Bazerman (Ed.), *Handbook of research on writing* (pp. 401–419). New York, NY: Erlbaum.

Solsken, J. (1993). *Literacy, gender, and work in families and in school*. Norword, NJ: Ablex.

Street, B. (1995). *Social literacies: Critical approaches to literacy in development, ethnography and education*. London: Longman.

Thomas, W. P., & Collier, V. (1997). *School effective for langauge minority students* (NCBE Resources Collection Series 9). Washington, DC: National Clearinghouse for Bilingual Education.

Chapter Two
Possibilities, Purposes, and Goals for Writing

"I dwell in possibilities." Ms. J has this title of an Emily Dickinson (1951) poem posted near her teacher's space. Completed by a calligraphist several years ago, the words are surrounded by endless circles overlapping, bleeding into one another, bold in orange and then softening to an almost imperceptible halo of pinks. It is a mantra of Ms. J's: dwell in possibilities of what might be, could be, is but is not seen. Learning and teaching as possibilities open worlds, create visions—keep Ms. J from falling into dogma or despair. As a writer and as a teacher of writing, Ms. J conceives of writing as possibility: everything she reads, lives, engages with, are possibilities for writing topics, the act of writing is possibility (who knows what might unfold?), sharing writing provides possibilities in relationships, growing identity, understanding the writing-self. And so when Ms. J considers purposes and goals for writing, she is also thinking about "possibilities." How can she expand the vision of what writers do, and what writing can do for writers during each Writing Studio? How might this "new" writing strategy be used to create different possibilities and purposes for young writers? Where are the possibilities in children, curriculum, required assessments, and mandates that she may at first resist, or dread, or even fear? How can she see what appears not to be there?

Dwelling in possibilities is a powerful place to live.

––––––––––––––

April is 5 years old and busy and likes soccer balls and bubbles and hide-and-seek and the ShowMe (Learnbat, Inc., 2013) application on her Mom's iPad and talks and is *in* motion (whew!) all the time. And April knows the possibility of writing to name her. Ask her about her writing, and she proudly points to a self-portrait on the refrigerator and will show you how she has written her name underneath (the *A* is the only recognizable letter): "This is me!" It is her first autobiography.

Roger, a third grader, is showing his friends his writing about how snakes shed their skin. Roger has a pet snake, so he and his mom keep a snake journal at home, and when his own snake began to shed, they documented the process. His mom helped him with an Internet search to learn how to care for his snake. The librarian at his school suggested a good book with lots of pictures. Roger views himself as an expert on snakes. He has designed his piece to look like a page from the Internet with headings, pictures, and a small graph. He hopes to publish the piece using a Google webpage. (The media specialist at his school has promised to help him with this!) Roger believes his piece will be informative to others who want to own snakes as pets. Writing makes Roger an expert and from this identity, he writes to inform others.

Prior to Grade 5, Sebas was considered a resistant reader and writer. The only books he had truly enjoyed reading were Jeff Kinney's (2007) *Diary of a Wimpy Kid* series, told through diary entries. What Sebas truly loves is all things military, which is reinforced by his grandpa's service in the Army. Not long after his grandpa was deployed for a tour of duty in Iraq, Sebas began requesting that his mom read him war stories—lots of them, especially graphic novels about battles. His mother cannot begin to count the number of times she read Sebas the graphic novel *The Battle of Iwo Jima: Guerilla Warfare in the Pacific* (Hama, 2007). During this time, Sebas had to be coaxed and cajoled to write almost anything and then produced only the required bare minimum. At other times, he would choose to be sent to the office or miss recess just to avoid writing. But then, something happened: Sebas came alive during a fiction-writing unit in May of his Grade 5 school year. Sebas wrote a multipaged story about a fictional character, Andrew Pettison, Ace Platoon Sergeant of the 501st Airborne, deployed to Afghanistan to get revenge after the 9/11 attacks. (See Appendix E.) There's lots of action, dialogue, and details building to the climax of the story. Sebas' story is told through a series of diary entries, similar to the structure of the *Diary of a Wimpy Kid* series. When asked, "How did you do this? How did you accomplish all this writing?" Sebas replied, "That's what happens when you read a lot of books."

April, Roger, and Sebas are learning what writers do and what writing can do for them. They are learning about the possibilities inherent in *becoming-writer*. As teachers of writing, we want to expand the possibilities of what writers do and what writing can do for children. One way to expand such possibilities is teaching with mode and through genre. Understanding mode and genre can be a powerful factor in establishing possibilities, purposes, and goals for writers.

Teaching With Mode and Through Genre

Here is a definition of *mode*: "An unspecific critical term usually designating a broad but identifiable kind of literary method, mood, or manner that is not tied exclusively to a particular form or genre" (Baldick, 2008, p. 213). We had to read that twice: an "unspecific" yet "critical term" that identifies a "literary method, mood, or manner" that may or may not be tied to a genre? And this is, of course, the difficulty with mode! If we say, "Students are to write an expository text," what do you visualize? Can you quickly name an example of "expository writing"? Because we have used the word *students*, you may associate this with school, and therefore, you may visualize a five-paragraph essay that does some kind of explaining or provides some kind of information. That does not foster much possibility or motivation!

We resonate with Katie Wood Ray's (2006) definition of *mode*: "Mode describes the meaning work that a piece of writing is doing at any given place in the text" (p. 57). "*Meaning work*" at "*any given place in the text*." Okay, so mode isn't just a categorical definition. Mode is *meaning work*, and if it can be in any given place in the text, then any single text may have more than one mode. Now the idea of mode is getting interesting! Mode implies general categories like narrative (telling a story), expository (explaining), descriptive (describing, often related to the five senses), and argumentation (persuading, giving an opinion, using evidence to support an idea, action or theory). But the beauty of understanding mode is *not* in its definition but in knowing the "meaning work" that it is doing—or knowing the purpose of the writing. The nuanced understanding of mode is realizing that while the meaning work of an argument may be to persuade, the writer may use description, information, stories, even poetry, to make his or her case—and that is an interesting possibility.

While mode is a broad classification of the *meaning work* of texts, genre denotes a *specific category of literary composition* identifiable by a common set of characteristics. There is not a single agreed-on list of genres. Some common children's and young adult literature genres include realism, formula fiction, fantasy, traditional tales, poetry, informational books, and biography (Lukens, 2007). Within each of these genres are various subgenres. For example, subgenres of realism are identified as realistic stories, animal realism, historical fiction, and sports stories (Lukens, 2007). Some books can be categorized in a single genre whereas others can be categorized as multi-genre. Ray (2006) describes genre as "what we say when someone asks, '*What kind of writing is it?* [emphasis added]'" (p. 54).

Often writers transition between modes and genres in a single text. Mode and genre are fluid categories, and our point here is for you to be able to read books and identify potential categories the books may fit, yet not allow these categories to be static. The goal is to teach *with* mode and *through* genre to expand possibilities, purposes, and goals for writing. Teaching elementary writers the language of mode and genre invites them to participate in the language of the "literacy club" (Smith, 1987), empowering them with words to describe the purpose of their work.

As teachers of writing, one way to make mode and genre come alive for us it to specifically search for texts that represent the work of mode and genre. Children can then use these texts as mentors in their writing. Ray (2006) encourages teachers to make "stacks" of books to read and use as mentors for writing.

Stacking for Genre

For example, let's take a small stack of books sitting on Mindy's desk: *March: Book One* (Lewis & Aydin, 2013), *Alia's Mission: Saving the Books of Iraq* (Stamaty, 2004), and *Mother Jones: Labor Leader* (Miller, 2007).

The first book in Mindy's stack, *March: Book One* (Lewis & Aydin, 2013), tells the story of Representative John Lewis' involvement with the 1965 march from Selma to Montgomery, referred to as "Bloody Sunday" with flash-forwards to President Barack Obama's inauguration day in 2009 and flashbacks to John Lewis' life from a young boy in rural Alabama to his college years and his leadership with the Student Nonviolent Coordinating Committee. The second book in Mindy's stack, *Alia's Mission: Saving the Books of Iraq* (Stamaty, 2004) centers on the story of Alia Muhammad Baker, the chief librarian of the Central Library in Basra, Iraq, in 2003 when the war was moving closer to Basra. The third book in Mindy's stack, *Mother Jones: Labor Leader* (Miller, 2007) tells the story of Mary Jones, later known as Mother Jones, and her life's work supporting labor rights.

This stack of books can be categorized under the genre of *biographies* because they are all stories that give "accurate, verifiable facts and authentic picture of a period; [of a] subject worthy of attention; and sources of information shown or listed." (Lukens, 2007, p. 34). This stack of books can also be categorized under the genre of *graphic novels* because they are all told through comics with speech bubbles, narrator boxes, and illustrations in panels. In addition, each of the books slides between three modes: they all *inform* the reader about a real period in world history; they all *tell a story* through narrative; they all *persuade* the reader to take action.

 Expand your understanding of mode and genre by trying this activity: (1) Choose a day and declare it a particular mode day; for example, Wednesday is Information Day. (2) Beginning with your morning activities and continuing throughout the day, note every kind of informational text (including multimodal text) you encounter. The "seeing" mode takes practice—we suggest you do this more than once! (3) After collecting different examples of the informational mode, analyze your lists. Could some of what you have identified as "informational" also be considered a different mode? How many different genres of "informational" texts do you have? How could these different genres be writing possibilities for writers?

Teaching *with* mode and *through* genre is empowering when we understand the fluidity and possibility within each term and allow this understanding to focus our thinking and teaching on the "meaning work" (Ray, 2006) of writers. Teaching elementary writers how meaning is made and works through mode and how many purposes for writing exists with genre engages them in embracing what writers can do and what writing can do for them.

In the next section, we turn to the Common Core State Standards (CCSS; National Governors Association [NGA] Center for Best Practices & Council of Chief State School Officers [CCSSO], 2010a). Key to seeing the CCSS as descriptive (rather than prescriptive) and establishing a wide variety of possibilities and purposes for writing is knowing the meaning work of mode and genre.

Introduction to the Common Core State Standards (CCSS)

Let's start this section with an activity: take a moment and make a list of everything you know about the CCSS. Once you have made this list, return to it and underline everything you understand to be fact. Draw a line from this "fact" and note how you know it is "true." Evaluate your sources. What might most influence the opinions and experiences of the "sources" you have identified? Include how you personally feel about each "fact" you listed. Reread your list again, and write down any questions you have about the CCSS.

If there is one thing Ms. J knows, it is the importance of critically deconstructing, questioning, and seeking multiple perspectives as she learns about district, state, and federal mandates. It is not enough to simply listen to what others have to say, to attend district in-services or publishing company seminars, or take *carte blanche* the content of your professors' lectures (or what we write here!). All teachers own this responsibility for thinking hard, and this is particularly important regarding the CCSS. Calkins, Ehrenworth and Lehman (2012) write of the CCSS,

It is safe to say that across the entire history of American education, no single document will have played a more influential role over what is taught in our schools. The standards are already affecting what is published, mandated, and tested in schools—and also what is marginalized and neglected. Any educator who wants to play a role in shaping what happens in schools, therefore, needs a deep understanding of these standards. (p. 1)

Developing a "deep understanding" of the CCSS begins with a close reading of them. If you have not yet independently read the CCSS, we encourage you to take a break now, go to www.ccss.org, and read for yourself what the CCSS have to say. This will provide a backdrop for the next section of this text.

In this text, our goal is to present a reading of the CCSS illustrating how they can be used to provide possibilities, purposes, and goals for the elementary writer. In the interest of full disclosure, we are skeptical of the CCSS. To be more concise, it not the College and Career Readiness Anchor Standards for Writing with which we are concerned so much as other areas connected with the CCSS. We are concerned about the testing associated with the CCSS (Partnership for Assessment of Readiness for College and Careers, 2013; Smarter Balanced Assessment Consortium, 2013); the publication of later documents by the authors of the CCSS contradicting their original work (Coleman & Pimentel, 2011, 2012); and the amount of corporate wealth generated by the CCSS (Ravitch, 2013). We are greatly concerned about the interpretation and implementation of the CCSS by states and local school districts. Perhaps our greatest concern, as it relates to this text, is the grade-level expectations, or the grade-level progressions, outlined for children, especially for young children. The grade-level progressions are not based solely on research—in some instances, they appear to disregard what is known about young children's writing development. These grade-level progressions were developed using a consensus process among the authors, meaning the CCSS authors used (a) research readily available to them (not an exhaustive review of research), (b) best practice as seen in state standards, and (c) professional experience (Pearson, 2013). We hope with Pearson (2013) that the CCSS are a "living document" and that teachers like those of you reading this book will gather data that can be used to revise grade level progression.

Despite our concerns, the CCSS has more than likely come to the state where you are or will be teaching writing. To that end, we want to highlight the empowering pieces of the CCSS to focus our discussion on how they can be used to create possibilities, purposes, and goals for writing instruction.

The CCSS describe a "vision of what it means to be a literate person in the twenty-first century" (NGA Center for Best Practices & CCSSO, 2010a, p. 3). They argue that students who have met the CCSS will demonstrate the "cogent reasoning and use of evidence that is essential to both private deliberation and responsible citizenship in a democratic republic" (NGA Center for Best Practices & CCSSO, 2010a, p. 3). Let's keep this vision: as teachers of writing, we are fostering writers who will be able to engage, debate, move our democracy by understanding what writing can do for themselves and for others, by knowing and being able to use the power of words to shape decisions and choices in personal and public life.

Let us also focus on the power and responsibility given to teachers by the CCSS (NGA Center for Best Practices & CCSSO, 2010a):

> By emphasizing required achievements, the Standards leave room for teachers, curriculum developers, and states to determine how those goals should be reached and what additional topics should be addressed. Thus, the Standards do not mandate such things as a particular writing process or the full range of metacognitive strategies that students may need to monitor and direct their thinking and learning. *Teachers are thus free to provide students with whatever tools and knowledge their professional judgment and experience identify as most helpful for meeting the goals set out in the Standards* [emphasis added]. (p. 4)

This commitment to teacher prerogative is further supported in the stated limitations of the CCSS: "The Standards define what all students are expected to know and be able to do, *not how teachers should teach* [emphasis added]" (2010a, p. 6). Furthermore, the CCSS are clear that "while the Standards focus on what is most essential, they do not describe all that can or should be taught. A great deal is left to the discretion of teachers and curriculum developers. The aim of the Standards is to articulate the fundamentals, not to set out an exhaustive list or a set of restrictions that limits what can be taught beyond what is specified herein" (2010a, p. 6).

Furthermore, the CCSS support an integrated approach to literacy, calling for proficiency, complexity, and integration across curricular disciplines (Calkins et al., 2012). Writing is not relegated to only the language arts but a necessary component of *all* discipline areas: writing is to be done all day long in all disciplines. The CCSS acknowledge limitations: they do not describe advanced work for students, intervention models or how to support English learners and students with special needs (NGA Center for Best Practices & CCSSO, 2010a, p. 6). But they do give us as teachers the authority to call into question practices that deny a rich literacy education to *all* children and to use our professional knowledge to ensure that all children are given authentic purposes to write and to envision possibilities of what writing can do for them as citizens of a democratic republic. This combined with the CCSS's support of critical and creative thinking and problem solving, as well as adequate time for writing process, allow us to use the CCSS to imagine writing instruction where elementary writers have and learn to exercise choice, are permitted to experiment with form and design, build writers' vocabulary, develop a writers' craft-tool collection for multiple forms of writing, collaborate as they most certainly will in a future workplace, and assume responsibility and ownership for their work.

From this broad framework, then, we can begin to see how the CCSS can be used to create possibilities, purpose, and goals for elementary writers.

The CCSS as Possibility

Let's begin this work with the College and Career Readiness Anchor Standards for Writing. The first broad category is *Text Types and Purposes**.

1. Write arguments to support claims in an analysis of substantive topics or texts, using valid reasoning and relevant and sufficient evidence.
2. Write informative/explanatory texts to examine and convey complex ideas and information clearly and accurately through the effective selection, organization, and analysis of content.
3. Write narratives to develop real or imagined experiences or events using effective technique, well-chosen details, and well-structured event sequences.

Take note of the asterisk, which clarifies the category title in this way: "These broad types of writing include many subgenres" (NGA Center for Best Practices & CCSSO, 2010a, p. 18). You will recognize, then, that these "text types" are *modes*. "Purposes" describes the *meaning work* of the writer (Ray, 2006). The text types of the CCSS are *arguments*, referred to as "*opinions*" for Grades K through 5; *informative/ explanatory*; and *narratives*. As modes, these broad categories in and of themselves do not define what a writer will do or the kind of writing decisions that must be made. This comes when we use our knowledge of genre to further explore possibilities within each mode or text type.

The CCSS honor the nuances and complexities of mode in their definitions of each text type found in Appendix A of the CCSS English Language Arts document. Of narrative writing, the CCSS Appendix A (NGA Center for Best Practices & CCSSO, 2010b) notes, "Narrative writing conveys experience, either real or imaginary, and uses time as its deep structure. It can be used for many purposes, such as to inform, instruct, persuade, or entertain" (p. 23). Remember our discussion of mode? While a mode defines the meaning work of the writer, the writer may use multiple kinds of modes within a mode to get that meaning work accomplished! Or, in the words of the CCSS, "skilled writers many times use a blend of these three text types [opinion, informative/explanatory, narrative] to accomplish their purposes" (NGA Center for Best Practices & CCSSO, 2010b, p. 25).

Why is this so important? The CCSS provide teachers of writing the mode, the broad text type, or general areas where writers must demonstrate competence, but as teachers, we are given the authority to find possibilities in the many and varied kinds of genres within each mode. The CCSS are not prescriptive—they are descriptive. It would be wrong to plan the Writing Studio by privileging traditional kinds of school writing alone: the five-paragraph essay, the report, the letter arguing for more of anything in the lunchroom! Equally wrong would be to declare a unit "informative writing" and not allow writers to learn to choose and use mixed modes such as the power of a personal story to do the meaning work of the piece. For this reason, we agree with Ray (2006) that genre words do a better job of setting out possibilities, purposes, and goals for writing. Put your knowledge of mode and genre together as you read and implement the CCSS!

Remember also that the CCSS do not purport to cover everything. A text box in the CCSS English Language Arts Appendix A reads, "The narrative category does not include all of the possible forms of creative writing such as many types of poetry. *The Standards leave the inclusion and evaluation of other such forms to teacher discretion* [emphasis added]" (NGA Center for Best Practices & CCSSO, 2010b, p. 24).

Besides text types or modes, the College and Career Readiness Anchor Standards for Writing honor the work of real writers, providing direction for establishing possibilities, purposes, and goals for our elementary writers. The following are three additional anchor standards:

Production and Distribution of Writing

4. Produce clear and coherent writing in which the development, organization, and style are appropriate to task, purpose, and audience.
5. Develop and strengthen writing as needed by planning, revising, editing, rewriting, or trying a new approach.
6. Use technology, including the Internet, to produce and publish writing and to interact and collaborate with others.

Research to Build and Present Knowledge

7. Conduct short as well as more sustained research projects based on focused questions, demonstrating understanding of the subject under investigation.
8. Gather relevant information from multiple print and digital sources, assess the credibility and accuracy of each source, and integrate the information while avoiding plagiarism.
9. Draw evidence from literary or informational texts to support analysis, reflection, and research.

Range of Writing

10. Write routinely over extended time frames (time for research, reflection, and revision) and shorter time frames (a single sitting or a day or two) for a range of tasks, purposes, and audiences.

Production and distribution of writing speaks to the process of writing: "planning, revising, editing, rewriting, or trying a new approach" (NGA Center for Best Practices & CCSSO, 2010a, p. 18)—the stuff of playing and working with language to get our writing "right," in order to communicate our intentions to others. Here, there is also language about organization, writing design and collaboration, and the development of style—all choices we make as writers based on the purposes and goals of our writing. The CCSS describe the writer as a researcher—drawing from experiences, multiple print and digital sources, searching for relevant and credible information. Each such source presents more possibilities for writers! There is emphasis on "range of writing," and thus writing practice. Writing practices includes writing "routinely over extended time frames" as well as composing shorter more focused pieces in a single setting.

Together, the writing standards support writing practices, process, and craft, the authentic work of writers in composing meaning. They open up possibilities, purposes, and goals for writing when we read them descriptively and use them in fostering writing instruction that prepares writers to powerfully engage as global citizens.

Writing Traits as Possibilities

Writing traits can further expand possibilities for a writer and help to establish purposes and goals for writing. Although the CCSS Anchor Standards for Writing provide a description of what and how much students should write, writing traits focus on the craft of the writer or on how a writer develops his or her work. The traits can expand a writer's view of him- or herself as a writer, provide direction for learning, and act as a way for a writer to track his or her writing growth. The writing traits as defined by Education Northwest (2013) are as follows: ideas, organization, word choice, voice, sentence fluency, conventions, and presentation.

Ideas

Ideas are the main message, the content of the piece. (Education Northwest, 2013)

Ideas grab the reader and produce a reaction: "Ohhhh!" "Interesting—I didn't know that" "LOL!" Jon Scieszka's (2008) story "Buyer Beware" in *Knucklehead: Tall Tales and Mostly True Stories About Growing Up Scieszka* tells about a time when he ordered 100 toy soldiers from an advertisement placed in the inside cover of a comic book. The details Scieszka employs make us "see" the ad: "Two-way radios for sixty-nine cents, joy buzzers, trick black soap, prank onion gum, even X-ray specs" (p. 51).

Organization

[Organization] is the internal structure of a piece of writing, the thread of central meaning, the pattern and sequence, so long as it fits the central idea. (Education Northwest, 2013)

There are almost infinite ways to organize writing. Let's go back to our stack of biographies. *Mother Jones: Labor Leader* (Miller, 2007) is told chronologically from the time Mary Harris (Mother Jones) was an 8-year-old girl living in Cork, Ireland, in the 1840s to the day she died in 1930. *March: Book One* (Lewis & Aydin, 2013) is told through a series of flashbacks and flash-forwards from President Barack Obama's inauguration day on January 20, 2009, to various moments in John Lewis' life up until 1965. *Alia's Mission: Saving the Books of Iraq* (Stamaty, 2004) focuses on a key moment in Alia Muhammad Baker's life when she helped move 30,000 books from the Basra Central Library to safe locations during the Iraq war in 2003.

Voice

Voice is the writer coming through the words, the sense that a real person is speaking to us and cares about the message. (Education Northwest, 2013)

In many ways, voice is the composite of all the other traits. Listen to this excerpt from *More Than Anything Else*, by Marie Bradby (1995). She is describing Booker T. Washington's first experience hearing a Black man read:

I see a man reading a newspaper aloud and all doubt falls away.
I have found hope, and it is as brown as me.

I see myself the man. And as I watch his eyes move across the paper, it is as if *I* know what the black marks mean, as if *I* am reading. As if everyone is listening to *me*. And I hold that thought in my hands. (p. 12)

The rhythm of the words, the repeating "I," the imagery of holding a thought in one's hands—all of this combined gives this piece *voice*.

Molly Bang and Penny Chisholm's (2012) *Ocean Sunlight: How Tiny Plants Feed the Seas* is a clear example of how nonfiction books can exhibit voice. The story is told from the sun's first-person perspective. Read an excerpt:

Dive into the sea! Now flip over slowly, and look up. The water is shimmering with light—my light. I am your sun, your golden star. All ocean life depends on me; so does all life on land. In your forests, prairies, and your gardens, green plants catch my sunlight-energy. They pump in water from the ground and pull in carbon dioxide from the air. Plants use my energy to build these molecules into . . . SUGAR! (pp. 1–3)

The personification of the sun fills the text with *voice*. The sun begins by talking directly to the reader. Throughout the book, the sun is full of personality and agency, engaging our imagination.

Word Choice

Word Choice is the use of rich, colorful, precise language that communicates not just in a functional way, but in a way that moves and enlightens the reader. (Education Northwest, 2013)

Laban Carrick Hill's (2010) book *Dave the Potter: Artist, Poet, Slave* begins:

To us it is just dirt, the ground we walk on. Scoop up a handful. The gritty grains slip between your fingers. On wet days, heavy with rainwater, it is cool and squishy, mud pie heaven. But to Dave, it was clay, the plain and basic stuff upon which he learned to form a life as a slave nearly two hundred years ago. (pp. 1–3)

The simple, yet poetic language draws the reader into the story; we want to know more about Dave the Potter. Hill's word choice gives us sensory images of touch, sight, and smell: "scoop" and "gritty grains slip between your fingers."

Sentence Fluency

Sentence Fluency is the rhythm and flow of the language, the sound of word patterns, the way in which the writing plays to the ear, not just to the eye. (Education Northwest, 2013)

Steve Jenkins's (2011) *Just a Second: A Different Way to Look at Time* is an excellent example of sentence fluency. He begins each segment of time with a description followed by examples from nature. For example, on the pages describing "one second" Jenkins (2011) writes,

The second doesn't relate to any cycle in nature—it's a human invention, and the shortest interval of time most of us use in our daily lives. The Babylonians came up with the idea of the second about 4,000 years ago, but they had no way to measure such a short interval of time. (p. 3)

This is followed by:

In one second . . . A vulture in flight flaps its wings once. A pygmy shrew's heart beats 14 times. A bat can make 200 high-pitched calls. A rattlesnake shakes its tail in warning 60 times. A humming-bird beats its wings 50 times. A bumblebee beats its wings 200 times. A midge, a kind of gnat, beats its wings 1,000 times. A woodpecker hammers a tree trunk with its beak 20 times. (pp. 3–4)

The story begins with background information on the human-created measurement of time we call "second." These informational sentences are longer, employing compound sentencing. Jenkins follows this with a series of four short sentences describing things various animals can do in a second followed by three sentences that each describe how many times three different kinds of animals beat its wings each exponentially more than the previous. While the longer sentences introduce the concept of time as a "second," the shorter sentences make us feel the second as a time construct as we read them. Sentence fluency, used in this way, conveys the meaning of "second."

Conventions

The Conventions trait is the mechanical correctness of the piece and includes five elements: spelling, punctuation, capitalization, grammar/usage, and paragraphing. (Education Northwest, 2013)

The Conventions trait is the one trait for which the Education Northwest makes specific grade-level recommendations. Conventions in many ways represent cultural norms. Conventions have an impact on readers' ability to make meaning of texts. For example, authors sometimes include comments in parentheses to indicate a snarky aside the writer is trying to convey to the reader. This is why when teaching English learners, we take care that the cultural clues of such words and the parentheses that enclose them are taught as meaning-making signals to the reader.

Mo Willems is a master at using conventions, especially punctuation to convey emotion and tension in his stories as well as to develop both the plot and characters. Read the excerpt from *I Love My New Toy!* (Willems, 2008):

Hi, Piggie! What are you doing?
LOOK AT MY NEW TOY!!!
I love my new toy.
What does it do?
I have no idea (pp. 2–7).

Piggie's excitement over his new toy is seen through the use of all CAPS and triple exclamation marks. His friend's curiosity is evident by the questions he asks Piggy.

Presentation

Presentation combines both visual and textual elements. It is the way we exhibit or present our message on paper. (Education Northwest, 2013)

Presentation speaks of design, of exercising writer's choice in how a piece of writing is displayed for the reader. Louise Borden's (2005) multi-genre book *The Journey That Saved Curious George: The True*

Wartime Escape of Margret and H. A. Rey is a wonderful example of presentation. The book has a biographical narrative strand that runs throughout each page telling the story of Margret and H. A. Rey, the authors of the *Curious George* series. The narrative is layered with both primary documents such as photographs, Margret's birth certificate, stamps from the countries they lived in, early manuscripts of *Curious George* books. There are also pen and ink illustrations throughout the book. In addition the author wrote a foreword telling the background of how she "found" the story and an afterword telling more about the lives of Margret and H. A. Rey. The end pages are pen-and-ink maps of all the countries the Reys lived in when they escaped during World War II.

Develop your own examples of writing traits as possibilities by spending time in the children's literature collection of a public, a university, or an elementary school library. Browse through books and find examples as we have done in the preceding section. Once you have established such a document, add to it with each new book you read and watch your collection of writing trait examples for use in the Writing Studio grow! Conversely, this is an excellent activity to do with elementary writers to develop their understanding of the writing traits.

Writing traits do not cover everything a writer does or all that is involved in the act of writing. The traits are constructs to think about writing—they are not definitive. It would be silly to think otherwise. Nor is it our intention to suggest that there is universal agreement on *the* writing traits—more than likely this is why no one set of traits can fully describe writing. However, the traits are yet another set of language that allows young writers to become part of the writing club. Listen to these snippets of conversation:

Writer to teacher: I asked for a writing conference today because I can't quite figure out design. I have all this information and all these pictures. How to I get them on the page to look good?
Teacher to writer: I wonder if we might brainstorm other possible word choices for "really awesome"? What other possibilities might there be to give your reader a picture of what it is like to play this video game?
Writer to writer: It's an exclamation mark! It's a convention! Make him "scream" like this!"
Teacher to parent: Lize has excellent ideas. [Reads aloud from child's writing.] What we are working on now are possible ways Lize can better focus and organize her writing by developing one or two related ideas.

The language of writing traits expands possibilities, purposes, and goals for writers and writing instruction when used judiciously. Writing traits become dangerous if we use them to reduce writing to a quantifiable skill and even more dangerous if teachers and administrators see them as a skill only and do not understand the depth and richness embedded in each trait as writing craft. Sometimes, too much time is focused on the traits, as if that is all there is to teach in writing and at the expense of writing itself. Furthermore, the abstractness of the terms can lack meaning especially for young writers if they are not approached with developmental expertise and care. Yet used with a deliberate focus on possibilities, purposes, and goals, writing traits provide language for developing writing practices, process, and craft.

Practice your understanding of mode, genre, CCSS, and writing traits and how they can be applied to a teaching event. Read "Teaching Event with March: Book One" found in Appendix F and see if you can identify places where the teacher discusses explicitly or implicitly the concepts from this chapter: writing goals, genre, mode, and writing traits. Read the excerpt a second time with the CCSS ELA standards next to you. Highlight the Reading, Writing, Language, and Speaking and Listening standards that are addressed in this lesson. How did you know? How might you revise the lesson to more fully develop a specific standard?

An Illustration: Developing Writing Possibilities, Purposes, and Goals With Sebas

We return to Sebas . . . you met him at the beginning of this chapter. If you haven't had a chance, read his story "Middle East Revenge" (Appendix E). If we apply our knowledge of mode and genre to Sebas' story about a solider seeking revenge after the 9/11 attacks, we can work with Sebas to name the genres his story encompasses: realistic fiction, historical fiction, and war stories. "Middle East Revenge" is an example of the genre realistic fiction because it centers on a character, Andrew Pettison, and his desire to stop terrorism in the Middle East. The genre of Sebas' story could also be categorized as historical fiction because the fictional character, Andrew Pettison, is placed in the Middle East after the 9/11 attacks. In addition, Sebas' story is the genre of war stories because he focuses solely on the military life of army airborne platoon sergeant, Andrew Pettison's deployment to Iraq in 2001. With Sebas we could talk about the purpose or mode of "Middle East Revenge." Was he trying to tell a story by using a narrative mode? Was he also trying to persuade his readers by using an argument mode? If so, how was he hoping to influence his readers?

Because Sebas has such a keen interest in military weapons, aircraft, and wars, we can capitalize on his interests and expertise to encourage Sebas to pursue other possible genres and modes. We can collect additional pieces of writing that represent new genres and modes. For example, we can give Sebas several magazine feature articles about war. Sebas could read them, and together we could discuss the following questions: "What do you notice about feature articles? How are feature articles different from your story? What is the purpose of these feature articles? What aspects of the feature articles do you want to try using as a writer?"

Directing Sebas toward feature writing will expand his repertoire of "Text Types and Purposes," thus supporting his journey toward meeting the CCSS. By introducing a new mode of writing, we provide Sebas another purpose for writing. Such writing provides Sebas with an authentic reason to "Research to Build and Present Knowledge" as he composes this next piece.

We can also use our discussions to teach Sebas about writer's craft as represented by writing traits, and from this discussion, we can set specific goals for him as a writer. We can compliment Sebas for his engaging ideas and content as well as his vivid word choice in "Middle East Revenge." Then, we can set goals for Sebas as a writer. One goal might be to develop Sebas's skills with conventions, specifically learning how to punctuate dialogue. Another goal might be to develop strategies for organizing his writing. Both goal-areas support Sebas toward his mastery of CCSS "Production and Distribution," which includes organizational and editing skills.

Taken together, we are practicing integrated language arts teaching, combining reading, writing, listening and speaking, to create possibilities, purposes, and writing goals for Sebas. Although Sebas has been ascribed labels within medical and school settings—Attention Deficit and Hyperactivity Disorder (ADHD) and prior to his fifth-grade fiction-writing unit, "noncompliant writer"—these labels faded away during the fiction-writing unit. His teacher, Ms. Widmer, allowed Sebas choice to write about a topic of interest and choice in the form of his fiction story. Ms. Widmer understands the importance of taking a student where he is and knows she can expand his range of writing in the future, if he has just one successful writing experience to build on.

Watch an interview with Sebas discussing his writing "Middle East Revenge."

Possibilities, Purposes, and Goals in Writing

You may find yourself in a school context where standards and/or writing traits are applied in a prescriptive way. If so, then to read and implement them as possibilities is a way to resist and practice subversive teaching. In other schools, this framework of reading the standards and/or traits as possibilities is actively adopted in one form or another, and you will grow many more interpretations and possibilities. Regardless of your teaching context, we encourage you first and foremost to grow your own knowledge of writing: know what writing can do for you and for children, know how it works, and develop a deep understanding of the language of mode/genre, the CCSS or other state-adopted standards, and writing traits. Tweak and twist but re-frame mandates as *possibilities* and see what you may discover. In *Letters to a Young Teacher*, Jonathan Kozol (2007) writes:

> the point is not to lose your job! It is to find a way to navigate the contradictions it presents without entirely forfeiting one's personality or undermining the ideals that make our work with children a 'vocation' in the truest sense rather than a slotted role within a spiritless career. (p. 203)

Dwelling in possibilities is a powerful place to live as a writer and as a teacher of writing. Let us find these possibilities, define them with our young writers, and use them to foster authentic writing, purposes, and writing goals.

Problematizing Practice

The goals of Problematizing Practice are to deconstruct assumptions and beliefs and to consider multiple responses and implications of teaching decisions. It is best to do this in the company of colleagues and your instructor:

1. Read the scenario.
2. Quickly write down assumptions about the scenario. *Study your assumptions.*
3. Discuss and problematize assumptions with others and your instructor.
4. Discuss and write possible responses to the scenario.
5. Discuss the possible consequences (intended and unintended) of each response.

Scenario

In the faculty lunchroom, you overhear teachers saying the following about the CCSS. How might you reply?

- "Because of the CCSS, we are required to purchase an approved writing curriculum."
- "Under the CCSS, we can no longer teach anything but informational and opinion writing."
- "The CCSS mandates the use of graphic organizers for all writing modes."
- "The CCSS is an initiative of the federal government."

References

Baldick, C. (2008). *Concise Oxford dictionary of literary terms* (3rd ed.). Oxford, England: Oxford University Press.

Bang, M., & Chisholm, P. (2012). *Ocean sunlight: How tiny plants feed the seas.* New York, NY: Blue Sky Press.

Borden, L. (2005). *The journey that saved Curious George: The true wartime escape of Margret and H.A. Rey.* Boston, MA: Houghton Mifflin Harcourt.

Bradby, M. (1995). *More than anything else.* New York, NY: Orchard Books.

Calkins, L., Ehrenworth, M., & Lehman, C. (2012). *Pathways to the common core: Accelerating achievement.* Portsmouth, NH: Heinmann.

Coleman, D., & Pimentel, S. (2011). *Publisher's criteria for the Common Core State Standards in English language arts and literacy, grades 3–12.* Washington, DC: CCSSO & NASBE.

Coleman, D., & Pimentel, S. (2012). *Revised publisher's criteria for the Common Core State Standards in English langauge arts and literacy, grades 3–12.* Washington, DC: CCSSO & NASBE.

Dickinson, E. (1951). *The poems of Emily Dickinson* (R.W. Franklin, Ed.). Cambridge, MA: Belknap Press.

Education Northwest. (2013). 6+1 trait definitions. Retrieved from the Education Northwest website: www.educationnorthwest.org/resource/503

Hama, L. (2007). *The battle of Iwo Jima: Guerilla warfare in the Pacific.* New York, NY: Rosen.

Hill, L.C. (2010). *Dave the potter: Artist, poet, slave.* New York, NY: Little, Brown.

Jenkins, S. (2011). *Just a second: A different way to look at time.* New York, NY: Houghton Mifflin Harcourt.

Kinney, J. (2007). *Diary of a wimpy kid.* New York, NY: Amulet Books.

Kozol, J. (2007). *Letters to a young teacher.* New York, NY: Crown.

Learnbat, Inc. (2013, October 15). ShowMe interactive whiteboard 4.2.2 [Mobile application]. New York, NY: Author.

Lewis, J., & Aydin, A. (2013). *March: Book one.* Marieta, GA: Top Shelf.

Lukens, R. (2007). *A critical handbook of children's literature* (8th ed.). Boston, MA: Pearson/Allyn and Bacon.

Miller, C.C. (2007). *Mother Jones: Labor leader.* Mankato, MN: Capstone Press.

National Governors Association (NGA) Center for Best Practices & Council of Chief State School Officers (CCSSO). (2010a). Common Core State Standards for English language arts and literacy in history/social studies, science, and technical subjects. Washington, DC: Authors.

National Governors Association (NGA) Center for Best Practices & Council of Chief State School Officers (CCSSO). (2010b). *Common core standards for English language arts & literacy in history/social studies, science, and technical subjects. Appendix A: Research supporting key elements of the standards and glossary of terms.* Washington DC: Author.

Partnership for Assessment of Readiness for College and Careers. (2013). Partnership for Assessment of Readiness for College and Careers. Retrieved October 24, 2013, from www.parcconline.org

Pearson, P. (2013). Research foundations for the Common Core State Standards in English language arts. In S. Newuman & L. Gambrell (Eds.), *Reading instruction in the age of Common Core State Standards* (pp. 237–262). Newark, DE: International Reading Association.

Ravitch, D. (2013). *Reign of error: The hoax of the privatization movement.* New York, NY: Knopf.

Ray, K.W. (2006). *Study driven: A framework for planning units of study in the writing workshop.* Portsmouth, NH: Heinemann.

Scieszka, J. (2008). *Knucklehead: Tall tales and mostly true stories about growing up Scieszka.* New York, NY: Viking.

Smarter Balanced Assessment Consortium. (2013). Smarter Balanced Assessment Consortium. Retrieved October 24, 2013, from http://www.smarterbalanced.org/

Smith, F. (1987*). Joining the literacy club: Further essays into education.* Portsmouth, NH: Heinemann.

Stamaty, M.A. (2004). *Alia's mission: Saving the books of Iraq.* New York, NY: Dragonfly Books.

Willems, M. (2008). *I love my new toy!* New York, NY: Scholastic.

Chapter Three
Creating Place, Time, and Routines for Writers

Ms. J recently hosted a teacher candidate, Lydia, from the local teacher education program. Lydia spent a week observing and interacting with children just after winter break. At the end of this time, Ms. J and Lydia chatted about the experience.

Lydia exclaimed, "The amazing thing about your classroom is how everything just happens! I think you have an exceptional group of children. These are not like the children I have seen in other schools. They are so responsible! They actually behave! During writing they write and work pretty much on their own! That is just amazing! Kids don't just do that!"

Ms. J was taken back by Lydia's words. On one hand, it seemed to be a compliment. On the other hand, did Lydia really think learning and teaching in her classroom "just happened"? Did she truly believe the children in her classroom were extraordinary for "behaving"?

"Lydia," Ms. J said, "may I tell you a story? It comes from the first month of school. During that first month of school, I teach expectations and routines and dwell in possibilities. Beginnings matter. Beginnings make October through June productive, enjoyable months of living and learning. Use your imagination with me and allow me to walk you 'behind the scenes' of this classroom. Trust me, nothing 'just happens.'"

What do you think of when you hear the words *structure*, *routine*, *responsibility*, and *choice*? How do you or don't you see them related? At this point, how do you imagine them being important to the Writing Studio? Take a moment and consider your responses.

Veteran teacher of writing, Nancie Atwell (1998), tells a story about a time when Donald Graves, a noted professor and teacher of writing, came to visit and observe in her classroom. Here is how she records the conversation:

He [Graves] said "You know what makes you such a good writing teacher?"

Oh God, I thought. Here it comes: validation from one of the world's most famous writing teachers. In a split second I flipped through the best possibilities. Was he going to remark on the piercing intelligence of my conferences? My commitment to the kids? My sensitivity to writing language?

"What?" I asked.

He answered, "You're so damned organized." (p. 89)

Organization—it turns out that possibilities and purposes don't just happen. It takes deliberate planning to organize the Writing Studio, the classroom environment, and writing materials to honor writers and the work they do. Donald Graves (1991) advises "classrooms need careful structuring so that children can function more independently. Structure also helps to integrate the enormous range of differences among children in any classroom. Structure and responsibility must be carefully developed throughout the school year: what is possible in January may not be possible in September" (p. 44).

Return to your earlier musings on the word *structure*. Did you define it as something inflexible? Structure used here by Graves is not something inflexible but evolving, a verb, adapting based on the needs of developing writers in our classrooms.

In this chapter, we explore deliberate and purposeful schedules and routines, organization, and structures of the Writing Studio, the classroom environment, and the careful selection and organization of necessary materials to support developing writers. The chapter serves to organize later chapters of *Becoming a Teacher of Writing in Elementary Classrooms*; return to it often as a resource.

Schedule, Routines, and Structures of the Writing Studio

We know writers need routines to grow writing perseverance and stamina so they can develop a piece of writing from beginning to end. A predictable schedule triggers specific behaviors and supports children in transitioning from one classroom learning activity to the next. The Writing Studio's predictable schedule provides a creative safety net for children and, within this creative safety net, a space to practice choice and individual and collaborative responsibility as writers (Graves, 1994).

The Writing Studio Schedule

Writing Mini-lesson (10–20 Minutes)

Teacher-directed lesson focusing on one or two objectives based on ongoing classroom assessment and overall unit goals. The mini-lesson can be many things, including a teacher demonstration, a shared learning activity eliciting and engaging writers, or a writer share or demonstration. The purpose of the mini-lesson is to directly teach writing practices, process, and/or craft to the whole class. As a routine, children come to anticipate the mini-lesson as the beginning of the Writing Studio.

Status of the Class (2–5 Minutes; Atwell, 1998)

Think of this as a "roll call to action." While there are many ways to do a Status of the Class, the purpose is for children to declare their goal for the individual and collaborative writing time and for the teacher to note these and follow up with writers as necessary. The purpose of this routine is to focus writers.

Independent and Collaborative Writing Time (30–60 Minutes)

The soul of the Writing Studio, this is time when writers use various writing practices, process, and craft to develop as writers. Writers work both independently and collaboratively talking, drafting, researching, revising, reading, editing, and sharing their work. The teacher is engaged in individual teacher–student conferencing and guided writing groups.

Sharing (5–20 Minutes)

The Writing Studio concludes with sharing, celebrating the work that has and is being accomplished by writers.

Schedule and Structures of the Writing Studio: Snapshots

The following are snapshots of kindergarten, Grade 3, and Grade 5 Writing Studios. Actively read for routines and expectations being taught, language the teachers use, and how choice, creativity, experimentation, and adaptation of writers' needs are explicitly or implicitly included.

Snapshot: Kindergarten

Ms. Furgison sings out, "Time for writing, time for writing, come to the rug, come to the rug," and the kindergarteners jump, dance, and scurry to surround her as she stands by a writing pad mounted on an easel in the rug area. It is September and most of the children are still learning routines for being a member in the Writing Studio community. Ms. Furgison uses signals and songs to cue the children and remind them of appropriate behaviors.

Ms. Furgison begins, "Writers, we have been learning how to s-t-r-e-t-c-h out sounds to write words to go with our drawings." She begins a quick sketch on the writing chart. A picture emerges of Ms. Furgison slurping an ice cream cone. Ms. Furgison talks as she draws, "This is me, and I am drawing about this weekend when I took my son and we bought ice cream cones!" Children are delighted, and some remember they, too, had ice cream cones on the weekend. Ms. Furgison says, "I want to write, 'The ice cream cone was delicious!' But I don't know how to spell *delicious*. Can you help me?"

The children use their best phonics skills to help Ms. Furgison s-t-r-e-t-c-h out the word.

Ms. Furgison thanks the children for their help. "Writers, I challenge you to s-t-r-e-t-c-h out your letters today to create words and sentences to describe your stories!"

Ms. Furgison hands children their Daily Writing Folders. This is a signal to the writers that they may leave the rug area and go to their writing tables. It is a way of doing Status of the Class at the kindergarten level. This is a routine she has been deliberately teaching. Skillfully, she differentiates in small ways during this time, sometimes physically pointing a child directly to his or her seat and at other times offering a word of encouragement, "Remember, you were going to write about trains today," or reinforcing directions, "You are going to start writing as soon as you find your table." Children do find their seats quickly. They select colorful markers situated in the middle of the writing tables with which to write. Paper for writing is already in their writing folders.

The mini-lesson lasted just about 5 minutes—perfect timing for this group of writers and their 5-year-old attention spans. The mini-lesson length will lengthen as the year progresses and children mature as writers. Children write for approximately 15 minutes. During this time, Ms. Furgison moves around the room, kneeling beside every child and providing writing instruction and encouragement. Stephen writes about a new toy; he labels his drawing with words. Madeline writes several sentences, sounding out words well as she describes shopping with her mom. Jabon draws three colorful blocks and announces that they are dragons. The only word on his paper is his name. Marcus writes a complete sentence describing a rocket and sounds out the words beautifully—he writes from right to left. These children represent the range of abilities in Ms. Furgison's classroom, all within the expectations for September in a kindergarten classroom.

After individual writing time, Ms. Furgison again sings and signals for children to gather at the rug. They have learned to bring their writing folder with them. Ms. Furgison says, "Writers, I saw such good writing today. I heard you s-t-r-e-t-c-h-ing out those words and using your phonics skills to spell. Everyone open their writing folder and just take a few seconds to look at your good work!" She pauses. "Now close up your folder carefully. This is your beautiful work in the folder, so make sure not to crumple any of your pages. Let's work now to put away your folders in a way that honors your hard work as writers."

Closure is short at the beginning of the year. Ms. Furgison notes that writing comes just before lunch. Children are hungry and ready to eat and play so long closures are not appropriate. Later, children will begin to share their writing with one another but most likely as a mini-lesson or during independent writing time to account for the lunch schedule. At the beginning of the year, Ms. Furgison uses this closure to reinforce children's identities as writers and the routine for care and storage of writing folders.

Snapshot: Grade 3

It is October, and Ms. Lomas' Grade 3 writers are in the middle of a writing unit on the writing process. Writers are able to write in any genre and on any topic. Some writers are writing narrative stories about a recent school-sponsored fun run, others are writing imaginative stories about unicorns while others are writing informational stories about their families. Ms. Lomas has noticed that writers are moving from drafting directly into publishing. She decides it is time for a mini-lesson on revision.

As writers are sitting in their table groups, Ms. Lomas stands in the center of the classroom and begins her writing lesson. "I thought today we should have a mini-lesson on how to move from a draft piece of writing to a final, published piece of writing. It appears many of you really want to type up your books and create a published piece of writing. But when we write a story for the first time it doesn't automatically look like this." She shows one child's final "published" book. "George Lucas wrote drafts of *Star Wars* in notebooks just like this." She holds up Adan's writing notebook. "He didn't write one draft and send it to a studio."

"So, together let's look at my piece of writing and make revisions to improve the writing so it can be ready to publish. First, I will read the draft writing straight through. Then, I will model how I make revisions to a piece of writing. Then you can join in with me to make additional revisions. Okay, let's get started—here is my first draft of writing."

Teaching Writing

Teaching writing can be a challenge for a teacher. I noticed yesterday a lot of you love free writing time where you write about any you choose. I also noticed that many of you want to publish your story. You want to pick up that ward paper off the printer, fold it into a book, illustrate it, and share it with your friends and family. Believe me, I like that feeling, too. I started to wonder if sometimes some of you might be rushing through the writing of your stories? So, I asked myself, "What should I do?"

This question made me think about what writers, like Kate DiCamillo, do when they write. So, I did research and read books published writers. I found out what published writers do:

1. Published writers reread their writing aloud to hear if their story will sound right to their readers.

2. Published writers ask someone else to read their writing aloud to see if their story will make sense to a reader.

I wonder if you might be willing to try these ideas from published writers today before you print your story?

"Well the first thing I want to do is change the second sentence so it will make sense. I'm going to revise it to say, 'Yesterday I noticed a lot of you love free writing time when you can write about any topic you choose.' Oh, and I see that in the next sentence the word should be *warm*, not *ward*. Am I done revising?"

"No," several writers answer.

"How do you know?" asks Ms. Lomas.

"You need to keep reading all the way through your writing," replies Emma.

"What am I looking for when I read all the way through my writing?" asks Ms. Lomas.

"C.O.P.S.," responds James.

"Sure, I will look for C.O.P.S.: capitals, omissions, punctuation, spelling," Ms. Lomas replies, "but revising is different from editing. Editing is looking for C.O.P.S. Revising is looking at the words, the sentences, and the whole piece of writing to see if it makes sense to the reader. For example, I'm going to look back at the first sentence of the paragraph because it doesn't really match the rest of the paragraph. Please talk with a partner and brainstorm some different sentences I might want to use to start my writing." She pauses as children confer with one another before saying, "Yes, Lauren," inviting children to provide sample introductory sentences.

"Teaching kids to stop and slow down can be a challenge for a teacher," Lauren suggests.

"Another sentence that could start my story?" Ms. Lomas inquires. Hands burst into the air. Ms. Lomas calls on Alejandro.

"I've been observing, and I am noticing that writers have been rushing to publish," Alejandro says, offering another introductory sentence.

"Interesting," Ms. Lomas replies. "I can tell you are thinking about writers that you know and how they start their writing to get you interested in the writing and letting you know what the writing will be about. One more topic sentence that I might use to start my story?" As hands are raised around the room, Ms. Lomas calls on Erica.

"Rushing to publish can be difficult for teachers to teach their children," Erica offers.

"Wow. Now," Ms. Lomas says, "I have three topic sentences from three friends. This tells me that you are all thinking about my writing and you care about making my writing better. I'm considering all three of your topic sentences as I revise this piece.

"Now I'm thinking I may need to have a better ending. I'm thinking I may want to end my writing with questions writers can ask themselves and their friends to revise their writing. Turn and talk to your partner about questions I could use to end my writing."

Children visit with one another.

Ms. Lomas says, "Let's share out some of our ideas. Melissa, share your idea."

Melissa comments, "You could ask yourself if the story sounds right."

"Yes, that it is a great idea, and it connects back to what we know published writers do when revising their writing. We could end our writing with the question, 'Could you reread your story out loud to see if it sounds right?' I am also going to add, 'Could you ask someone to read your story to see if it makes sense?' Let's read our revised writing."

Rushing to Publish?

When I teach writing I observe you and take notes in my head about what I notice. Yesterday, I noticed a lot of you love free writing time when you can write about any topic you choose. I also noticed that many of you really, really, really want to publish your story. You want to pick up that warm paper off the printer, fold it into a book, illustrate it, and share it with your friends and family. Believe me, I like that feeling, too. I started to wonder if sometimes some of you might be rushing through the writing of your stories so you can print your stories? I asked myself, "What should I do?"

What should I do? This question made me think about what writers, like Kate DiCamillo, do when they write. So, I researched and read books about published writers. I found out that published writers do a couple of important things:

1. Published writers reread their writing aloud to hear if their story will sound right to their readers.

2. Published writers ask someone else to read their writing aloud to see if their story will make sense to a reader.

I wonder if you might be willing to try these ideas from published writers today before you print your story? Could you reread your story aloud to see if it sounds right? Could you ask someone to read your story to see if it makes sense?

"Today I modeled revising my writing and you helped me find more ways to revise my writing. During writing today, I would like you to let me know what you will be accomplishing. When I call your name you can come up to the board and move your magnet to indicate what you will be working on during writing time. You can put your magnet under (1) writing my draft, (2) reading my writing aloud to yourself, (3) meeting with a classmate to read our writing aloud looking for places to revise, (4) having a writing conference with a teacher, or (5) typing my final draft. Turn to your neighbor and repeat the instructions."

The children repeat the instructions to each other.

"All right, please head to the board when I call your name: Adan, Carolina, Claire, Cristian . . ." Ms. Lomas continues until each writer has moved his or her magnet.

After moving their magnets, writers head off to independent and collaborative writing time. Some continue draft writing; others begin reading their writing aloud to see if they need to make any revisions. After some time passes, a few children begin to pair off to read each other's writing aloud. Ms. Lomas moves around the room conferencing with writers, primarily helping writers with revision.

As the Writing Studio comes to a close, Ms. Lomas asks, "Are there any volunteers willing to share revisions they made to their writing after they read their story aloud or had a classmate read their story aloud?" Many hands burst into the air. Cristian shares how he added a topic sentence to his story about his birthday party and how he crossed off most of his *ands* and has inserted periods and capitals to start each sentence so the reader could take a breath while he reads the story. Morgan shares how she added an important detail to one of her sentences so it would make sense to the reader.

Ms. Lomas concludes for the day, "The strategies I modeled and we practiced today will help you as a writer. You can use these strategies with any piece of writing. Great work today, writers."

Snapshot: Grade 5

Ms. Widmer's Grade 5 class is in the middle of an integrated language arts unit focusing on theme. It is mid-November, and today's mini-lesson connects to the reading lesson, completed earlier in the day on "finding theme," to the writing lesson about drafting a storyboard comic with a clear theme. Ms. Widmer has read aloud picture books and has shown short videos to her class, modeling how to identify the theme of a story or video.

Ms. Widmer starts her writing mini-lesson asking her class, "What are we learning about in reading? It starts with *th*. Tell your partner. What is it?"

"Theme," the class replies in unison.

"When we look for theme do we look at small story details or do we look at big-world ideas that are developed through character and plot?" Ms. Widmer asks.

"Big-world ideas," the children reply.

"Right," Ms. Widmer continues, "We have been reading books and discussing theme. We have watched videos and discussed the theme of the videos. Today we are going to continue working on our comic storyboards related to a theme. Everyone wrote the theme of their comic on the back of their comic storyboard. We want to make sure our comic storyboards have a theme, big ideas developed through character and plot. Let's read through a couple of examples to see if you are on the right track. Okay, on the back of this comic storyboard it says, 'The little boy who got in trouble by jumping the school fence.' Is this a theme, or is this a detail from the story? Talk to your neighbor. Yes, Alyssa, what do you and your partner think?"

"It is a detail from the story," Alyssa replies.

"Take a look at this storyboard. What might the theme of this comic be? Talk in your table groups."

The table groups quickly begin discussing possible themes.

"Blue table," Ms. Widmer says, inviting the children of that group to respond.

"Follow the rules at school or at home," Megan suggests.

"Does someone else have another theme idea?" Ms. Widmer asks. "Somebody at yellow table."

"Maybe like being responsible?" Nick contributes.

"Can you explain your thinking?" Ms. Widmer asks, pushing him to expand his answer.

"Well, the kids in the comic are not responsible, and that gets them into trouble," Nick answers.

"I like your reasoning," Ms. Widmer says and then selects another writer's draft comic storyboard and places it on the document camera. "This one says 'Friendship.' Is this a theme? Why?"

"It is a big-world idea, and the characters are getting to be best friends," responds Colby.

"Yes," Ms. Widmer answers. "Please take 20 seconds to look through your writing folder and decide what you will be working on today. When I call out your name please tell me how you intend to spend your writing time today. You can respond with one of the following options: (1) revise my theme, (2) read my theme to my writing partner to be sure he or she agrees with me, (3) conference with a teacher, or (4) continue writing and illustrating my comic storyboard." Ms. Widmer points to a chart with these options as she lists them. "Alyssa?"

"Read my theme to my writing partner," Alyssa quickly responds.

"Ashlyn?" Ms. Lomas continues.

"Revise my theme," Ashlyn answers.

Ms. Widmer calls out each name and jots down the writers' responses on her Status of the Class sheet attached to her writing clipboard.

After the Status of the Class, writers get right to work, reading their theme and discussing their themes with their writing partners. Soon writers are quietly writing at their desks as they listen to classical music. Ms. Widmer makes her way around the room, checking with a couple of her English learners first to be sure they understand the concept of theme and are able to apply their knowledge to their own comic storyboards. She noted earlier that two of her English learners had incorrectly identified a detail from their story as a theme. Then, Ms. Widmer transitions to meet with writers indicating they wanted a writing conference with her during Status of the Class.

At the conclusion of writing, Ms. Widmer signals writers to gain their attention. She calls on two writers to come up to the document camera and share their theme and comic storyboard. After the two writers share the theme of their comic storyboard with the whole class, Ms. Widmer asks the class to check in with their writing buddy to see if their writing buddy identified a theme and if the theme matched their buddy's comic storyboard.

"Writers, I appreciated the way you were able to work with your writing buddy to make sure you had a theme for your comic storyboard. Tomorrow we will continue developing our stories so we can publish them as an iMovie on our iPads."

 Pause and think about these snapshots. How do the snapshots grow your thinking about the structures and routines of the Writing Studio (mini-lesson, status of the class, independent and collaborative writing time, sharing)? What other routines do you see in these snapshots? How are the teachers deliberate in organizing writing instruction (planning, preparation, classroom environment)? These teachers are successful in teaching writers with a wide range of abilities. Based on these snapshots, why do you think this is?

Beyond the Writing Studio: Writing All Day Long

The Writing Studio is a focused, consistent time for writers to develop as writers. But writing isn't bound to the 30 to 60 minutes of writing during this Writing Studio! Writing happens all day long—not just by accident or decree ("Every child must write in science this year!") but because writing is thinking, and thinking happens all day long as an act of learning. By writing all day long, children come to know how demands on the writer and writing itself changes based on context, writing purpose, and audience. How do scientists write? Why do they write? What about mathematicians? What kind of writing happens in social studies? The arts? Inherent in each of these questions, is also an invitation to join the language clubs of each of these academic areas. The Writing Studio and writing in all discipline areas ought to compliment and support one another. For example, Ms. Lomas in the earlier snapshot is teaching writers to slow down and revise their work. Later in the day during science, she emphasizes to children as scientists to slow down their work and record written observations carefully.

 Are you curious about how writing happens all day long? Check out the companion website for writing schedules for kindergarten and for upper grades.

Organizing the Classroom Environment: Creating Places for Writers

Mini-lessons, individual and collaborative writing, and sharing writing all take place in a physical space. Creating a place for writers *matters*. Colors, desktops, desk size, wall charts, and writing materials available—all send messages inviting, dissuading, encouraging, naming children as writers and participants in the classroom. Twenty-nine (or more!) possible children and one teacher, plus additional volunteers and/or teacher aides, all sharing space, all potentially needing something different as writers and teachers within this space. Because so many classrooms are crowded, making the most of physical space is critical.

Think for a moment what you may need as a writer: Do you prefer a quiet spot, a bustling coffee shop, music (and what kind?), a desk, or a couch? Here are voices from elementary grade writers describing their favorite places to write:

Ashley: In my backyard because I have a deck and it is quiet and I can concentrate or inside in my room.

Zoa: At school I like to sit on the floor or the couch, it is so comfy.

Nic:	I like to write in my desk. I write at home in my room on my brother's bed. We have a bunk bed.
Ezekiel:	Probably in quiet places. When it is really loud I can't concentrate and remember my ideas.
Madison:	Well sometimes I go to my grandma's house. She has upstairs, a little room, a table and I write and listen to music and sometimes the music gives me ideas.
Colton:	My house. If it is an assignment I do it on the computer. If it is a free write then I just like to write on notebook paper or regular paper so I can draw pictures on the back.

Children do not often see the classroom as the best place for writing. In fact, many of the children we survey enjoy writing most outside of school—and that is the dilemma: how do we create classroom space that is inviting and inspiring and sustaining for writers with so many different interests, preferences, and needs?

Graves (1991) advises "the highly structured classroom is a functional classroom 'What is this for?' and 'How does it enhance the quality of classroom living for learning?' are questions you regularly ask of yourself and the children" (p. 45). We have found these questions to be useful as they recognize that classrooms are places where teachers and children *live* and learn, where children grow up: where they develop socially and find identity. Given this, what kind of living for learning spaces do we design? What guiding principles can we employ for the diversity of spaces our classroom may occupy?

Although there is no one right way to organize a classroom, the key is that such space is deliberately and thoughtfully arranged to be in the service of all day learning. We describe specific kinds of necessary spaces to support this goal in the following sections.

Classroom Spaces for Learning

Every classroom needs a space where children as writers can gather to share one another's work, see a teacher demonstration, and engage in shared writing and reading. In kindergarten through Grade 3 classrooms, this is often floor space, designated by a rug. For older grades, because of limited space and larger bodies, children typically remain seated in their desks or tables.

Guided Writing Instruction Area

The guided writing instruction area can be used for all forms of teacher directed small-group teaching and learning. Writers may also gather here to do collaborative work (see Figure 3.1, "Guided Writing Instruction Area").

Teacher–Student Writing Conferences

Teacher–student writing conferences are a mainstay of writing instruction (and are useful in teaching other disciplines as well). Where and how will you meet one-on-one with children? Consider either a separate space with a desk and chair or a moveable teacher's chair, allowing you to meet at the writer's desk or table.

Quiet Space

Some children need quiet, alone places in order to do their writing. Think creatively: where and how might an individual station be arranged to allow a child to work without all the distraction of the classroom? Some writers need music—decide how iPods and earbuds might create quiet space. For other writers, noise distraction headphones do the trick.

Figure 3.1 Guided Writing Instruction Area

Children's Personal Storage Space

Children need a space for their personal things: cubbies, crates, or desks. What other creative options can you think of? Children learn independence and responsibility in organizing personal storage space.

Classroom Library

Developing a classroom library of 500 to 1500 books and then organizing them takes time! (see Figure 3.2, "Classroom Library").

Figure 3.2 Classroom Library

The payoff is worth the effort because the writers and readers of the classroom have access to a wide variety of books to read at their reading level and to use as mentor texts for writing. Become a garage sale sleuth, watch for public library sales, check out secondhand stores, and take advantage of book sales. We like organizing by genre but other possibilities exist: what will serve the writers and readers of your classroom best? (see Figure 3.3, "Classroom Library Key").

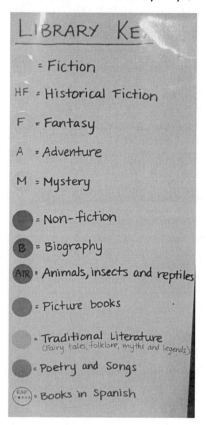

Figure 3.3 Classroom Library Key

Children's Work Area

When working collaboratively or designing page layout, writers need to spread out their work. For example, writers may be designing a large persuasive poster, a big book for younger children, or a mural with narrative text.

Teacher's Space

Honest question: Do you need a desk as a teacher? How does a teacher's desk support teaching and learning? Some of us have found giving up a big teacher's desk provides more classroom space for other more important instructional purposes. Consider other options! Perhaps a small table and a closet to keep personal items secure is all you will need!

A Special Note About Kindergarten Classrooms

Kindergarten classrooms in particular need to be arranged to allow children to play. Children learn through play (Paley, 2005) and there must be space for the youngest writers to move about, explore, and discover. The Reggio Emilia approach to learning is based on principles of community and discovery in a rich and supportive environment (Edwards, Gandini, & Forman, 2010). The concept of atelier, a place of discovery, is critical to kindergarten. The atelier includes many supplies for creative expression and cognitive development.

Not only must class space be organized and structured for learning; children also need to respect and learn about living in these spaces; growing up includes learning how to negotiate shared space. What are the expectations for each of these spaces? How do you envision children behaving, talking, and moving in such space? Plan whole class meetings to discuss the spaces and to collaboratively develop guidelines for each area—and then revisit these guidelines and let them evolve as the year and the needs of children change.

 Interested in learning more about creating a classroom environment to support writers? Visit the companion website and watch a guided tour of Ms. Furgison's kindergarten classroom and Ms. Lomas' Grade 3 classroom.

Stocking the Writing Classroom With Meaning

Writers need access to supplies—sometimes, a writer needs just the right color pen for a specific word to make her writing *POP!* in all the right places. Ms. Furgison, a kindergarten teacher, notes how supplies change based on writers' needs. For example, in December the children in her classroom are interested in list making (wonder why?), so Ms. Furgison provides lined notepads for list making. New supplies are always accompanied with modeling and mini-lessons on how to use and keep such supplies.

Three overall categories of supplies are necessary to the writing classroom in order to support the writer: writing supplies, bookmaking and art materials, and technology resources. Recall Graves' (1991) guiding questions "What is this for?" and "How does it enhance the quality of classroom living for learning?" as you read the brief descriptions that follow and imagine them in your own Writing Studio.

Writing Supplies

Writing supplies includes appropriate pencils and pens, lined paper according to grade level, small blank booklets, cards and envelopes, colored pencils, sticky notes, and spelling aides (personalized dictionaries, dictionaries—paper or electronic.) The instructional purpose of writing supplies is to support writers as they write for different purposes and audiences. Supplies also serve to develop writer's voice, by allowing writers to emphasize text in creative ways (see Figure 3.4, "Writing Supplies").

Bookmaking and Art Materials

Bookmaking materials includes binding supplies (stapler, coil binding machine and coils); cardstock for covers; markers, colored pencils, crayons, and markers; Sharpies; stickers; scrapbooking paper; a variety of papers with different sizes and textures; scissors (including scrapbooking scissors); glue and tape; and other craft items such as ribbons and stamps. Young writers begin the writing process through illustration (Ray, 2010). Through bookmaking, young writers identify writing with the books they are learning to read and discover how writing is meaning making. Conversely, a final book becomes a piece that can be shared and broadcast to others, providing an authentic reason and purpose for writing. Different kinds of books teach writers about different genres and purposes for writing.

Figure 3.4 Writing Supplies

Technology

Technology includes word-processing technology, publishing technology (both software to create attractive final publications and Internet capabilities for creating websites or adding to classroom blogs), applications for tablets such as those that make cartooning easy and fun or allow children to author a digital story with either their own drawings or photographs they produce, interactive technology such as blogs, and moviemaking applications and software (see Figure 3.5, "Carolina Writes With Technology").

Figure 3.5 Carolina Writes With Technology

Technology supports many instructional purposes of the writing classroom and components of the CCSS. Technology allows writers to work with and produce different kinds of text types for different kinds of audiences. Word processing allows writers to revise and edit without simply copying text and can be used to create colorful and informative reports that can be uploaded easily to the Internet. In addition, writers learn to use technology to research and find information to enhance, support, and develop writing.

We carefully select supplies based on who the writers are in our classroom and the writing purposes we hope to achieve. This is particularly important since so many teachers purchase these kinds of supplies with their own money! There may be, for example, several applications for creating comics on an iPad, but which ones will be easiest for a fourth grader to use and will support his or her writing goal to create a story with expanded details and are free? Equally important with all supplies is teaching writers how and when to use them and how to negotiate shared supplies with peers. Finally, a deliberate act of organization is considering the placement of supplies in the classroom. Do you envision writers using supplies at their desks, or do you see writers moving to different areas of the classroom to use shared supplies? If most everyone in the class is ready to do bookmaking, how will supplies be distributed around the classroom? Be intentional in planning and developing routines for the use and care of supplies.

Walls, Walls! Filling Wall Space With Meaning

It is all too easy to tack an inspirational poster on the wall of our classroom, but as with all classroom decisions what goes on the wall is yet another deliberate and thoughtful choice. It isn't just about "decorating" the room. Beautifully teacher-constructed bulletin boards, for example, miss the opportunity to broadcast the good work of writers. Graves (1991) refers to the way walls are organized as a "studio-like atmosphere" (p. 35), with necessary reminders, tools, samples of work, and celebrations of work professionally hanging on classroom walls.

What are options for filling wall space with meaning? We describe a few "essentials" in the following sections.

Word Walls

Word walls (Cunningham, 1995; Pinnell & Fountas, 1998) can take many forms: lists of high-frequency words; interesting "found" words in alphabetical order; commonly misspelled words; discipline-specific theme words, such as "family words"; root words; and prefixes and suffixes to name a few (see Figure 3.6, "Family Word Wall").

Word Sorts, categorizing words by themes or uses, can also be useful. Word walls may represent specific vocabulary study units. Word walls that combine graphics, with definitions collaboratively written by children, are particularly good for English learners. In the Writing Studio, word walls provide easy access to useful resources writers may need. Word walls allow children to operate with independence. They do not need to "ask the teacher"; rather, they need to "read the wall."

Figure 3.6 Family Word Wall

Alphabetic Awareness Charts

Charts that build alphabetic awareness (Bear, Invernizzi, Templeton, & Johnston, 2004; Pinnell & Fountas, 1998) are essential to young writers, including rhyming words, alliteration play, and rhyming charts (see Figure 3.7, "Rhyming Chart").

Figure 3.7 Rhyming Chart

Such charts are used for whole-class, small-group, and individual instruction as the teacher models their use, teaching children how to use them as resources for their independent and collaborative work.

Writing Helps

Writing helps include scaffolds and suggestions that writers can reference easily to maintain the flow of writing. These include genre charts, punctuation reminders, writing organizational schemas ("Three possible ways to begin a persuasive letter"), and process charts ("When I am Done" chart), among many others (see Figure 3.8, "Writer's Reminder: 'When I'm Done' Chart").

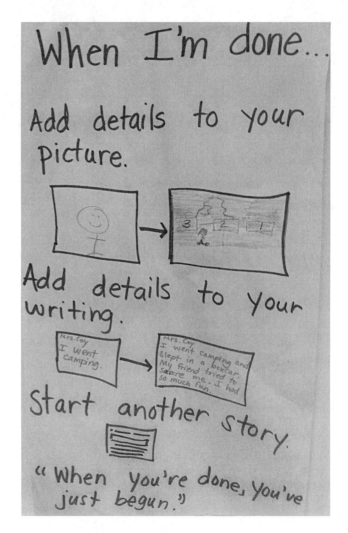

Figure 3.8 Writer's Reminder: "When I'm Done" Chart

Again, be deliberate and thoughtful in selecting the resources writers need at any given time. Because writers are developing and changing throughout a school year, it follows that the kinds of writing resources found on classroom walls will change as well. Writers embarking on informational writing may need reminders on how to find and check sources accurately while young writers just learning to be a member of a writing community might need a wall reminder about Writing Studio routines (see Figure 3.9, "Writing Studio Reminders").

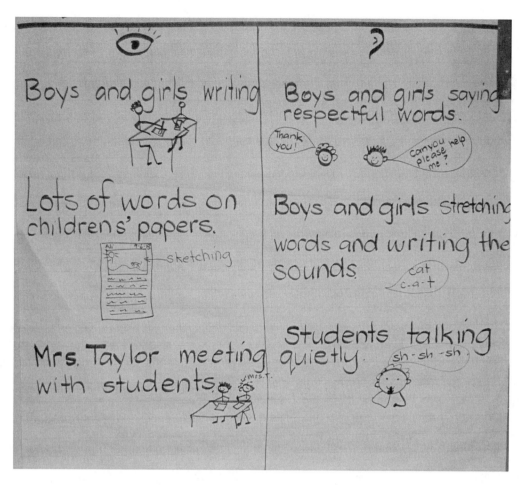

Figure 3.9 Writing Studio Reminders

Displaying Writers' Work

Displays of children's work broadcast "Learning happens here!" Such displays ought to be carefully arranged to honor the work of the writer. Select background color for display boards so that the writing is emphasized. Recycled mat board from art framing shops adds a professional quality to the work of writers. Photos of the author further emphasize an author's importance. A clothesline strung across the room can be an alternative way to display written work. Highlighting children's writing in the hallway or at a local retail store is another way to broaden the audience. Collaborate with children in designing public displays. Such instances can even become math lessons as children measure and design space.

Daily Writing Folders

A final step in organizing the Writing Studio is to prepare the Daily Writing Folder. Each child will need his or her Daily Writing Folder. A plastic folder with pockets (more durable than paper) works well; however, it could be a child-made folder with cereal box covers or a manila folder. Discover what works best for you and the writers in your classroom. Make the folder prior to the first day of school and have them ready for writers the first day of the Writing Studio. Alternatively, in upper grades, have all supplies readied for making the folders and have writers assemble folders the first day of the Writing Studio.

Writing support forms are best stapled in the folder so they are not lost. Again, be deliberate in choosing the best forms for the Daily Writing Folder: Does the form actually scaffold or hinder writing practices and process? How do the forms support writers' independence? For example, not all writers will need a peer conference form—it will be one more step that takes away time from peer conferencing or from writing independently or collaboratively. Yet, other writers need such a form to be accountable. How can forms be differentiated?

The Daily Writing Folder is both invitation and announcement of writing expectation. The purpose of the daily folder provides tangible evidence of writing practices, processes, and developing craft. It also serves to organize the writer for independence. Therefore, the Daily Writing Folder includes the following:

- Current Writing. This includes a record of all the dates a writer has worked with the piece. Expect children to be working on more than one piece of writing; therefore, expect multiple pieces of "current" writing.
- "Possible Writing Topics." This is a formal place for a child to write down different topics he or she may write about in the future. Having a list of ideas for writing keeps the writer motivated and looking forward.
- "My Writing Goals." This is an individualized goal sheet for each child. Writing goals are established based upon writing assessments described in Chapters 4 and 5. Writing progress is tracked through the writing goals form.
- "Spelling Words to Remember." Having a list of high-frequency words is an essential resource for writers of all ages.
- "My Spelling List & Spelling/Grammar Reminders." This is an individualized list of spelling words, taught spelling strategies, and conventions. This list also serves as a way to track writing progress.
- "My Writing World" (optional). This daily log of writing activities records the writing practice of each writer. In this way, the log serves as an assessment for writing practice and development of writing as a process. This is an optional tool for teachers who are not using Status of the Class. For some writers who find the act of writing difficult, completing a daily log can actually distract from writing. Yet, the form can also give directionality and agency to the writer as he or she marks the progress they are making in writing a piece.
- "Peer Response" (optional). The writer records on this sheet responses, suggestions, and questions from peers. This form demonstrates how a writer collaborates with others.
- "Edit Checklist" (optional). While there are general editing reminders useful to every writer, this checklist can be individualized to meet each writer's needs. Alternatively, teachers often create editing checklists for specific genres that are the focus of the Writing Studio.

 Visit the companion website to watch a video of kindergarten teacher Ms. Furgison sharing about Daily Writing Folders.

 Continue your exploration by searching the Internet for additional ways teachers of writing organize and create Daily Writing Folders and the various forms available for the previously mentioned categories. Pinterest is a good place to see what other teachers of writing are using. Experiment with your way of setting up these forms. Discuss options with your colleagues.

Status of the Class or My Writing World charts and the writer's Cumulative Writing Folder are two additional pieces to organize prior to the first day of the Writing Studio. See Chapter 5 for a description of how to organize these essential pieces of assessment.

 On the companion website, you will find a "Beginning-of-the-Year To-Do List" for teachers of writing setting up their Writing Studio's for the first time.

Well-reasoned predictable schedules and routines, deliberate and meaningful organization of classroom space, and attention to detail in folders, forms, and supplies acknowledges that *things* influence who we are and what we can do as writers.

And So It Matters

"And so, Lydia," Ms. J said, "nothing just 'happens' in the classroom. Nor are the children in my classroom somehow extraordinary for 'behaving.' If there is a magic bullet—and it isn't very magical; it is mostly hard work—it may be organization: finding the structures that work for you as a teacher with each new group of children; having a meaningful predictable schedule that allows for exploration, curiosity, and wonder; being deliberate in setting up and maintaining the physical space of the classroom; and taking time to teach expectations and routines. Knowing how to 'mix things' up just enough to keep it interesting, but not enough to turn things into a circus."

Ms. J sighs. "It is a compliment to the children and me that you see this classroom as being extraordinary. We all work hard to keep it this way. However, I do believe that learning really is a very natural human endeavor—I want to create a classroom atmosphere and space that fosters such learning, instead of getting in the way of that learning."

Problematizing Practice

The goals of Problematizing Practice are to deconstruct assumptions and beliefs and to consider multiple responses and implications of teaching decisions. It is best to do this in the company of colleagues and your instructor:

1. Read the scenario.
2. Quickly write down assumptions about the scenario. *Study your assumptions.*
3. Discuss and problematize assumptions with others and your instructor.
4. Discuss and write possible responses to the scenario.
5. Discuss the possible consequences (intended and unintended) of each response.

Scenarios

- A teaching colleague excitedly says, "There is a sale at the local craft store! They have tons of premade bulletin board items on sale! There are things for each season! Let's shop it!"
- When you direct writers to retrieve their Daily Writing Folders from a crate situated in the work area of the classroom, there is a collision of bodies and a bone fide traffic jam. It is chaos!
- You have two computers and four tablets in your classroom. How do you organize their use?

References

Atwell, N. (1998). *In the middle: New understandings about writing, reading and learning* (2nd ed.). Portsmouth, NH: Heinemann.

Bear, D.R., Invernizzi, M., Templeton, S., & Johnston, F. (2004). *Words their way: Word study for phonics, vocabulary, and spelling instruction* (3rd ed.). Upper Saddle River, NJ: Pearson.

Cunningham, P. M. (1995). *Phonics they use: Words for teaching and writing* (2nd ed.). New York, NY: HarperCollins.

Edwards, C., Gandini, L., & Forman, G. (2010). *The hundred languages of children: The Reggio Emilia experience in transformation* (3rd ed.). Santa Barabara, CA: ABC-CLIO.

Graves, D. (1991). *Build a literate classroom.* Portsmouth, NH: Heinemann.

Graves, D. (1994). *A fresh look at writing.* Portsmouth, NH: Heinemann.

Paley, V.G. (2005). *A child's work: The importance of fantasy play.* Chicago, IL: University of Chicago Press.

Pinnell, G., & Fountas, I. (1998). *Word matters: Teaching phonics and spelling in the reading/writing classroom.* Portsmouth, NH: Heinemann.

Ray, K.W. (2010). *In pictures and in words: Teaching the qualities of good writing through illustration study.* Portsmouth, NH: Heinemann.

part II
Assessing Writers: Determining Strengths, Needs, and Instructional Directions

Meaning is not packaged neatly into words.

—Frank Smith

Figure PartII.1 Who Is This Writer? The Importance of Parental Insight

Playing Around With Form – Developing the Idea

Lower your standards and keep writing.

—William Stafford

When we were last together writing (at the beginning of Part I of *Becoming a Teacher of Writing in Elementary Classrooms*), you found an idea for a personal narrative, talked it over with a friend, and experimented with getting that idea on paper by writing and/or sketching. Maybe you finished getting all the thoughts from your head onto paper—maybe you didn't. Either way, before you commit to revising a piece, let's play with your story a bit more. The play involves experimenting with form and perspective to see how your personal narrative might sound, how it might look, and how it might work.

Remember Donna wants to write about her only pet as an adult, a dog named Morgan. After talking about this idea with Mindy, she realized her story of Morgan, and of adopting him out, was more than just about giving up a pet. Morgan's story represents a major transition in her life: a time of moving her home from the high desert and rural country to a city where rain prevailed; it is about leaving a teaching position she loved so her spouse could accept a promotion; it is a story of passion, grief, love, anger, adulthood—ah!—the stuff of life and living. After visiting with Mindy, Donna sat down at her computer and pounded out a four-page draft.

Then, Donna talked with Mindy again because the writing in front of her was an outpouring of emotion spreading across the page like a Rorschach inkblot. "Now what do I do with this *thing*?"

"Play around with perspective and form," Mindy advised. "Maybe if you play with perspective and form, you will find the focus. Play before you commit to revision."

And so she did . . .

Forms to Play and Experiment With as a Writer of Personal Narrative

Remember—this is about *play*. It is not about "finishing" a draft or a product. Play to experiment with form and perspective, to further develop your idea; commit later to more serious composing.

Seeking Perspective and Finding Inspiration From Wallace Stevens

Find and read a copy of Wallace Steven's "Thirteen Ways of Looking at a Blackbird" (a quick Internet search will result in several websites with the poem). What are the different ways you might look at your personal narrative? Play around with different perspectives. You may actually begin to write short poetry stanzas or try a cluster map of different perspective or even write possible (if not so great) first lines.

Modeling: 13 Lines About Leaving Morgan

- *We were young . . .*
- *The dust engulfs, obscures the view, but it doesn't mean it is not there . . .*
- *"How could you?"*
- *The city seduced us . . .*
- *And now, you are an adult, Responsibility whispered . . .*
- *He runs, those small legs pounding the ground, ears alert, silly dog: when will you learn you are so small?*
- *First night apart: where is he sleeping?*
- *"Really, I don't much care. They feed me, too."*
- *If guilt were a tattoo . . .*
- *He creeps in close, in the nexus of bent arm and beating heart . . .*
- *"And now would you cage another to placate your own needs, wants, desires?"*
- *The beagle finds the scent. It always leads him home.*
- *Twice again—he died.*

In taking different perspectives, a writer discovers a variety of ways to focus the piece. Perspective taking is a journey in finding a possible center. Finding a center gives a writer a place to begin and a place from which to travel.

Six-Word Memoirs and Three-Minute Fiction

How much can you say in just six words? Check out *Smith* magazine's Six-Word Memoirs (www.six-wordmemoirs.com/). Is it possible you might be able to capture the moment, the emotion, the lesson, the action—your personal narrative in just six words? Read and enjoy the many six words memoirs on the website. Play around with this form. Does it hold possibility for your personal narrative?

Alternatively, National Public Radio's weekend edition of *All Things Considered* challenges readers in this way: write an original story that can be read in three minutes or less (www.npr.org/series/105660765/three-minute-fiction). Take a break and listen and read some of the stories that have won this contest. What do you notice about them? How do they work? How many words does it take to create a Three-Minute spoken story?

Go ahead: take the challenge. Play with a Six-Word or Three-Minute personal narrative. How do these forms help you as a writer communicate the essence, the heart, of your personal narrative?

Modeling: Donna Plays With Six-Word Memoirs

- *We gave him up—now what?*
- *He runs fast. Can't catch up.*
- *What else did we leave behind?*
- *Dust chokes, hides, swirls: still there.*

- *It may have turned out differently.*
- *A door closes, opens, somebody said.*

Write a Letter or a Letter Poem

Re-conceptualize your personal narrative as a letter. Whom would you write to about your story? Why? Would you write to share this as a common memory? Would the purpose be to thank someone? Or perhaps the letter would be an apology, a rant, or a rave? Maybe the letter is not to a person but to an object, an animal, the weather, or some other being. Or—change the point of view. Rather than you writing the letter to someone or some other being, maybe another person or being is writing back to you about the event you have chosen. Have fun with this idea—go play!

Modeling: Donna Plays With the Letter Format

Dear John & Donna,

I didn't forgive you for a very long time. I mean, really, how could you? We were the best of friends, weren't we? I slept on the bed with you, stayed by your side when you were sick, bounced all over in the old truck you drove everywhere—even barked to help you get it started. We did everything together. So why were your city jobs all that important . . .

Dear Morgan,

We are not going to come and see you anymore. It isn't fair to any of us. You are content, I think. You have open spaces, other dog-friends, and Cathy and Lenny are so good to you. Lenny tells us he has to hold you or you will chase us down the drive—yet again . . .

Making a Writing Decision

So what do you think? Will your personal narrative be a poem? A letter? A more traditional story format? From whose perspective will the story be told? Do any of the alternative formats seem to work for you?

The heart of this writing decision is about what you want this writing to first do for you. The second decision is about audience. How do you want your audience to react? What do you want your audience to hear? What form will best accomplish this? You may need to walk away from experimenting with form and perspective to think about these questions. More than likely you will want to talk with a colleague about your decision. Possibly, you will need to play and experiment more, perhaps even in other ways.

There is yet another possibility: in the act of playing and experimenting with perspective and form, you've decided you don't want to live with the topic you have chosen. That's okay, too. If you find yourself unwilling to work anymore with the original topic, go back to the different kinds of quick writing you did in section *Becoming-Writer: Getting Started*. Choose another topic. Find a topic to which you can commit time and energy to revise.

Writing Goal: Draft Completion

We are asking that by the time you finish reading Part II of *Becoming a Teacher of Writing in Elementary Classrooms*, you complete a first draft of your personal narrative in whatever format you choose. You may end up with more than one completed draft. That's okay, too. Meanwhile, take a little time now to consider what it was like for you to play and experiment with perspective-taking and writing form.

Metacognition Practice

Consider the following questions—chat with a friend (or friends) who also completed these writing exercises and compare experiences:

- Have you ever done this kind of playing with form and perspective before? If so, describe how you have used a strategy like this and how it worked for you.
- Why might playing with form and perspective be important for writers? Would it always be important? What might make the difference?
- Did playing with form and perspective seem interesting, a waste of time, useful, or . . .? Try to describe why.
- What do you learn about yourself as a writer from playing with form and perspective?

Donna Practices Metacognition

I have done this exercise before, however, this time I followed the directions more carefully. I actually had fun with it! It is just play—so I felt like I could be a bit flippant, not so serious with the subject. In doing this, I realize the different ways I might focus my personal narrative. (Actually, I think it is becoming a memoir.) On the other hand, having all the choices is a bit overwhelming, too. I don't know where to focus. Six words doesn't seem quite enough; my four-page draft is sappy and goes everywhere. The good thing: I am going to study my first lines from the "13 Ways of Looking at a Blackbird" and see if I can identify a focus or even if I want to go the route of a poem with different perspectives. I think this tells me I write to discover my writing purpose.

Reference

Stafford, W. (n.d.). William Stafford biography. Oregon History Project website. Retrieved February 23, 2014, from http://www.ohs.org/the-oregon-history-project/biographies/William-Stafford.cfm

Chapter Four
Getting Started: Who Are These Writers? Assessments to Begin Teaching Writing

Ms. J loves how possibility is inherent in assessment. As a teacher of writing, she anticipates how assessment results unfold, how they often surprise, puzzle, or even confound her. Assessments done well, according to Ms. J, are like a narrative, so beginning-of-the-year assessments are the first chapter in the developing writing biography of each child in her class. This is why after a recent school district meeting, Ms. J feels as if the word "assessment" is being hijacked, as if its life is being sucked out by the Dementors of a Harry Potter novel. "Something gets lost in all the language," Ms. J whispers to a colleague, "POWER data, formative, summative, progressive, universal, performance, comprehensive, balanced. All seems like some kind of judgment foisted on children comparing them to an unknown and unnamed norm." Ms. J wearies of the adage "assessment drives instruction," knowing that children drive instruction, the learning needs and interests of children, and the overarching goal that children become literate, inquiring global citizens. "Assessments are tools to learn about children, research tools that assist in writing their learning biographies. Assessments ought to be about what children can do," Ms. J insisted during the district meeting. Although it is true that Ms. J is required to do certain assessments, Ms. J's primary motivation to do assessments doesn't come from the government, or the school district, or to make herself look good as a teacher: Ms. J plans assessments to inquire about what each child can do, might do, might become as a writer, and to plan and individualize instruction that will open up for each child the power of what writing can do and be for them.

Beginnings. We've talked about these before. And it is a reason we love teaching: every new school year is a do-over, another beginning, another uncharted journey with a new group of children discovering what *becoming-writer* means and what writing can do for them. We imagine possibilities, purposes, and goals for writers and we create a physical inviting environment for growing up: growing up as learners and growing up as writers. And then they arrive: all those anxious, excited children, bringing with them the narratives of their homes, their play, and their dreams. How do we get to know these children and their writing lives? Beginning-of-the-year assessments are vital—they provide the data we need to plan and individualize instruction. We can know what a "typical Grade 3 writer" is supposed to do or be able to do according to standard rubrics developed by professionals, but those professionals have never met the specific class of children in a contextualized school and district. And these rubrics are useful, but "typical" may not be the writers seated in any given classroom during any given September, in any given place in the U.S. While children as writers are generally and statistically normed, individually these same children haven't all read the script that defines them. So as teachers of writing, it is critical that we spend the first month of school not only teaching children routines, processes, expectations, and responsibilities but also inquiring what makes each child uniquely "them," writers-in-residence in our specific classroom.

To do so, we borrow strategies from teacher action research because assessment represents an *inquiry*, a desire to find something out, a question we want answered. We speak of triangulating data by collecting observations, artifacts, and interviews (Phillips & Carr, 2014). Other qualitative researchers envision this not so much as triangulation, but data as a crystal reflecting and creating new perspectives (Richardson, 2003) or even as the work of a bricoleur, who like a quilt maker assembles pieces to put together a whole (Denzin & Lincoln, 2007). The point here is that *not just one assessment will do*. Just looking at writing scores from a standardized test will not provide an accurate image from which instruction can be tailored, nor will a review of the previous year's writing scores even if they are from an "authentic" writing sample. (Consider how much children change over the summer). No *one* assessment can provide an accurate portrait of a writer. And so as teachers of writing, we seek triangulated assessment data, or multiple points of assessment data, that best describe the writer and allow us to then envision purposes, possibilities, and goals for that writer.

To this end, we find four basic assessments useful in beginning the narrative of what will become a chapter in each elementary writer's writing biography: (1) a writer survey, (2) a parent/guardian survey (surveys are considered interviews), (3) writing observations, and (4) a writing sample (artifact); (see Figure 4.1, "Triangulated Beginning-of-the-Year Assessments").

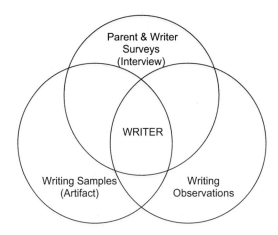

Figure 4.1 Triangulated Beginning-of-the-Year Assessments

Each of these assessments is described in this chapter, along with ways to manage the assessments. We use data from four Grade 3 students, Daniel, Marc, Marisol, and Harper, and model how to analyze data generated by each assessment (see Appendices G–J for the sets). Daniel, Marisol, Marc, and Harper are real students and this is real assessment data. It is not that their work is "representative" of all Grade 3 writers. It is simply the writing data from the beginning of their third grade year—it is where they are at this time in their writing lives. And that is what this chapter is about: taking children at the beginning of the year as they enter our classrooms, inquiring about their writing lives, and planning instruction based on this assessment data, not assuming or insisting they should be at a "normed" level of Grade 3 writing proficiency. We have, however, selected Daniel, Marc, Marisol, and Harper, because they do represent the writing range of development within their particular classroom. This is important for considering whole class instruction, which we do at the end of this chapter.

We invite you to read this chapter through the lens of inquiry: how does each assessment add to the individual writer's biography? Taken together, how do the assessment data answer the questions: Who are these writers? What can they do? How do I individualize instruction for them?

 Apply and practice as you read: Appendix K includes a data set from assessments of Peyton, a Grade 5 writer. After studying the Grade 3 assessments and analysis in this chapter, read from Peyton's data set and complete your own analysis of this assessment data. Find samples of Grade 5 writing at the Education Northwest (2014) website (to gain a sense of fifth-grade writing, as needed): http://educationnorthwest.org/traits/scored-examples. Work with one or more colleagues; collaboration and multiple viewpoints will deepen the experience. Share your analysis with mentor teachers and teacher educators for additional experienced insights.

Who Are These Writers? Writer Surveys

Writer surveys seek the perspective of children in telling their own story about their writing histories. Surveys provide for the teacher of writing a glimpse of how the child sees him- or herself as a writer. A writer who, for example, keeps coming back to spelling as being the most important aspect of writing perhaps needs to learn that while spelling is an important communication tool, writing is more than just being able to spell correctly. Another writer may bring in her writing folder overflowing with fairy tales, covered with pink stars, rainbows, and unicorns. The teacher of writing certainly knows what this writer can do and the genre she is most proficient and interested in writing!

The following key questions can be adapted for surveys across grade levels. Time constraints may shorten the list; choose and adapt questions that get to the heart of your questions about children in your Writing Studio as writers. The purpose of the questions is to inquire about a child's sense of writer identity:

1. What is easy about writing?
2. What is hard about writing?
3. What kind of writer are you?
4. What is a favorite piece of writing you have written?
5. Where do you get your ideas for writing?
6. Are you working on a piece of writing? If yes, what is it about?
7. Where do you like to write?
8. What makes someone a good writer?
9. Is there anything else I should know as your teacher about you as a writer?

Nuanced responses to Questions 1 through 3 often reflect a writer who sees writing as more than a school activity. When a child can proclaim, "I am a fiction writer," then we immediately know the writer has a knowledge of mode and identifies as a writer. We learn from the responses to Questions 4 through 6 whether a writer has had positive writing experiences in the past and how these experiences are influencing his or her present sense of self as a writer. The longer the response to Question 5, the more the writer understands that everything in his or her life is a possible writing topic. A writer's response to Question 7 provides clues on how as teachers of writing we might best meet writers' needs in organizing our classrooms; it also informs us whether a child writes outside of school. Again, the more nuanced response to Question 8, the more likely it is a child identifies as a writer. It is the difference between "a good writer uses complete sentences" and "a good writer makes the reader want to keep reading." We learn from the last question how a child identifies with the title of "writer" and how well he or she can articulate his or her needs as a writer.

Managing Writer Surveys

There are multiple ways to manage this survey. The survey can be handed out to the entire class and time can be allotted for writers to complete it all at the same time. The dilemma here is that writers require differing amounts of time to think and respond to the questions, meaning some writers will finish early and others may feel rushed. One question a day may be posted for writers to respond to as a journal prompt or for younger grades, children can be gathered at the rug area and a teacher can ask children to answer one to two questions daily until all questions have been asked and data have been collected. The teacher can record responses as they are given using an easel chart, a notebook, or a tablet device or even by audio recording the session and transcribing the information later. If a child does not respond during the whole group session, the teacher can follow up individually. A teacher might also have children complete the survey during a small-group session either orally with the teacher writing down responses or by writing their responses individually.

With older children, "clicker" technology may be used. To do this, change the questions so they can be answered with "yes," "no," or "maybe" or provide multiple-choice answers. The teacher can read each question aloud and children "click" their answer into the system. Advantages of this are "instant" results that the teacher can then use immediately as a discussion about writing with her students. Disadvantages are in the nature of the response: "yes," "no," or "maybe" are not as descriptive.

Shorten the list for kindergarten and Grade 1 children and give them the option of drawing or telling their answers. For example, just the questions "Are you a writer?" "What kind of writer are you?" and "What is easy about writing?" can generate insights into a child's writing identity. Children might also be prompted to draw themselves as a writer and then asked to tell an adult about the drawing. Notes can be taken from these sessions, or they can be audio recorded.

We like it best when we are able to ask these questions at any grade level as a one-on-one conversation with each writer. Conducting the interviews individually provides a good opportunity to establish the routine and expectation for one-on-one teacher–student conferences. (Teacher–student conferences are described in Chapter 8.) Alternatively, a teacher's aide or parent volunteer might be recruited to complete one-on-one interviews with writers. Keep the writer survey in the Cumulative Writing Folder established for each child. (The Cumulative Writing Folder is described in Chapter 5.)

Interpreting Writer Surveys

In reading and interpreting writer surveys, follow these steps:

1. Read all of the survey data. Make notes on a separate document. It is nice to organize the survey assessment data into charts, but it is not necessary.
2. Look through your notes: What strikes you as interesting upon your first read? What are your hunches? What else do you want to know?
3. Try grouping the surveys into like-categories of writer identity. After doing this once, regroup in another way to gain perspective. Ask yourself, Why these groupings? What is the common theme? Name the theme or group (and the naming may change). What do these groupings mean to you as a teacher of writing?

How Interpreting Writer Survey Data Might Look (and the Thinking It Inspires)

What we find interesting in our first read through of the Grade 3 survey data is how writers are starting to notice and name the importance of writing conventions and structures and are thinking about what this has to do with being a "good writer." These writers talk about a good writer being someone who uses good details and a topic sentence and includes a beginning, a middle, and an end to the story. These are all topics stressed in early grades. One writer notes that what makes writing both easy and hard is "spelling and making up the story," reflecting an overall theme among all the surveys of these Grade 3 writers as they learn to merge formal structures of writing with their own writing style. There is a difference between teaching what is "correct writing" to a Grade 3 writer and how a writing convention or structure can be useful in making a piece about a superhero come alive. And so a question that emerges from our reading of these assessment data is, "As writers are learning standard writing conventions are they also learning what these writing conventions can do for them in developing writer's style and voice? Are they learning how conventions are in the service of meaning making?" We want to learn more about this.

Next we move to reading writer survey data from Daniel, Marisol, Marc, and Harper.

Daniel's Survey

Daniel answers that he is a "slow writer." When asked about a favorite piece of writing, his first response is "I don't know what it's called." He names a topic, "Christmas," but the lack of enthusiasm and detail in his response may be a signal that this is a piece of writing he remembers completing but that it is not necessarily a favorite. When asked where he gets ideas for writing, he says, "Sometimes books." We hope this is true; however, there is no evidence that he has used this strategy for finding writing ideas in his other responses. Daniel simply says, "It is hard to write a lot," and lists nothing as being easy about writing. As an English learner, he may struggle with English; if so, writing in Spanish could be a good option. We wonder if he has had this opportunity. It could be that too much attention to writing conventions and structures are getting in the way of Daniel taking writing risks. We theorize that Daniel needs a writing success; he needs to tap into a writing topic that can engage his interest and passion enough to carry him through completion of the piece.

Marc's Survey

Marc, in contrast to Daniel, quickly identifies himself as a "fiction writer." Then, with detail, he tells about a favorite story he wrote last year, "Super Donut." He talks about getting the idea for this story from a video game. This tells us that Marc has a good idea of mode (fiction) and genre (Humor/Superhero). However, Marc doesn't have a current piece of writing he wants to talk about, and he doesn't write at home. He describes a good writer in school terms, as one who uses a "topic sentence, facts, details, and a conclusion." While Marc finds thinking of stories to write easy, he finds it hard to make stories longer. We wonder if he has difficultly finishing a piece of writing. It may be that Marc had enjoyed writing in the past, but perhaps he is finding requirements for school writing not to necessarily mesh with the kind of writing he enjoys. Maybe Marc needs to see how "facts and details" can make his "Super Donut" story truly funny. Marc doesn't mention publishing or sharing his writing with others. We wonder if Marc has had the opportunity to have his peers enjoy his work? How might this develop his writer's identity?

Marisol's Survey

Marisol like Marc is quick to provide an answer to what kind of writer she is. She is a "fairy-tale writer." She describes in detail a favorite fairy tale she has written and describes another fairy tale in the works, one called the "Smart Princess." We love her enthusiasm for writing fairy tales. Marisol's responses indicate to us that she identifies herself as a writer. She twice notes that good writing has a problem and solution. She is working on this with her own writing—this is positive: Marisol is learning how a problem and solution can make her fairy tales more meaningful! Marisol notes that "freewrites" are easy, but those 10 sentences her teacher asked her to write at the beginning of the year? Those were hard. This is a caution to us: Is prompted writing the best way to grow Marisol's writing identity? How might requiring a minimum number of sentences have an impact on her identity as a writer? We also wonder what other kinds of genres might spark Marisol's imagination. She mentions watching movies as a way to get writing ideas. What other movies besides fairy tales might she watch that could move her into another genre of writing? And how much is she reading, and can reading also give her ideas for writing? We know Marisol is an English learner who has recently exited from English language development services. From her survey responses, she appears to be mastering academic English, but we know oral fluency can be deceptive and we need to explore her written work further.

Harper's Survey

Harper identifies herself as a writer who usually writes fairy tales but sometimes "real stories." Harper sees herself writing for more than one purpose and is distinguishing the difference between fiction and nonfiction. Harper describes her favorite piece of writing as something completed at the request of her mother, a piece for her scrapbook about the first day of second grade. This informs us that Harper is supported at home as a writer and has enjoyed positive feedback from sharing her writing with others. Even as Harper identifies a writer as one who "gets to think of stories and how to make them funny," she also is learning the importance of spelling alongside good ideas. "You have to learn how to write— you have to learn all the letters and the sounds they make, like *sh* and *ph* and capitals and vowels." Harper has a sense of what writing can do for her: "I like to write because you get to write about your own story and its fun." Writing is a personal adventure for Harper, allowing her to escape into a world of unicorns and fairy tales. In what other ways can Harper learn what writing can do for her?

As teacher of writing at the beginning of the school year, we read these writers' surveys and feel a sense of anticipation in introducing children such as Daniel, Marc, Marisol, and Harper to new genres of writing, exposing them to a wide variety of purposes and possibilities for writing without having them sacrifice their love of unicorns and Super Donuts. These are all places of beginning.

We can read across the entire classroom set of assessment data and find these four writers are representative of three broad groups of writers in this Grade 3 classroom: Hesitant Writers, Willing Writers, and Eager Writers. We theorize that Hesitant Writers need an immediate writing success by tapping into their personal interest. Willing Writers need encouragement to see how the standard writing conventions they are learning can make their own stories more exciting for readers; they may need a bit of direction in finding meaningful topics. Eager Writers are ready to have their writing repertoires expanded, to find new purposes for writing. Because few of the writers in the entire classroom mentioned publishing their writing or sharing it with others, we theorize that such an experience could provide an early and critical experience for these Grade 3 writers. But we want to know more—we can only theorize (not generalize) based on these surveys. So we turn to parent/guardian surveys to continue our work as a bricoleur, piecing together the writing biographies of children to best plan possibilities, purposes, and goals for individual writers in our class.

Return to Appendix K. Using the preceding example, complete an analysis of Peyton's survey data. Include questions in your analysis. What additional information do you need to know?

Who Are These Writers? Parent/Guardian Surveys

A parent/guardian assessment tool is any activity that can bring to the teacher the wealth of home–life knowledge. Parents/guardians can provide cultural context and meaning past stories of learning and can articulate dreams and goals they have as a parent/guardian for their children. Parent insight can provide surprises: "Lania had a tough year writing in school last year. She seemed bored with school writing, but she loves writing fantasy stories and uses different iPad apps to publish these. I wish you could see what she does at home and with her friends."

Furthermore, parent/guardian surveys can shape purposes for writing and writing instruction throughout the year: "I want my child to learn to love writing. I would like for him to see writing more as a form of creative self-expression. (Too bad you can't see him with Legos, though! He is a budding engineer!)," or "My child struggles with being a perfectionist. He doesn't like revision. He wants to do it 'right' the first time. This is the area where he really needs support." The parent/guardian perspective is a critical perspective and a beginning-of-the-year parent survey can be the first step toward a teacher–parent/guardian partnership and thus a positive yearlong learning experience for children.

The following basic questions can be adapted but represent the essence of a beginning-of-the-year parent/guardian survey:

1. Do you see your child as a writer?
2. What have you noticed about your child as a writer?
3. How has your child changed as a writer?
4. Does your child write at home? What does he/she write?
5. What goals would you like your child to have as a writer this year?
6. Is there anything else you would like me to know as your child's teacher about who he or she is as a writer?

Managing Parent/Guardian Surveys

A parent/guardian survey is often sent home with a letter describing writing instruction in the classroom and inviting parents to partner in this instruction in specific ways (see Appendix L for a sample parent survey letter). Surveys often go home with homework or in the school's weekly communication folder. Check with children daily to collect surveys. Teach the routine of taking home a classroom newsletter with this first survey. In early grades, take advantage of the fact that often parents/guardians drop off their children at school. Use this opportunity to personally hand the surveys to parents; give them an opportunity to complete them on the spot. Phone parents as necessary to either encourage them to return the survey or to talk through the survey on the phone. Sometimes, teachers use e-mail or upload surveys to class websites, but this limits the surveys distribution to those parents with Internet services. If languages other than English are spoken in homes, make sure to have a quality translation available for parents/guardians. (Note: Do not depend on Google translation for this type of thing!) Parents/guardians need to know that the assessment data they provide are going to be thoughtfully read and used. During the first parent conference, refer back to the data parents provided, discuss the data with parents, and be able to show how you have used the data in planning instruction for their child. Keep the parent/guardian survey in the child's Cumulative Writing Folder (see Chapter 5 for a discussion of the Cumulative Writing Folder).

How Interpreting Parent Survey Data Might Look (and the Thinking It Inspires)

Data from parent surveys can verify and expand hunches and emerging theories about writers in our classroom. In the assessment data set we are working with, parents/guardians of the Grade 3 children were asked, "Does your child write/draw at home? If so, what does he or she write/draw?" "What have you noticed about your child as a writer?" and "What are your goals/hopes for your child as a writer this year?" Parents/guardians were also given space to write additional questions and comments.

Insights From Daniel's Parent Survey

Daniel's parent chooses to respond in Spanish, so we know that Spanish is the language of the home. This is a critical data point. Daniel's mother notes that Daniel draws and paints at home. We read this a second time (!) and return to Daniel's survey. He does not mention drawing or painting, but if he is doing this at home, if he likes to draw and paint, then particularly as an English learner, having Daniel draw or paint illustrations first and write text later could be an excellent writing strategy. We wonder about teaching Daniel how to storyboard. We consider introducing him to the catalog genre, using pictures and short text around a chosen theme. In response to the question, "What are your hopes/goals for your child this year?" Daniel's mother writes, "I hope it is better than last year." We want to know more. We *need* to know more. What happened last year? This data point provides a sense of direction for us: as teachers of writing, we need to visit more with Daniel and his mother. We need to understand his story of writing and being a writer in order to best scaffold his learning.

Insights From Marc's Parent Survey

Marc's parent identifies him as a writer of fiction, and we quickly note in the margins that Marc also identified himself as a writer of fiction. We might infer that Marc does write at home, or at least he shares his fiction writing with his parents. We wondered if Marc experiences sharing his writing with others. This response may indicate that Marc does have an audience: his family. And this is a good place of beginning. Marc's parent also notes that Marc enjoys writing and "He can describe step-by-step instructions well." We find this useful. If we want to expand the kind of writing Marc does, then we could capitalize on this strength his parent has mentioned. What kind of step-by-step writing might Marc do?

Insights From Marisol's Parent Survey

Marisol's parent responds in Spanish, so once again, we understand Spanish to be the language of home. Marisol, her parent says, is a hardworking student. She writes daily in her journal and she brings books home from the library. She does this intentionally so she can become a better writer. Now we know that Marisol is using books to support her writing—an excellent strategy. Marisol has a good imagination—her parent has seen this in her work. We can infer from this that Marisol's parent is involved in her homework, reading her work, and praising her for a job well done. In all of her schoolwork, her parent notes, Marisol gives her best. Marisol, she says, brings joy to her family. From her parent's description, we gain insight into Marisol's eagerness to do well in school, to learn English, and to make her parents proud. As teachers of writing, we want to analyze Marisol's writing and provide the necessary scaffolding so that her academic English continues to develop alongside her sense of story and imagination.

We want to continue to seek insights from Marisol's parent throughout the year to validate Marisol's progress and to make sure she continues to enjoy learning.

Insights From Harper's Parent Survey

Harper's parent validates how Harper sees herself as a writer. Her parent notes, "Harper likes to write make believe stories usually about princesses or animals. She spends a lot of time writing or typing these stories up in her room." Her parent also writes, "She uses writing and drawing as her quiet down-time in her room. It seems like something that she enjoys because it is not something we have had to force or prompt her to do." When we analyzed Harper's survey, we theorized Harper wrote at home—now we know that Harper not only writes at home but also that she has a sense of what writing can do for her: she can use writing as "quiet downtime." Writing gives Harper a place to think and find herself. Harper's parent notes that it would be good if Harper could develop "precise" sentencing so we now know that when Harper expresses concern in developing writing conventions and structures, this is something being stressed at home along with support for her make-believe writing. "I want her to continue enjoying her time writing and feel comfortable putting down on paper what she is imagin-ing in her head," her parent writes. "I love her imagination!" It is easy to understand why Harper sees herself as a writer. She is supported at home in her writing efforts, with both an audience and a place to write. As teachers of writing, we want to stay in contact with Harper's parents and partner with them to deepen Harper's sense of writer identity and her writing craft. We love Harper's imagination as well: how can we continue to encourage this even as we nudge her into other genres of writing?

Insights provided by parents/guardians are critical and necessary data we need as teachers of writing. When paired with writer survey data, the writing biographies of each child grow deeper. Given this background, we next collect observational data to further inform us as teachers of writing.

 Return to Appendix K. Read through Peyton's parent survey and complete an analysis of the data using the model above. Remember to connect Peyton's survey data with the data provided by his parent.

Who Are These Writers? Observations

Observations of writers at work provide yet another critical perspective of children as writers at the beginning of the year. Some items to observe include the following:

- How do writers get started?
- Where do writers seem to get stuck? What strategies do writers use for getting out of "stuck" places?
- How long do writers stay with the writing task?
- What kinds of writing do writers stay with the longest?
- Do writers collaborate with others? If so, how?
- Are writers open to suggestions?

One of the tricks to successful observations is not to jump to conclusions too soon. Sometimes as writers, we may need to *think* and thinking may look like being distracted. It could be talking with a friend, finding a different pencil, staring into space, or even asking for a restroom break. It is one of the reasons why having more than one observation provides better assessment data about the writer.

Data over time can affirm what may be "distraction" and what may be "need." We can also use writer and parent/guardian survey data to guide some of our observations by taking our early theorizing and forming questions that then guide our observations.

Managing Observations

There are several possibilities for collecting observational data. Every teacher needs to experiment and figure out what works best for him or her. A chart on a clipboard with each child's name listed in the left column with several cells to the right allows a teacher to take quick notes as he or she walks around the classroom over the course of a week. Sticky notes can also be efficient. A teacher can later group sticky note observations for each writer and quickly analyze results. iPads or other tablets or even cell phones can be used to record data as well. Some teachers use photography, taking snapshots of children's writing and then recording notes next to the photos. Important to any observational data is to document the date, time, and context (writing lesson, genre of writing, and any "outside" influences, such as an upcoming assembly, that may be distracting for writers).

How Interpreting Observational Data Might Look (and the Thinking It Inspires)

Observational data continue to develop the beginning-of-the-year writing biographies of each of the Grade 3 children we are highlighting: Daniel, Marc, Marisol, and Harper.

Observations of Daniel

We begin with Daniel. The writer and the parent/guardian survey seem to suggest that Daniel is a hesitant writer. We wonder how confident Daniel will be during independent and collaborative writing time. How does he get started writing? Can he come up with an idea? Observational data show Daniel appears distracted during mini-lessons. We check and find his notes from a mini-lesson are incomplete. When it is time to write, Daniel usually sits at his desk. He appears lost. Across observational data, Daniel only begins writing with the teacher's help. Now we have concerns. His mother indicates there was some kind of a struggle last year in writing. And here at the beginning of this year, Daniel is not writing independently. What can we do as teachers of writing to engage Daniel with writing?

Observations of Marc

Remember Marc's parent (and Marc himself) described Marc as a fiction writer. His parent also notes his skill at writing step-by-step instructions. This is important because the beginning-of-the-year observations come from a writing unit on personal narratives. How does Marc perform as a writer of personal narrative? Can personal narrative capture his attention and motivate him to write? Across the observational data we find that while Marc is a willing writer, he may see writing as a school activity that just needs to be completed. He copies down everything the teacher says during mini-lessons. He quickly begins writing. What he writes is a direct reflection of the teacher's mini-lesson, but the primary goal seems to be to get the writing done quickly, not particularly thoughtfully. He often asks the teacher for affirmation. He does respond to teaching prompts: is he concerned about being "correct" or because he wants to improve his piece? Would this be different if he were writing fiction?

Observations of Marisol

Marisol's parent described her as a hardworking student. Observational data confirm this. Marisol is very attentive during the teacher's mini-lessons, copying down word by word what is modeled. Because

Marisol is an English learner, it is important to check with her and make sure she understands the notes she has taken. We find Marisol often looking in Spanish-language books for other ways to write her sentences. We are reminded that her parent said she brought home books from the library for this very purpose. This is an effective strategy: Marisol is finding and using authentic examples of writing in Spanish to guide her as a writer. We want to support her in doing this. We note she is using a fiction book during the personal narrative writing unit. *Note to us as teachers of writing:* provide her with good examples of Spanish-language personal narrative writing to further support her in writing.

Observations of Harper

Given Harper's strong sense of writer identity and her parent's description of Harper as a writer, we wonder if Harper finds writing in the classroom conducive to her needs as a writer? Observational data confirm Harper is an active writer in the classroom, and they give us additional information into her sense of how writing develops: we discover that she is an active collaborator as a writer and that she seeks feedback from others. We observed Harper and her writing buddy sitting knee to knee discussing and revising their writing. They were both using the conference form provided by the teacher. We observed Harper following up on her conference, immediately revising her writing based on the feedback her writing buddy provided. When Harper is writing intensely, she is "in the zone" and appears focused on producing writing that she finds meaningful. As teachers of writing, we plan to continue to support Harper as a writer, including checking with her about her perceived needs, giving her the agency to name her strengths as a writer, and in providing direction in where she would like to travel next in her writing journey.

Observational data as illustrated provide knowledge of how writers go about the work of writing and confirm or disaffirm survey data. Based on these observational data, we can further plan purposes and possibilities for each individual writer. Gathering observational data allows a teacher to slow down and step aside in the busy days of the classroom with the deliberate intent of seeing just what writers are doing and how they approach writing. This deliberate pause in our day as teachers allows us to reframe and redirect writers in meaningful ways.

 Return to the data in Appendix K. Find the observation data of Peyton and analyze these data according to the model above. How does the observation data continue to develop the writing biography of Peyton? What additional information do you want to know about Peyton after analyzing the data thus far?

Who Are These Writers? Writing Sample

We deliberately saved analyzing a writing sample as the last assessment in our work as a bricoleur. "Why wait?" you may ask. "Why not start with the writing sample?" The quilt maker, as bricoleur, applies knowledge of design when piecing together the many fabrics stitched together as a whole. That bright orange final star applique, for example, stands out on this blue patterned cloth; fades on the multi-pink-colored background, overwhelms the soft solid green. In this metaphor, the context of the applique, the material background where it is placed, *matters*.

The same is true when reading and analyzing beginning-of-the-year writing samples: context matters; background matters. Reading writing samples with the writer and the parent survey and observational data provide context for the sample. We have a sense of who the writer may be—we allow the writing itself to speak to this sense and develop it further. Analyzing a single writing sample is useful—we hope to illustrate this—it can also be dangerous. It is still a *single* writing sample. As with all of the beginning-of-the-year assessments, we should use writing samples to develop our knowledge of each writer in our classroom with the goal of creating purposes and possibilities. It is not our goal to generalize or lock a writer into a box. After all, it is just one writing sample: who knows what the future may bring?

Managing Writing Samples

There are many ways to collect an initial writing sample. We find the following to be trustworthy guiding principles:

- *Collect samples during the first month of school.* The first two weeks is best!
- *Allow writers choice in a topic and genre.* This gives insight into writer's preference and can be cross-referenced with the writer survey question about current and past writing.
- *Allow time for writing.* Use this writing time as an opportunity to collect observational data and to follow up on writer surveys by visiting one-on-one with writers; conversely, conduct writer surveys during this time.

Allow up to 2 weeks for Grade 3–5 writers to complete a first writing sample and gather a 1-week collection of stories from kindergarten through Grade 2. This provides assessment data to analyze by the end of the first month of school.

We like taking notes on a separate piece of paper for each writing sample. The writing sample is placed in the Cumulative Writing Folder, as a first writing benchmark, because the purpose of the folder is to demonstrate writing growth over time. (The Cumulative Writing Folder is discussed in Chapter 5).

How Interpreting Writing Sample Data Might Look (and the Thinking It Inspires)

In reading the beginning-of-the-year writing sample, we avoid using standardized rubrics such as state or national or the 6+1® writing trait rubric (Education Northwest, 2013). Our goal at the beginning of the year is not to find out how the writer might measure against other writers of his or her grade; our goal is to find out "Who is this writer?" To this end, we read beginning-of-the-year writing samples with these guiding questions:

- What does the writer know how to do?
- Has the writer taken any writing risks: made an interesting writing/drawing attempt, played with structure, words, or ideas?
- When reading the piece, is there a sense of *voice*, of the personality or passion of the writer?

In our work as teachers of writing-bricoleur, we place our reading within the context of the survey and observational assessment data we have collected.

 You will find it useful to review the writing samples in Appendices G through J prior to reading the analysis in the next section.

Analyzing Daniel's Writing Sample

As Daniel said in his writer survey, his beginning-of-the-year writing is about Halloween. It is still September, so either this must be a holiday that Daniel anticipates or this is one holiday that he knows is an acceptable school writing topic. (He indicated his favorite piece of writing was about Christmas.)

Daniel can identify and use supporting details: he includes four reasons for liking Halloween. He is learning about topic sentences; he added a topic sentence after a conference with his teacher. He is also learning about writing conventions: after a conference with his teacher, he returned to his piece, deleted extra "ands," and made new complete sentences, with periods. Phonetically, his spelling is accurate. He now needs to learn the nuances of spelling in English. We do not see evidence that Daniel has risked much; this is a play-it-safe, write-for-school piece with its topic sentence and supporting ideas. We wonder about the part of Daniel's writing that he erased and why he did this. Maybe Daniel needed more time to delve into his topic and find its center. Perhaps beneath those erased words is his voice. (We can see he began to write, "I'm going . . .," and we want to know what he was planning to do.) We have a sense that the real story is somewhere in the erasure.

Daniel said he is a slow writer during his survey. Observational data confirm he is a slow starter—often appearing lost at the beginning of the writing period and needing teacher assistance. His parent noted that he draws and paints at home. We wonder, again, how might drawing help him get started as a writer? Perhaps using graphic novel techniques or even a tablet application for comics might be useful to Daniel? Within this genre, he could use both Spanish and English. We come back to the notion that Daniel needs a writing success early on that causes a change in his writing biography trajectory. He does have a sense of writing structure. He can sound out words, and his English can develop with writing practice. He needs time to write. How can we support Daniel in finding a topic he wants to write about and then provide the time he needs to complete such a piece using his drawing and painting and Spanish/English-language abilities?

Analyzing Marc's Writing Sample

Marc has two pieces of writing he started. Both are personal narratives. Right away, we notice that in the second piece, Marc tells his story in chronological order using signal words to show a change in time: "The first thing we did . . .," "The second thing we did . . .," and "After . . ." Marc has a sense for order; we remember his parent writing that Marc did well with step-by-step instructions. His sense of writing structure is also evident in his second piece where he ends the paragraph with a topic sentence—this is a nuanced use of the topic sentence because most Grade 3 writers would only begin a paragraph this way. In his shorter first piece of writing, we notice his word choice: "A tree got split by lightening." *Split* works well in this sentence. There is an emerging sense of voice. Voice is faint, yet when Marc describes good times with friends and his dad, and ends with "It was the best day ever," we have no reason to doubt him.

In considering Marc's sense of order and remembering his description of his favorite piece of writing, the Super Hero Donut, we wonder if Marc might benefit from using drawing, too. Storyboarding might appeal to him; he could layout an entire piece, revising the storyboard prior to writing. This would allow him opportunity to expand his ideas more, a goal his parent stated. Marc, in his survey, said it was hard to write longer pieces, but if he had a developed storyboard, he would know where he was going as a writer and provide a scaffold for writing stamina. Using graphic novel techniques might also appeal to Marc. After all, a Super Donut Hero cries for a dialogue bubble accompanied with a "Bam!"

Analyzing Marisol's Writing Sample

One of the first things we notice about Marisol's paper is how she has carefully erased her name and date (once located on the left side of the paper) and has moved this to the right side of the paper, as modeled by the teacher. We smile at this. Marisol's parent noted how Marisol works hard to be a good student. We see this extra care on Marisol's part as attention to detail. She has written the day's mini-lesson topic in the proper place on her paper, "Author's craft Dialog." We cross-reference this to the observational data demonstrating how Marisol is very attentive to the teacher's mini-lesson; she copied down exactly what the teacher had said. Marisol's parent wrote how Marisol used books from the library to improve her writing, and the observational data illustrated her use of library books to find a word or a correct spelling. Indeed, it is strength that as an English learner, Marisol has no spelling errors in her paper. There is a kind of breathlessness to her paper as she repeats her friends' names several times. We can hear her saying rapidly, "Susana, Andrea, Julissa, Morgan, Emma," while waving hands in the air. Authors use such repeating lines to build their pieces. Showing Marisol how authors do this, we could direct her into a more nuanced use of repeating lines. Interestingly, while the mini-lesson was on dialogue, Marisol's piece lacks dialogue. Because Marisol is eager to do her work well and has copied down mini-lesson notes, this could signal that she does not understand the concept and needs a follow-up lesson on writing dialogue.

Marisol's writer survey was marked with enthusiasm; her parent characterizes her in the same way, calling her a source of "joy and cheer." She is an eager learner and is ready to be nudged into new levels of writing. Her parent mentioned her imagination and Marisol called herself a "fairy-tale writer." In her writing sample, she tells about playing pretend, she and her friends imagining to be other people. Marisol appears ready for a new challenge. She may be ready for chapter-book writing, mirroring her reading at this time. In this genre, she could show playing pretend rather than telling about it and take her readers on an imaginary journey. What might Marisol be able to do with chapter books?

Analyzing Harper's Writing Sample

Harper's writing sample is what we might expect based on the other data collected. We know Harper sees herself as a writer. We know from the parent survey she writes at home of her own volition and has a wonderful imagination. Harper's writer survey tells us that she loves to write fairy tales. And so we are not surprised Harper's writing sample is a delightful four-page fairy tale. She begins with "Once upon a time," the trait of a classic fairy tale. She has a strong sense of narrative with harrowing events coming right after the other: a treasure box, wolves, a dark cave, a boy, a magical flower, and a magical eagle. And amid all the action, she circles back at the end to the treasure box that begins the story. Without a doubt, Harper knows the fairy-tale genre! Her written text is sprinkled with little drawings tucked into the text, with words wrapping the text as might be seen in a picture book. Imaginative details fill the piece: a dog with a flower in his mouth and dramatic pauses, "It was a . . . boy!" There is a kind of rush of detail throughout the story. In the observational data, it appeared that Harper found a "zone" where nothing could distract her from the task at hand. This writing sample appears to be written in such a zone with words tumbling and perhaps Harper's hand just two steps behind where the ideas in her head were taking her.

Harper knows what writing can do for her: she can use writing to "quiet down" in the evenings; she knows that writing can entertain and that stories have conflict. This strong sense of writer identity is a foundation for further developing her genre repertoire and writing skills. Her parent hoped that Harper might learn more "precise sentencing," and perhaps this comment is related to the many details and sentences Harper links in the rush of her narrative. For different reasons than Marc and Daniel, Harper might also benefit from storyboarding. She could draw out all of her ideas and then select the events that most make sense to organize and develop in more depth. Harper is a reader; this is clear with her sense of narrative. The same picture books she enjoys could also teach her paragraphing and dialogue writing skills. Clearly, her illustrations inspire her as a writer and her story. How can Harper use drawing to select events, slow down the action, and make her stories even more dramatic? Harper is ready to author her own picture book!

 Take time now to return Appendix K and to read a writing sample from Payton, the Grade 5 writer you have been following. Read the samples using the questions posted at the beginning of the section on Writing Samples. Combine your analysis of the writing sample with the interview and observational assessment data. What do you now know about Payton as a writer? What do you still need to know?

Planning With the Beginning-of-the-Year Assessments

Who are these writers? What can they do? How do I individualize instruction for them? These inquiry questions drive our desire to gather beginning-of-the-year assessment data. Through writer and parent/guardian surveys, observational data, and writing samples, we do the work of the bricoleur, piecing together data to gain a more complete, if still partial, portrait of each writer in our classroom. Such data inspire us, move us to action, and allow us to plan writing instruction wisely and thoughtfully.

Planning for instruction is tentative, even when based on data. This is how our teaching is a continual inquiry: we gather the best data we can; we plan instruction knowing our data is incomplete; we "test" our plan. Are writers growing in their writer identity, developing writing practices, process, and craft? Are they taking writing risks? We pause, gather data again, tweak, adjust, and start all over (again).

We have gathered the data for Daniel, Marc, Marisol, and Harper. Now we synthesize these data into learning plans.

Daniel's Learning Plan

We describe Daniel as a hesitant writer. Our goals for him are to connect with a topic of interest, to allow him time to work out his thoughts, and to produce an expanded piece of writing that he can be proud of and share with others. We propose to do this by tapping into his interest in drawing and painting. We plan to phone his parent and learn more about his artistic abilities and his less than positive experience as a writer last year. We will introduce storyboarding to him as a strategy for thinking through drawing, planning his writing, and expanding his writing with details. We will encourage him to write in both Spanish and English. Collaborating with Marc could build enthusiasm for writing. Both boys may find graphic novel techniques motivating. In reading, we will introduce the boys to graphic novels of different genres to support their writing. We will make sure Daniel's final product is published and that he receives positive feedback.

Marc's Learning Plan

Marc appears to be a for-school-writer, concerned about being "correct" and "doing it right." We want to capitalize on his strong sense of chronological order and combine this with his Super Donut writing to develop not only his confidence as a writer, but to give him a sense of what writing might do for him. As with Daniel, we plan to introduce him to storyboarding, thus building on his strength in organization. We want to "test" whether the combination of storyboarding and graphic novel techniques can increase his excitement for writing and grow his independence as a writer. We plan to propose collaboration between Marc and Daniel, knowing that talk can generate ideas.

Marisol's Learning Plan

Marisol is already using texts as mentors. She finds books from the library and uses them as a resource for vocabulary and spelling. We plan to ask Marisol to identify a book she really loves, one that she might want to use as a model for her own book, and then use the structure of the chosen book to help her organize and expand her writing. Marisol is reading simple chapter books, so *Henry and Mudge* (Rylant, 1996) or *Mr. Putter & Tabby* (Rylant, 2013) books could be inspiring models for her. We think Marisol will love using a favorite author as a model, and we hope to see her writing become more organized, include a better sense of narrative, and use expanded details to show rather than tell during this first writing unit.

Harper's Learning Plan

We want to support Harper's sense of herself as a writer—not get in the way of it! Our goal is for Harper to learn a more nuanced approach to developing a focused narrative. We will begin with her love of fairy tales and move towards other genres after beginning the year with what we hope will be a rewarding experience for her. Harper is a reader and we think the use of a mentor text will scaffold her learning. *Magic Box* (Cleminson, 2009) is a "Harper story." Illustrations are carefully intertwined with text—a strategy Harper is attempting to use in her writing sample. Eva, the character in the story, performs a series of magic tricks, each one bigger and better. Harper can learn from Cleminson (2009) how to select story events that develop the narrative through this model. We plan to introduce Harper to storyboarding to bring together her love of drawing and narrative and to help her strategize her story prior to drafting it.

 Take a step back and read again your analysis of Peyton as a writer. (The data are in Appendix K.) If you were the teacher, how would you structure beginning-of-the-year writing instruction for Peyton? What goals might you write? How does your plan and goals reflect the data? Share and discuss your analysis and your writing plan with your colleagues. And begin now developing the informal practice of observing, interviewing, and studying children as writers and their writing as a daily way of being a teacher of writing.

At the beginning of this chapter, we noted that we could cluster the other writers of this Grade 3 classroom into three groups as illustrated by Daniel, Marc, Marisol, and Harper. This means that the learning goals and plans we have for these writers are similar for other children within their cluster. We will use these data to plan small, guided-writing instruction (see more on guided writing in Chapter 8), as well as to plan our beginning-of-the-year writing mini-lessons and writing unit. (Mini-lessons are described in Chapter 7; see more on how to plan units in Chapters 10 and 11.)

 We have used Grade 3 writing data for this chapter, and if you have been completing the practice opportunities, you have also worked with data from Peyton, a Grade 5 writer. The companion website includes an illustrative analyzed data set of a kindergarten writer to better understand how beginning-of-the-year assessments are used with early writers.

Our inquiry into what each child can do as a writer, leads us to imagine who each child might become as a writer and to plan meaningful and powerful individualized and group writing instruction. We do this by taking time to collect beginning-of-the-year assessment data to guide us as teachers of writing. We don't just "start teaching" or plunge blindly into the curriculum published for the grade we are teaching, or risk making assumptions based on what we "know about third graders." Rather, we listen, observe, and begin the task of learning from each new group of children as writers—and this is what makes the difference that matters, differentiating writing instruction by focusing on writers, beginning where they are, and developing next steps to develop their writing practices, process, and craft.

 This chapter models and illustrates four basic beginning-of-the-year assessments we can use as teachers of writing. Delve a little deeper into the concept of beginning-of-the-year writing assessments by considering and dialoguing with colleagues and mentor teachers about any of the following: (a) What do you need to personally learn in order to use these writing assessments to their fullest potential? How do you plan to learn this? (b) What additional data do you think may be useful at the beginning of the year? (c) If time is limited, which of the beginning-of-the-year assessments seem most important to you? Why?

Problematizing Practice

The goals of Problematizing Practice are to deconstruct assumptions and beliefs and to consider multiple responses and implications of teaching decisions. It is best to do this in the company of colleagues and your instructor:

1. Read the scenario.
2. Quickly write down assumptions about the scenario. *Study your assumptions.*
3. Discuss and problematize assumptions with others and your instructor.
4. Discuss and write possible responses to the scenario.
5. Discuss the possible consequences (intended and unintended) of each response.

Scenario

Alonso is a Grade 5 English learner in your Writing Studio. Through beginning-of-the-year assessments, you learn that Spanish is the language of the home. Alonso's parent writes that he would "rather play than write." Alonso does tell you about writing a techno adventure story with a friend last year of which he is proud. During writing observations, you notice he does not stay with writing long unless he is working with friends.

A sample of Alonso's writing can be found in Figure 4.2, "Alonso's Writing Sample."

If you are not familiar with Grade 5 writing, you may find it useful to read sample writing found at the Education Northwest (2014) website: http://educationnorthwest.org/traits/scored-examples. Equally useful in analyzing this sample is the Grades 4–5 English Language Proficiency (ELP) Standards (Council of Chief State School Officers, 2013). You can find a copy at this website: http://www.ode.state.or.us/opportunities/grants/nclb/title_iii/elpstandards_gr4–5__elagr4.pdf.

How will you plan for Alonso's writing instruction?

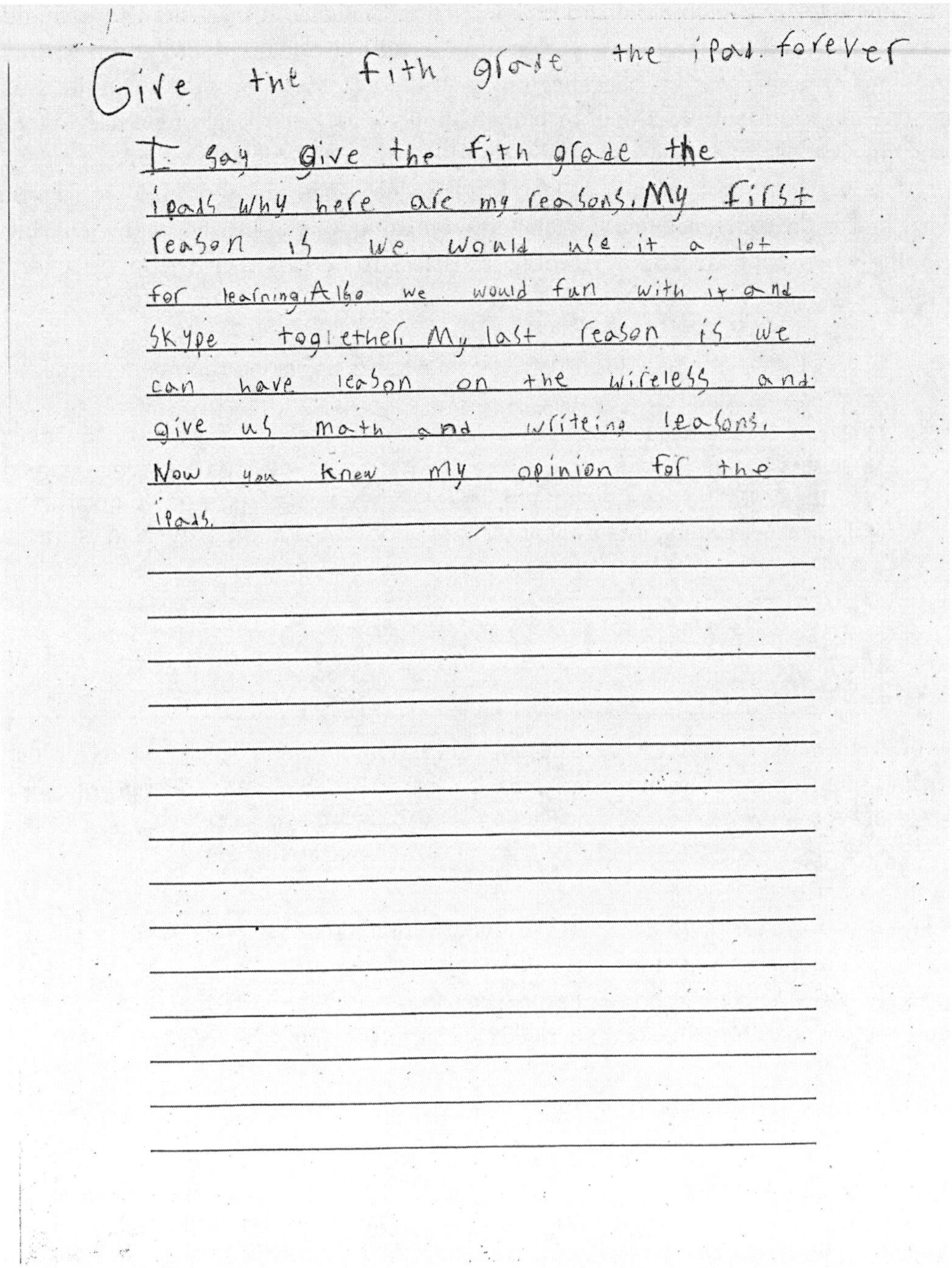

Give the fith grade the iPad. forever

    I say give the fith grade the
iPads why here are my reasons. My first
reason is we would use it a lot
for learning. Also we would fun with it and
Skype toglether. My last reason is we
can have leason on the wireless and
give us math and writeing leasons.
Now you knew my opinion for the
iPads.

Figure 4.2 Alonso's Writing Sample

References

Council of Chief State School Officers. (2013, October 17). Grades four-five English language proficiency (ELP) standards. Retrieved February 24, 2014, from Oregon Department of Education: http://www.ode.state.or.us/search/results/?id=36

Cleminson, K. (2009). *Magic box.* New York, NY: Hyperion.

Denzin, N. K., & Lincoln, Y. S. (Eds.). (2007). *The landscape of qualitative research* (3rd ed.). Thousand Oaks, CA: Sage.

Education Northwest. (2013). 6+1® trait rubrics. Retrieved from http://educationnorthwest.org/traits/traits-rubrics

Education Northwest. (2014). 6+1® trait writing scoring examples. Retrieved from http://educationnorthwest.org/traits/scored-examples

Phillips, D. K., & Carr, K. (2014). *Becoming a teacher of action research: Process, context and self-study* (3rd ed.). New York, NY: Routledge.

Richardson, L. (2003). Writing: A method of inquiry. In N. K. Denzin, & Y. S. Lincoln (Eds.), *Collecting and interpreting qualitative materials* (pp. 499–541). Thousand Oaks, CA: Sage.

Rylant, C. (1996). *Henry and Mudge.* New York, NY: Aladdin.

Rylant, C. (2013). *Mr. Putter & Tabby.* New York, NY: Houghton Mifflin Harcourt.

Chapter Five
Assessments to Inform and Celebrate Writers and Teachers of Writing

"New Teacher Accountability Measures Begin"

The newspaper headline riles Ms. J. "Teacher accountability" is one of those phrases that push all her buttons. As if teacher accountability was a new thing. As if teachers are not accountable. As if SHE is not accountable. As if "someone" has to force her to be accountable. She is going to need a run, a long run, with hills.

As a Teacher, one with a capital T as Nancie Atwell (1998) would say, Ms. J is always already accountable—not to some authority "out there," but as a Teacher, as one who knows her students, who understands their cultural context; as a Teacher who mentors, facilitates and directs learning; as a Professional Educator who is knowledgeable about disciplinary content, human development, pedagogy; as to teach, a calling, a way of being. Being accountable is her DNA as a Teacher. As a Teacher of Writing, she is first accountable to the writers-in-residence in the Writing Studio of her classroom. This means she is accountable to the work of writing—extending the invitation to make meaning, to think deeply, to create in many ways, to communicate widely—to make one's humanity visible. She is accountable to these writers' parents, guardians, extended families, and community because as writers and global citizens they will write a present and a future in which we are all part. Accountable? Ms. J pounds the table—absolutely, but long before "someone" decided that evidently she was NOT accountable and now needs to be "held accountable."

As her feet pound against the pavement, Ms. J breathes deeply and considers "accountability" all over again. Here is what she knows about accountability: it begins with organized, meaningful, and intentional assessments that matter. Of course, Teachers ought to know how, how much, and under what conditions children are learning. Of course, Teachers ought to be able to give an accounting of learning progress to the child first and then everyone else who loves and is interested in that child— and they ought to be able to do this quickly and efficiently. "Teaching isn't teaching without account- ability—without valid and reliable authentic assessments that allows me to be accountable," she gasps aloud on the uphill part of the run. Teachers use their skills of analysis to interpret assessment data *and plan accordingly—this is accountability. Ms. J dismisses statements that "teachers are too busy" when it comes to assessments. "Assessments are teaching so how can they be too busy? It is our job!" She also notes that some assessments do distract from teaching and learning—these are the assessments she resents. Ms. J dismisses the notion that assessments that really "count" are administered through standardized measures and must be graded by someone "outside" as a means of "objectivity". "Don't even get me started on that one!" she shouts on the downhill. She recalls a quote from author and teacher of writing Regie Routman (2005) talking about assessment: "There is no shortcut to helping students become effective writers, and there is no program you can buy that will do it for you" (p. 240). "Amen!" She puffs up another hill. "And furthermore, I don't want anyone to do it for me. I am the Teacher! And, yes, I am accountable!"*

Authentic assessments evaluate and value what writers do—and what is it that writers do? The work of a writer is one of *practice*, *process*, and *craft*. Practice speaks to the writing life of the writer. This is the daily habit of writing, sometimes for shorter and then longer purposes. It is the way a writer finds ideas, uses writing as thinking, seeks out information, and organizes and prioritizes writing tasks (CCSS Writing Anchor Standards 8 & 10). Process refers to the stops and starts and cycles of writing—the use of revision, seeking additional information, asking for and giving feedback, editing and choosing how a final piece is published and broadcasted (CCSS Writing Anchor Standards 5 & 6). Craft encompasses the wide variety of modes, voice, style, word choice, organization, conventions, use of sentencing, and creative twists and turns that capture the reader's attention (CCSS Writing Anchor Standards 1, 2, 3, 4, 7 & 9).

TABLE 5.1 Writing Studio Assessments

Types of Writing Assessment	Purpose	Frequency?
Status of the Class, My Writing World	Determines how each child's writing is progressing through the writing process (brainstorming, drafting, revising, editing, publishing, broadcasting).	Daily for Grades 3–5 Completed informally for Grades K–2
Teaching, Conferencing & Planning Notebook	Documents writing development. Used to prompt and document writing conferences and guided writing. Data used to plan writing instruction.	Daily. Goal to complete individual conferences with each writer every two weeks; guided writing as necessary.
Daily Writing Folder	Document writers' ongoing and developing writing practices, process, and craft.	Writers use daily. Assessed by teacher formally monthly or after each writing unit; informally during individual conferences as needed.
Cumulative Writing Folder	Writers and teacher select key pieces of writing to document writers' growth throughout the school year.	Select 3–5 (Grades K–2) or 1–2 (Grades 3–5) pieces of writing each quarter.
Self-Assessment	Provide time for students to think about their progress, future goals and to celebrate writing development in practice, process, and craft.	Every grading period (Grades K–2) or after each final piece of writing is completed (Grades 3–5).
Writing Sample	Assess a piece of writing using a writing rubric for genre criteria, writing traits, etc.	A minimum of one piece of writing per grading period.

Authentic writing assessment generates data that inform the writer, the teacher of writing, parents/guardians, and specialists how a writer is developing practices, process, and craft; the data is also used to celebrate what writers can do. The data generated from authentic writing assessments become the basis for intentional whole-group and individualized instructional planning. Writing assessment, as an ongoing practice of teaching, is in the service of the developing writer and should not distract from writing, burden the process, or impede the practice. Ask of every writing assessment, "Why am I doing this? Are the results of the assessment worth the time it takes to administer the assessment? Do the results energize and inform conversations about practices, process, and craft of writing, provide occasion to celebrate a writer's success?" It is our job as teachers of writing to ensure writing assessments result in improved teaching and learning.

In this chapter, six types of assessments to guide teaching and learning in the Writing Studio are described. These assessments include Status of the Class or My Writing World; Teaching, Conferencing & Planning Notebook; Daily Writing Folders; Cumulative Writing Folders; self-assessment; and writing samples. Each has a specific purpose and is collected at different times during the year. (See Table 5.1 Writing Studio Assessments.)

The assessments allow the teacher of writing to act as authoritative and professional bricoleur, the quilt maker piecing together the emerging biography of each writer-in-residence in his or her classroom. They honor writing as practice, process, and craft and, completed thoughtfully, provide living data over time that can be analyzed and synthesized resulting in agency for the writer and his or her teacher.

Status of the Class, My Writing World

Status of the Class is a term and procedure we borrow from Nancie Atwell (1998). It is a procedure to organize writers and scaffold independence during independent and collaborative writing time. The teacher cues writers, "Writers, it is time now to transition to our writing time. Please take a moment to open your Daily Writing Folder, look at your work from yesterday, and determine how you will use your writing time wisely today." Writers take about two to three minutes to consider their plan for the day. Writers whom teachers know will require more time to plan or need explicit instruction in finding a writing task for the day are best cued and prompted prior to the Writing Studio. The teacher then calls the name of each writer and records their plan on a Status of the Class chart that is organized to best work for them. The process must be taught and practiced to be efficient. Later, during the Writing Studio, the teacher holds writers accountable in part by referring to the Status of the Class: "You indicated you were working on a first draft of your fantasy. You are not. What has changed?"

Weekly or daily templates can be created and photocopied for easy use. Conversely, creating Status of the Class charts on a tablet allows a teacher to quickly include photos of writers' work or of the writer writing. The charts can be backed up to cloud technology and password protected. (See Mr. Mackie's Status of the Class in Appendix M for an example.)

In the primary grades, Status of the Class can be as simple as "Turn to your writing partner and tell him or her what you are going to write about today." The teacher listens in as writers share their plans for writing. The teacher might excuse writers from the carpet area by saying, "Stand up if you shared what you plan to write about today. Go ahead and head to writing. If you do not know what to write about today, please stay on the carpet." For any writers left in the carpet area, the teacher can help them brainstorm possible writing options.

Alternatively, My Writing World can be used for the same purpose as Status of the Class. My Writing World is a daily log writers complete at the end of the Writing Studio. Writers list the work they have completed usually at the direction of the teacher just before share time at the end of the period.

At the beginning of the Writing Studio, use My Writing World to focus writers by directing them to read their log and determine their writing intentions for the day. The key is making sure that each writer completes the log. For some writers, completing the log can take time away from writing; make sure to monitor and adjust for this.

 View a My Writing World example on the companion website.

Using either Status of the Class or My Writing World scaffolds writers' independence and decision making by providing time for writers' to set a writing goal, or goals, for the day.

Illustrations of Status of the Class: How It Works

The Status of the Class chart is daily documentation of developing writing practices and writing process. Study the Status of the Class for Mr. Mackie's Grade 5 class found in Appendix M. This Status of the Class was taken during one week of Writing Studio during a nonfiction, integrated science writing unit. Children were conducting an inquiry about disappearing songbirds in their community. Prior to this week, Mr. Mackie and his Grade 5 writers inquired into the nature of science writing in a variety of nonfiction genres. This is reflected in the kinds of writing writers are composing during this week in February: some are writing and designing an informative web page, others are creating picture books, some crafting chapter books, one writer is creating an educational game board, several are designing posters suitable for a classroom, and a few passionate writers are drafting letters to either the newspaper or their state senator. One writer requires more structure and is composing with a writing template on the computer.

As a daily assessment of writing practice, Mr. Mackie can quickly review the Status of the Class chart and see how writers Marcos and Francis; Xavier, Weston, and Rajesh; and Enzo, Joaquin, and T. J. are developing collaborative practices around web design and writing. This is a particularly good project for collaboration, reflecting the work of authentic web developers. Bella and Hallie are also developing collaborative skills. Mr. Mackie notes this is the first time either writer has worked collaboratively on a project. On the other hand, he notes that Esteban and Austin are once again collaborating, and while they are successful as collaborators, it may be time to challenge them to work on the next piece independently. Mr. Mackie will use this information to adjust their individual writing goals.

When Mr. Mackie looks across the weeks of the Status of the Class charts he has collected, he can find evidence of how writers such as Alannah, Jade, Ada, and Yolanda are developing independence in their practice. Yolanda, for example, was hesitant as a writer at the beginning of the year, depending heavily on Ada as a writing partner. But now, she is successfully writing independently. Her development is recorded in the Status of the Class charts.

Status of the Class charts, over time, also provide evidence of writing risk or of how writers are using a variety of text types and purposes in their writing process. Mr. Mackie can look back, for example, and see, to date, the various kinds of genres any given writer has experimented with and, based on this, guide writers to explore other text types and purposes. Furthermore, Status of the Class charts document the decisions a writer is making regarding research, revisions, and editing needed, given factors such as purpose and length of the piece. Mr. Mackie notes that Lilly, for example, requested a teacher conference on Monday to provide direction in her writing. Following the teacher conference, Lilly drafted a letter poem. Next, she requested a peer conference with Suelita, which prompted Lilly to complete additional research and another cycle of revision. The Status of the Class documentation demonstrates how Lilly is developing in writing process, making wise writing decisions in seeking feedback and using this feedback to further refine her work.

Mr. Mackie uses the data from the Status of the Class chart on a daily basis to determine with whom he will hold one-on-one writing conferences. Sometimes, such writing conferences are done at the request of writers. However, Mr. Mackie reads across the columns of his Status of the Class chart to check his pattern of conferencing and notes anyone he may have overlooked; he then schedules conferences with those writers. He also checks for writers who appear stuck in the process of writing. For example, he knows most writers in his class do not need three days to conduct research on their writing topic. So when he sees that Esteban and Austin have declared "research" as their intention for a third day in a row, he will check in with them. Colin and Kara require additional scaffolding because of writing learning disabilities; the Status of the Class chart allows Mr. Mackie to check in and monitor their progress daily. Most of the writers in Mr. Mackie's class are English learners. However, Caesar is still receiving English language development services, and Xavier, Yolanda, and Rajesh have recently exited this program. He is careful to note their progress and uses the Status of the Class to make sure he is regularly checking their progress. Status charts allow Mr. Mackie to continually develop writers' ability to research and present knowledge.

Mr. Mackie also uses the data from the Status of the Class chart to plan instruction for the Writing Studio. His planning reflects overall goals for writers' growth in practices, process, and craft as well as writers' individualized goals. During the week highlighted in the Status of the Class chart from February 10, Mr. Mackie conducted mini-lessons and one-on-one teacher conferences. It doesn't always work out this way, but the week before, Mr. Mackie had modeled and writers had practiced researching a topic and experimented with the writing genres present in the current week's Status of the Class chart. Mr. Mackie felt writers needed time to work individually and collaboratively with other writers to compose drafts. This allowed him time to conduct individual conferences with writers to make sure each writer had a writing topic and genre they were satisfied with prior to moving into the next week. The mini-lessons for the week of February 10, then, focused on the research and draft work writers do. By the end of this week, however, Mr. Mackie reviewed the Status of the Class chart and, based on these data, is making instructional decisions about guided writing, targeted small-group instruction, for specific instructional purposes, the following week (see Chapter 9 for a description of guided writing).

The Status of the Class chart and the My Writing World form documents writers' development of writing practices and process, providing daily assessment data for the teacher of writing in planning intentional instruction to scaffold writers. The data from these sources are particularly powerful when paired with data generated from the Teaching, Conferencing & Planning Notebook.

Teaching, Conferencing & Planning Notebook

The Teaching, Conferencing & Planning Notebook, as an assessment tool, is critical in prompting and documenting writing conversations, adjusting and monitoring individual writer's goals, and intentional planning of writing instruction. The Teaching, Conferencing & Planning Notebook provides further data about writing practices, how writers are using process, and are developing writing craft.

The Teaching, Conferencing & Planning Notebook must be portable as the teacher is most often moving around the classroom conducting mini-lessons, one-on-one conferences, and guided writing instruction with the notebook in hand. To be useful, conference notes must be dated and organized in a way to allow for both quick review and longer analysis. Here are some effective ways of organizing the notebook: (a) Create a 3-ring notebook with a page for each writer. Document the date and topic of teacher–student conferences, include notes for future teaching, include any summary reviews of writing samples, and salient observations of children writing. (b) Create a portable chart similar to a weekly Status of the Class. Use a clipboard and write quick notes after each conference—later organize these into a notebook. (c) Use sticky notes and a clipboard; organize the notes later in a conference notebook organized by writer. (d) Use tablet technology. This technology will allow for enhancing notes with photographs. For all these organizational methods, allow space for sifting through the data and using these data to plan for future instruction.

The teacher and the writer can collaborate in writing the conference notes: "Look here—just three weeks ago you didn't know how to write dialogue or show how people talk. Yet—look today—you did this on your own! How shall I record this in my notebook?" In this way, the notebook provides opportunities to increase a writer's sense of agency through celebrating what has been learned.

Illustrations of Teaching, Conferencing & Planning Notebook: How It Works

Read the following excerpts from Mr. Mackie's Teaching, Conferencing & Planning Notebook.

Mr. Mackie's Teaching, Conferencing & Planning Notebook: Lilly

Week of: February 10

Monday:

Lilly requested conference. Found notes on poetry formats (letter, diamond, found, haiku, free verse). Talked through which form would suit purpose best—wants to inform people of the plight of songbirds. (Great to see Lilly thinking about form and purpose together!) Decided on letter—can include more facts, be more convincing. Next step: write as letter and then work into poem.

Friday:

Lilly reports that Suelita thought she needed to focus on just one bird. Note: Using peer conferencing well. Found interesting facts about Junco. Now turning actual letter into poem form. Instruction: how free verse doesn't use complete sentences. Modeled. She did line on her own. Ready to go—considering poster as publishing—good she is thinking of this now. Guided writing group with Suelita, Caesar, Colin, and Kara on poster design.

Mr. Mackie's Teaching, Conferencing & Planning Notebook: Caesar

Week of: February 10

Monday:

Caesar requested conference—good decision. Read article in Spanish about cats killing urban birds. He is upset about this. Needs direction. Created graphic organizer for him to organize his thoughts.

Wednesday:

Caesar requested conference. Needed to determine next step. We discussed his purpose for writing: what does he want to communicate and how? Decided on poster: Save the Songbirds! Has research chart completed. Will create graphic illustrations to go on poster. Writing some dialogue bubbles in Spanish; some in English.

Mr. Mackie's Teaching, Conferencing & Planning Notebook: Kara

Week of: February 10

Monday:

Set Kara up on computer with headphones so she can focus. Reading from interactive website on birds. She is engaged.

Tuesday:

Talked about writing purpose: to inform. Set goal for Kara: Write five sentences describing five different birds. Set up template for her to complete on computer with sentences numbered 1–5. Took a bit of prompting but Kara completed four sentences! Note: Bella helped her several times.

Wednesday:

Helped Kara complete her fifth sentence. Created column on template for Kara to find a picture of each bird. Seems to like this task. Note: Xavier helped her with a picture.

Thursday:

Set up Kara on computer—she is still finding pictures. Doing well with task.

Friday:

Had printed and cut out Kara's sentences & pictures. She wasn't happy with these being cut up at first. But once she saw Colin is making his poster, got into the idea of matching sentences with pictures and gluing them on poster board. Pretty good day!

Mr. Mackie's Teaching, Conferencing & Planning Notebook: Enzo, Joaquin, and T. J.

Tuesday:

Want to complete a graphic novel type piece about this Super Bird who uses its superpowers to fight back and save the songbirds dying because of evil urban cats. Discussed what science fiction writers do. Asked them to make sure they had at least five solid facts about songbirds to base their fiction upon. Discussed how sci fi writers do this.

Wednesday:

Writers requested conference; wanted me to "okay" their facts. They did their research. They are off to storyboarding! Next week: guided writing instruction with Gabby/Maddie, Hallie & Bella; Austin/Esteban. Focus: checking for purpose (Are the pieces informative? Are the facts apparent?)

These conference notes were taken during the same week in February as the provided Status of the Class record (see Appendix M). From the Status of the Class chart, Mr. Mackie can quickly see Lilly's writing practices for the week and how she is using writing process. The conference notes further inform these data. Mr. Mackie can return to these notes and analyze how Lilly is also developing writing craft and growing in her independence as a writer. During the Monday conference, Mr. Mackie found Lilly engaged in decision making as a writer: what poetry form would best work for her purpose, to inform people of the plight of many urban songbirds? Mr. Mackie notes Lilly's thinking as a writer. Learning to connect form with purpose marks a critical point in a writer's development. On Friday, Mr. Mackie meets with Lilly again. We can deduce from his notes that he began by inquiring about her writing practices of the week. Lilly had a peer conference and is following up on the suggestions made by her peer, Suelita. This is documented in the Teaching, Conferencing & Planning Notebook to show Lilly's progress toward one of her individual writing goals: "I will seek feedback from my writing peers to revise my writing."

Mr. Mackie also records the targeted instruction he taught Lilly on this day, how sentencing is different for free-verse poetry. Once documented, Mr. Mackie can follow up on Lilly's progress and document her accomplishment of this writing craft. Through this kind of documentation, Mr. Mackie can give an accounting of what he has specifically taught Lilly and her progress at any time. Conversely, Lilly is accountable for her own learning as she notes this writing accomplishment on her individualized writing goal sheet.

A review of both Mr. Mackie's Status of the Class chart and his Teaching, Conferencing & Planning Notebook provide him data necessary for planning instruction not just for Lilly, but also for small groups of writers with the same writing needs. For example, a lesson with several writers on poster genre and design is on his radar.

Mr. Mackie's Status of the Class chart and his Teaching, Conferencing & Planning Notebook additionally demonstrate how instruction is differentiated in the Writing Studio. Take a moment to read the excerpts from Mr. Mackie's notebook for Caesar, who is developing English language skills and receives English language development assistance, and Kara, who is autistic and receives special education assistance. These can be found in the earlier excerpts from Mr. Mackie's Teaching, Conferencing & Planning Notebook.

Caesar is provided with a Spanish-language text; he has a choice whether to write in Spanish or English and sometimes uses a combination of both. He is hesitant of doing writing "wrong," and so Mr. Mackie scaffolds his learning with more graphic organizers to boost confidence prior to writing. A poster draws on Caesar's artistic abilities and, although it still requires the research and summary of research, does not require the amount of writing a letter might. This is a good English language project for Caesar. These instructional decisions, Caesar's use of English vocabulary and grammar, his risks, his successes, and his development are all documented in the Teaching, Conferencing & Planning notebook.

For Kara, writing is a difficult act, both physically and cognitively. The special educator and Kara's parents suggest explicitly scaffolding through the use of templates, the use of a computer to mitigate the challenge of handwriting, and the offer of noise-reducing headphones. Mr. Mackie's conference notebook records data on how this targeted instruction is working for Kara.

When Mr. Mackie attends meetings with the specialists of his school and the parents of Caesar and Kara, he will take his Teaching, Conferencing & Planning Notebook with him as evidence and data for discussing the next instructional steps and goals for both children.

The Teaching, Conferencing & Planning Notebook: Early Grades

The Teaching, Conferencing & Planning Notebook in the early grades can look many ways but serves the same function as it does in upper grades, documenting writing practices, process, and craft. The most useful assessments in early grades are anecdotal notes gathered through observation and conversation. An early-grade teacher needs to be exceptionally organized and intentional in collecting data that documents writing development. Kindergarten to Grade 2 teachers find that using the same system Mr. Mackie uses works well; however, being attentive to the writing development of young writers is critical.

Illustration of Teaching, Conferencing & Planning Notebook: Grade 1

Ms. Mekla practices careful observations as young writers compose, noting how writers are progressing according to the CCSS Writing Anchor Standards. She keeps a template of her Teaching, Conferencing & Planning Notebook on her tablet.

When she observes instances or examples of a writer demonstrating knowledge of any of these standards, she quickly enters notes and often snaps a photo to include in the documentation. Ms. Mekla makes a point of reviewing her Teaching, Conferencing & Planning Notebook informally on a weekly basis and more purposefully every four weeks when she synthesizes data and uses it to plan instruction. Table 5.2 is an excerpt from Ms. Mekla's notebook for writer, Gracie Lee.

TABLE 5.2 Grade 1 Excerpt: Ms. Mekla's Teaching, Conferencing & Planning Notebook

Gracie Lee	Text Types & Purposes (CCSS Writing Anchor Standard 1, 2, 3, 10)	Process of Getting Ideas on Paper (CCSS Writing Anchor Standard 5)	Ideas & Content (CCSS Writing Anchor Standard 1, 2, 3)	Conventions: Spelling, Grammar, Punctuation & Handwriting (CCSS Writing Anchor Standard 4, 5 CCSS Language Anchor Standard 1, 2)	Identity/View of Self as Writer
Sept	Personal narratives to be shared with the teacher and peers	Starts by drawing detailed picture about her story. Then transitions to writing.	Writes about recent events with family ■ State Fair ■ Visiting grandparents ■ Trip to the beach ■ Babysitting cousins ■ Soccer game	Handwriting developing Uses spaces between words Capital letters used instead of lowercase, specifically with B, D, P, W, G Spells a few high-frequency words accurately: *the, to, my,* and *man* Spells phonetically for unknown words: *satee/Saturday, plce/police, dag/dog, makik/magic*	Knows that writers write about what they know/do in their lives.
Oct	Personal narratives to be shared with the teacher and peers	Is beginning to write first and doesn't always include an illustration with her stories. Starts writing immediately because she has ideas about topics she is interested in writing about.	Writes about recent events with family ■ Pumpkin patch ■ Visiting greatgrandmother	Handwriting improving Spaces between words Incorrect use of capital letters less frequent, only with letters G, P Spelling more words conventionally: Yesterday, went, had. Uses the high-frequency word chart in her writing folder. Still uses phonetic spelling with unknown words, hearing more sounds: *apolcrip/applecrisp, wadfol/waterfall, swiming/swimming*	Eager to write about personal experiences. Is reluctant to share writing with friends or the whole class because she embarrasses easily and is a bit intimated by the older students in her 1st/2nd blend classroom

(Continued)

TABLE 5.2 *Continued*

Gracie Lee	Text Types & Purposes (CCSS Writing Anchor Standard 1, 2, 3, 10)	Process of Getting Ideas on Paper (CCSS Writing Anchor Standard 5)	Ideas & Content (CCSS Writing Anchor Standard 1, 2, 3)	Conventions: Spelling, Grammar, Punctuation & Handwriting (CCSS Writing Anchor Standard 4, 5 CCSS Language Anchor Standard 1, 2)	Identity/View of Self as Writer
Nov	Personal narratives Publishing books from her favorite drafts to share with peers	Writes some stories with illustrations and others without illustrations. Able to read through her story with a checklist to revise and edit her writing.	Writes about recent events with family ■ Bowling with her family ■ Playing the game Guess Who? ■ Playdate with friend	Improved handwriting Spells high-frequency words: *and, the, he, went, to my* Continues to use the high-frequency word chart in her writing folder Phonetic spelling for unknown words: *boling/ bowling, ale/alley, trkey/ turkey.* Occasionally adds sounds: *babey/baby, tabol/ table.*	Growing as a writer by adding more details to her stories.
Dec	Personal narratives Writing letters for the school post office to brother and friends	Has ideas for stories. Writes details including a beginning, middle and end. Writes interesting stories.	Writes about events with family ■ Birthday ■ Rock climbing ■ Getting a Christmas tree	Improved handwriting Correctly uses lowercase & uppercase letters Spells high-frequency words: and, *the, he, went, to my* Phonetic spelling for unknown words: *crecmes/ Christmas, suneing/ something, desuseing/ disgusting,* which makes her writing difficult to decipher	Beginning to adopt author's craft. For example, she used an ellipse to build anticipation in one of her stories.

Meaningful writing assessment informs the teacher in such a way that instruction can be differentiated for all writers. Status of the Class combined with the Teaching, Conferencing & Planning Notebook does just this.

Focus on the excerpt from Mr. Mackie's Teaching, Conferencing & Planning Notebook, taken from the collaborative writing team of Enzo, Joaquin, and T. J. Read these and the entries for each of the same writers in Mr. Mackie's Status of the Class chart located in Appendix M. Combined, what do the data suggest about Enzo's, Joaquin's, and T. J.'s evolving writing practices, their use of process, and their writing craft? What do the data suggest is the role of the teacher as he or she conferences with writers and plans for writing instruction?

The Daily Writing Folder

The writer's Daily Writing Folder, as the name suggests, is a collection of daily writing, writing notes, scribbles and drawings, lists, and reminders—all of the things writers keep as part of their writing practice. Such a collection also reflects the starts and stops and cycles of writing processes and the growing writer's craft. Chapter 3 described a number of possible forms that can serve to organize the Daily Writing Folder. Table 5.3 provides an overview of the Daily Writing Folder assessment.

TABLE 5.3 Daily Writing Folder Assessment

Writing Goal Area	Guiding questions for analysis	Possible Evidence
Writing Practice (CCSS Anchor Standard 10)	What strategies does the writer use to begin writing? How is the writer sustaining writing over time? Does the time writing reflect appropriately writing purpose and audience?	Prewriting strategies List of writing ideas Dates on drafts: total time to develop a piece of writing
Writing Process (CCSS Anchor Standards 4-8)	Is the writer using revision and researching strategies appropriate for writing development area? Is the writer learning to use feedback and give feedback?	Draft writing (includes learning to use editing symbols) Peer conferencing log or sheets
Writing Craft (CCSS Anchor Standards 1-3)	Is there evidence of growing writer's craft in revision work?	Specific revision samples, e.g., mastering proper sentence punctuation

To assess for writing practices, analyze the contents of the Daily Writing Folder to gain a picture of how the writer approaches writing (What strategies does the writer use to get started?), note how the writer is sustaining writing over time (What is left unfinished? What is returned to at a later date? What strategies does the writer use to keep writing?), and check to see how long a writer is spending on each piece of writing (Does the time spent appropriately reflect writing purpose?)

Writing process is documented by analyzing revisions appropriate to writing development (Pinnell & Fountas, 2011). For example, in a kindergartner's Daily Writing Folder, look for evidence of a writer adding details to their illustrations and then seeing the development of more words and sentences with less dependence on illustrations. By Grade 3, check for evidence of a writer drafting, rereading and revising content, making editing corrections, and even reorganizing information. By Grade 5, a Daily Writing Folder provides evidence of a deepening understanding of writing processes, and a more nuanced sense of the kind of process time necessary for different writing purposes. Editing for conventions and grammar will be demonstrated in draft work. (See Pinnell & Fountas, 2011, for a complete description of writing development across the grade levels.)

Part of developing writing practices and process is valuing feedback from others. Conversely, it is also about learning to give useful feedback to other writers. Peer response forms and notes are kept in the Daily Writing Folder providing evidence of this part of the writer's practice. (See Chapter 9 for more on peer conferencing.)

Developing writing craft is evidenced in the revision of drafts. Here is an example of how revisions provide data of developing writing craft from a Grade 5 paper:

Draft 1: *My mom yelled for us to stop*
Revision 1: *My mom yelled "Stop"!*
Revision 2: *Just then, my mom saw us balancing on the edge of the handrail and she yelled, "Stop!"*
Revision 3: *Just then, my mom saw us balancing on the edge of the handrail. Her eyes got the size of a pancake and she yelled, "Stop!"*

The revisions are evidence of this writer developing his writing craft: his ability to use dialogue to enhance his story and his growing control over the punctuation required for dialogue. A final paper, alone, will show his final use of dialogue, but not the process of *becoming-writer*.

The Daily Writing Folder provides evidence of a writer developing writer identity. Is the child taking risks as a writer? Is there a sense of energy, joy, and active meaning making in the writing? Is the writer developing a widening sense of writing purpose and audience? Analyze the Daily Writing Folder for these data. Identify it, name, and record the data. This is the kind of data that can be celebrated and can be used to grow a writer's sense of agency.

Illustration of a Daily Writing Folder: Grade 3

Ms. García Ramírez makes a habit of quickly leafing through each one of her Grade 3 writers' Daily Writing Folders whenever she conducts a teacher–student writing conference. Writers know she will most likely ask about their folders; they can often be seen doing a quick shuffle of papers prior to her coming to their desk, making sure everything is in order. They know that Ms. García Ramírez is a stickler (as she says) about organizing one's work. Ms. García Ramírez is clear in her purpose: "Your writing folders tell us about your writing practice, who you are becoming as writers. They are like a self-portrait! Make sure they tell your story well."

When she leafs through the Daily Writing Folder, she is looking for organization, revision work, and risk taking. Often, these are mental notes, but when Ms. García Ramírez sees something, like an attempt at independent poem writing or an obvious move by a writer to research and include new information in a text, she names this to the writer and notes it in her Teaching, Conferencing & Planning Notebook. Ms. García Ramírez keeps an eye on individual writing and spelling goals and purposefully watches for evidence of writer's progress in these areas. She makes a point of asking a writer about these goals and uses these to prompt teacher–student conferences. Listen in on this conference:

Ms. García Ramírez: Rainia, one of your writing goals is to learn strategies for organizing your writing. How does your work on this piece about how to make cookies show your progress towards this goal?
Rainia: I listed out things here [points to paper].

Ms. García Ramírez:	Let's take a look. So these are directions . . . or this is a recipe for making cookies?
Rainia:	Yes! These are my grandma's cookies!
Ms. García Ramírez:	What things are you listing out?
Rainia:	I listed out the steps for the cookies. See, I numbered them [points to numbering].
Ms. García Ramírez:	Yes—that is the way recipes often read and that is a good organizational strategy for a recipe. You have listed in number steps how to make your grandma's cookies. Anything else you may want to add? [Ms. García Ramírez is now tapping her finger on the goal statement. After "organization," (in parenthesis) it reads, "clear beginning, middle and end."]
Rainia:	Oh! I need a beginning! What can I do for a beginning of a recipe?

Ms. García Ramírez will follow the same pattern later during an editing conference with Rainia. Then, she will note Rainia's personalized spelling list along with the class list of "We Can Spell These Word" (high-frequency word list), pointing out any words Rainia has spelled correctly, noting words she needs to "check again" and finally determining if there are new words that ought to be added to Rainia's list.

There are no published tests that can provide the ongoing assessment data generated from a Daily Writing Folder. It is tangible evidence of ongoing learning toward targeted writing goals. The Daily Writing Folder communicates expectations, acts as an invitation, and marks progress. For these reasons, the Daily Writing Folder is beneficial during child-led parent/guardian conferences and meeting with specialists. The data allow the teacher and writer to be accountable to authentic writing goals and, therefore, be able to describe learning at any time. Furthermore, it serves to organize future instruction.

 Visit the companion website to listen to Eva, a Grade 4 writer, discuss her writing. What do you learn about children as writers listening to Eva?

Cumulative Writing Folder

While the Daily Writing Folder is evidence of ongoing learning, the Cumulative Writing Folder is a formal assessment that celebrates, broadcasts, and documents writing growth over time. While a final draft of the writing piece is the highlight of the folder, drafts showing revision, research, editing, and peer/teacher conferencing (how feedback was used), are also included to demonstrate the whole of writing practices and process. In determining what writing ought to be kept in the Cumulative Writing Folder, use required national, state, district, or school benchmarks. For example, pieces can be selected according to the CCSS for Writing:

- *Text Types and Purposes.* Select opinion, informative/explanatory, and narrative pieces, as well as other text types required by state, district, school, or teacher choice, such as poetry, book and video game reviews, lists, letters, and other genres taught throughout the year, to broadcast the way a writer is able to produce a variety of text types for differing purposes.
- *Production and Distribution of Writing.* Select pieces as evidence of a writer making decisions about text type and organization. Include pieces that demonstrate revision and editing appropriate for the grade level. Make sure some pieces showcase the use of technology in producing both final drafts and a variety of text types.

- *Research to Build and Present Knowledge.* Select specific pieces that have required the writer to complete research. Much of this standard begins in Grade 4, but evidence of young writers beginning to select and recall ideas and experience with the support of adults is included in the standard for early grades.
- *Range of Writing (this standard begins in Grade 3).* Select evidence of writers making decisions about writing tasks, purposes, and audience celebrating a growing understanding of the kind of writing requiring more or less time. Include writing completed in short and longer spans of time.

It is not necessary to save every piece of writing—it is necessary to be intentional in selecting writing that is evidence of learning that aligns with benchmarks and writing goals. Unlike a one time writing assessment, the Cumulative Writing Folder is longitudinal documentation of writing development. In the early grades (K–2), collect daily writing and at the end of each week or every other week (excluding shortened weeks) ask writers to select the one piece of writing they most want to save in the Cumulative Writing Folder. The actual piece of writing can be physically saved, photographed, scanned, or copied. Photographing writing saves time as a teacher and further celebrates the moment for young children through the act of picture taking. Additionally, children can take their writing home. Early-grade writing may include "transcription notes" completed by the teacher; this will be useful to other adults reading the piece. Having writers determine the writing piece to be documented grows their sense of agency and independence as a decision maker.

Teach writers the kinds of pieces to save: "All week, writers, we have been working on including more detail into our drawings to better tell our stories. Look through your Daily Writing Folder and find a piece where you have added details in your drawing. Make sure this is a piece you are proud of as a writer. Turn to your neighbor and tell them why you are choosing this piece."

Be equally intentional in Grades 3 to 5 in selecting writing pieces for the Cumulative Writing Folder. Again, teach writers how to make good selections. How a writer chooses to broadcast his or her work is an important decision. Return to the purpose of the Cumulative Writing Folder: it ought to provide evidence of developing writing practices, process, and craft. With this in mind, analyze the writing curriculum (see Part IV) and determine where in the writing year it may be best to collect final pieces of writing and related work. A guiding principle is to save a piece of writing from each writing unit or specific time frame.

In addition to final pieces of writing, other forms of documentation can demonstrate writing development and be included in the Cumulative Writing Folder. For example, include all beginning-of-the-year assessments. Repeating the beginning-of-the-year assessments at the end of the year can be a powerful demonstration of writing growth and sense of self as a writer. Some teachers and writers include lists of writing topics, peer conference notes, and selected anecdotal notes from the Teaching, Conferencing & Planning Notebook, the list of writing and spelling goals—all to provide evidence of writing growth and development in writing practices, process, and craft. Writer's self-assessment (see the following discussion) and scored writing samples (see the following discussion) are often included in the Cumulative Writing Folder.

One last caution: be mindful of where Cumulative Writing Folders are stored. As a special and celebrated folder of the writer's work and as documentation of writing development, plan for its safekeeping.

Illustration of the Cumulative Writing Folder

Jon's Grade 3 Cumulative Writing Folder contains evidence, by the end of the third quarter grading period, that he is able to write a variety of text types and is learning the purpose for these various text types. Jon has chosen for his folder a variety of pieces: a science report, a poem based on historical research, a superhero story, and a free-verse poem.

Jon's science report about frogs is six pages long and was typed on a computer. It includes pictures found on the Internet and a reference list of sources used. Each page introduces a new topic, with a title, a topic sentence, and supporting facts. For example, the paragraph on "frog appearance" begins with "This is what frogs look like. Frogs have NO NECKS!!!" The enlarged font is evidence of his attention to audience and design. Jon's report on frogs is evidence of his ability to organize informative writing, to complete and develop writing with research, and to use word processing.

A poem about Squanto is additional evidence of how Jon is learning how to research a topic. Stapled behind an illustration of Squanto Jon has drawn, is the final poem completed on a computer, which includes a drawing from the Internet. All the research and thinking he has completed (concept map, biography time line, and collected quotes) is also included. This research and revision work is evidence of Jon using writing as a thinking and learning tool.

Perhaps Jon's enthusiasm and his identity as an action writer is best illustrated in "Super Boy and the Curse of the Evil Pancakes!" The story is written in a breathless sort of way: "In a holtel it was 9:30 am when a few evil pancakes broke in the hotel. The few evil panckaes were sealing a lot of money this looks like a job for super boy." The superhero fights the pancakes, and arrests another robber along the way, before things become "bad guy free." Jon's writing has a lot of *voice*. You can hear him almost laughing at his own jokes. His voice is also noted in a poem titled "Boo-Boo"; he writes: "I write of / my stuffed animal / Boo-boo / in a flying tree / that is up in / space / I think of Boo-boo / running for president / and ordering / everyone to eat bananas / and forming a monkey army." These two pieces are evidence of Jon's ability to write narrative with imagined events, using descriptive details with a clear sequence of events. He develops character and plot, uses dialogue, and line breaks in his free-verse poetry.

Jon's teacher summarizes his writing progress as seen in Table 5.4.

TABLE 5.4 Summary of Jon's Cumulative Writing Folder

Cumulative Writing Folder: Jon Grade 3			
Selected Writing	CCSS Supported (S) or Met (M)	Individualized Writing Goal Supported (S) or Met (M)	Teacher Notes
Frogs Non-fiction Science Report	CCSS.ELA.W.3.2 (S) CCSS.ELA.W.3.10 (S) CCSS.ELA. L.3 (M) CCSS.ELA. L.3.3.2e (M)	Writing organization (M) Design layout (M) Word choice (S) Editing (S) Developing writing with details (M)	*Frogs* has voice—Jon selected fun facts and organized them well! He also selected great photos that match the text!
Squanto Biographical Poem	CCSS.ELA.W.3.2a,b,c,d (S) CCSS.ELA.W.3, 4, 6 (S) CCSS.ELA.L.3.7 (S)	Design layout (M) Word choice (S) Editing (M) Developing writing with details (M)	Lots of care selecting facts and organizing them in poem fashion; also careful attention to word choice.
Super Boy and the Curse of the Evil Pancakes Superhero	CCSS.ELA.W.3.3a, b, c, d (S) CCSS.ELA.L.3.2b, c, e, f (S)	Writing organization (M) Word choice (S) Editing (S) Developing writing with details (S)	Such voice! Excellent beginning, middle, and end: has a climax!
Boo-Boo Free-verse Poem	CCSS.ELA.L.3.5 (S)	Design layout (M) Word choice (S)	Writing risk here (and imagination) in composing this poem. Different than other pieces of writing.

This summary sheet is placed in the front of Jon's Cumulative Writing Folder. Jon's teacher or Jon can easily access the folder and give an account to others about his writing progress at any time.

Continued or future individualized writing goals can also be identified from an analysis of the Cumulative Writing Folder. For example, Jon has not yet completed an opinion piece. This becomes a teaching and learning focus for the last grading period. Jon is still working on some pieces of standard writing conventions (paragraphing), as well as learning how to use conventions usually associated with narrative writing (how to punctuate dialogue). Jon's enthusiasm and sheer sense of fun is apparent in all of the pieces in his Cumulative Writing Folder. His teacher imagines a lively opinion piece that continues to develop his abilities to find fun, related facts and that uses design layouts available on the computer. She imagines that Jon can employ his great sense of narrative to create this opinion and thereby continue to practice specific writing conventions.

Jon's Cumulative Writing Folder, as a collection of final pieces of writing and their associated draft work, illustrate how the Cumulative Writing Folder can provide authentic evidence for analysis of writing accomplishment and future writing instruction.

Writer Self-Assessment

Writer self-assessment is a pause in the action of writing that celebrates and takes note of writing development. Writing self-assessment done well is a practice in metacognition and gives writers a sense of agency as they consider both accomplishments and future writing goals. Writer self-assessment can be completed whenever a final piece of writing is completed, or it can be strategically positioned throughout the year, for example, at the end of each grading period; at the beginning and at the end of the year only or three times during the year to provide a pre-, mid-, and post-overview of the writer and his or her work. Self-assessments that are overdone tend to lose their importance and too often must be rushed because of a shortage of time. Self-assessments are often connected to the selection of pieces placed in the Cumulative Writing Folder.

Self-assessments most often are conversations in the early grades (K–2). These are recorded in the Teaching, Conferencing & Planning Notebook. In Grades 3 to 5, conversations, rubrics, checklists, letters, and even sticky notes can be used. In selecting the format, keep in mind the purpose: to document writing development and growth, to celebrate progress, and to set future goals and direct writing instruction. Which format will work best within the context of your Writing Studio? Not every writer needs to use the same format; differentiate as needed.

In early grades, invite children to respond to these questions about pieces they select for the Cumulative Writing Folder:

- Why did you choose this piece? What makes it good?
- What kinds of things did you do to check your work?
- What are one or two things you would like to work on next as a writer? (Owocki & Goodman, 2002, p. 91)

Record responses in the Teaching, Conferencing & Planning notebook or use sticky notes that will later be placed in the notebook. Conversely, tablet technology make audio files easy to create and preserve the actual talk of the writer. If using a tablet as the Teaching, Conferencing & Planning notebook, these audio files become part of the notebook instantly. Audio files add an extra level of authenticity for both the writer and the parent/guardian during conferences.

For Grades 3 to 5, a simple form can be constructed with all or a selection of the following questions, adjusting for grade level, self-assessment occasion, or specific groups of writers:

- What does this piece tell about you as a writer?
- What did you do in this piece as a writer that you could not do, or did not do, before?
- Did you take any writing risks in this piece that you would like to share? *Or*—did you practice any specific writing craft in this piece?
- As you consider your writing, what are two things you would like to work on next as a writer?

Writers can complete this self-assessment as a questionnaire, or they might use color-coded sticky notes to highlight places in the final piece and make notations. If the piece is completed on a computer, Grade 5 writers can be taught to insert comments into the text itself. Alternatively, writers may use these questions as a prompt and write a letter to parents/guardians, or to themselves ("What I want to remember about myself as a writer at this time and place"), or to classmates (the letter is read aloud or could be made public using technology). Rubrics and checklists can also be developed. These can be specific to text type, practices, or process and mirror what a teacher may be using to assess a piece of writing.

Illustration of Self-Assessment

Jon's teacher (see earlier Cumulative Writing Folder discussion) asked writers to self-assess after completing the research writing for their integrated science unit. The questions were deliberately written by Jon's teacher to gather data for future writing units requiring research and word processing. (See Table 5.5 Jon's Self-Assessment, "Frogs!")

TABLE 5.5 Jon's Self-Assessment, "Frogs!"

Learning goals for science reports	Circle the best answer . . . or just choose to write in the Author's Personal Note section!			Author's personal notes
I learned how to find important facts on the Internet.	(Yes!)	I did pretty well.	I want to practice this more.	
I found pictures on the Internet for my report that I like.	Yes!	I did pretty well.	(I want to practice this more.)	*I really like the pictures I found! It was fun looking for pictures. I want to do more of this!*
I organized my piece using a topic sentence and related facts.	Yes!	(I did pretty well.)	I want to practice this more.	
I used peer conferencing to check my facts.	Yes!	(I did pretty well.)	I want to practice this more.	
I am learning word-processing skills.	Yes!	I did pretty well.	(I want to practice this more.)	

What I like best about my science report is . . .
I like the pictures and the facts I found. I like how I designed them on the page. It looks really awesome!

Take a break from reading and study Jon's self-assessment found in Table 5.5. How does this self-assessment inform you as a teacher? If you were Jon's teacher, what additional questions might you ask him during a writing conference? How would the responses to these questions further inform you as a teacher?

Self-assessments require risk and confidence as a writer. We suggest that you conduct a self-assessment of your own writing to "test" out any rubric you create. Make sure as a teacher you have intentionally taught the items to which writers are being asked to self-assess. Self-assessment is a writing practice—teach, reinforce, and allow time for writers to develop their responses. Then writers and teachers of writing will discover potential and possibilities of self-assessments.

Scored Writing Sample

While rubrics can be generally defined as any set of criteria specifying expectations for a specific paper, there are also rubrics designed for the purpose of evaluation. For example, the 6+1® Writing Traits (Education Northwest, 2013a) introduced in Chapter 2 form an evaluative assessment rubric. For these kinds of rubrics to be valid, grade-level teachers need to read widely and deeply children's work, collect examples of "anchor" papers to define the individual traits, and share in the task of evaluating papers for interreliability of final scores. Often, the task of determining anchor papers, or examples of each trait and scores for that trait, is done at the state or district level. With the advent of national assessment, this work is being done through assessment consortiums such as the SMARTER Balanced Consortium (2012) and the Partnership for Assessment of Readiness for Career and College (2014a, 2014b) Routman (2005) writes,

> I worry that conscientious teachers will spend hours scoring papers against a rubric only to have the writing remain stagnant because they are looking primarily at word choice or skills in isolation, such as spelling or sentence fluency, and not at the big picture, at what the writing is trying to say. (p. 242)

This is a legitimate concern. Rubrics can be useful and no one rubric can define and encompass all that writing is or does. When we read a powerful novel or informative piece, we rarely step away and say, "Oh, what amazing use of conventions! I would give this a 5!" We are more likely to say something like "This book is changing my lifestyle. I will make different decisions after reading this book." It is the totality of writing, the way the work connects with the reader's personal schema and place in life, the full press of language working its way into the reader's way of being, the imagery, page design, perhaps the jarring use of conventions, the moment of transaction with the text as reader that defines the writing. And it is worth noting the obvious: not all writing appeals to all readers, so even the most "standardized" rubric and its anchor pieces reflects a subjective view, an opinion about what counts and gets counted as "good writing."

This is not to say a teacher of writing should not use rubrics. Use rubrics—most of you will be required to do so—but keep the focus on the writer, improving writing and writing instruction. Not every piece of writing needs to be evaluated with a rubric (and you will be exhausted if you try to do this). We recommend that you score three or four papers over the course of the school year. It will be most rewarding if this work is done with other grade-level teachers, using the scoring to spur discussion about what writers do, how writing it is made meaningful, and revising writing curriculum and instruction. While writers need to learn the language of writing rubrics, they also should not be so inundated with this language that they cannot conceive of writing beyond the framework of the rubric. If using rubrics, remember to have "kid-friendly" rubrics, especially for younger grades, so children can understand and use them. Finally, remember that officially scored writing samples represent *one* time, *one* place, and *one* effort by a writer. Who the writer is and what the writer can do is best determined over time, as is documented in the Daily Writing Folder and the Cumulative Writing Folder. The "official" scored paper is an important piece of the total writing assessment plan—it does not warrant a place of preeminence.

Select different text types (modes) to score throughout the year. Choose to score a final paper the writer has had sufficient time to draft, revise, receive feedback, edit, and finalize, because this reflects the authentic work of writers. After scoring the paper, consider the paper in the context of the Daily Writing Folder and the Cumulative Writing Folder: Is the scored paper representative of this writer's abilities and skills? In what ways? How is the scored paper not representative of the writer's abilities and skills?

Teach writers how to score their own writing as an exercise of self-assessment. You can also use this as a prompt for a teacher–student writing conference. How do the scores reflect what the writer can do? How do the scores reflect next steps for the writer? Discuss how the scored paper "fits" with other data generated by formative assessments and the Cumulative Writing Folder. Use the scores to point out how a writer has grown in writing practices, process, and craft and set future writing goals.

An Illustration: Using a Rubric to Score a Writing Sample

Emme is an enthusiastic Grade 3 writer. We use a narrative she wrote as a response to a writing prompt given to her by her teacher, Ms. Lomas, to illustrate using a rubric to score writing. Ms. Lomas is required by her district to periodically provide writers with a prompt and to score the writing as formal assessment. For this writing prompt, Ms. Lomas brought a most interesting bulky canvas bag into the classroom and set it on the front table. "What do you think might be in this bag, writers?" she asked. Increasing anticipation, she added, "What was that? Did you see the sack move? What if it did move?" After some discussion about the sack, Ms. Lomas wrote the writing prompt on the board: *One day Ms. Lomas put a sack on the desk and it started to move.* Writers were given multiple days to compose a draft, revise, edit, and finalize their stories.

 In preparation for our discussion of Emme's writing sample, please read her writing sample found in Appendix N. Additionally, visit the Education Northwest (2013b) website, http://educationnorthwest.org/traits/traits-rubrics, to review the 6+1® Trait Rubric for Grades 3 to 12 we used to score Emme's paper.

We find this to be a lively piece of writing. Emme is clearly a reader of fantasy. Her plot sequence includes vocabulary not often used by a third grader, "experaments," a "crechor from another demention," and to save the day, the heroes toss the "flu fall" (the kind of creature in the sack) into a "potal"! Vivid details are created through these word choices. Furthermore, Emme is to be commended for her use of active dialogue that drives the story. The sequencing of events are logical: the sack is discovered; there is action to discover what is in the sack, followed by a discussion about the kind of creature it is, and, finally, getting the creature to that portal so all is well! The ending is clever: "The end enles you think it is ah-ah-ah!" and reflects the kind of story that begs a sequel. While Emme's sentence fluency is somewhat uneven, there are places where she takes writing risk. For example, during one dialogue exchange, a character announces the character is a "flu fa," and another asks, "A flu fa?"

What stands most in the way of the reader, is Emme's use of conventions. There are a number of misspelled words. Most of these are spelled phonetically and can be easily decoded, for example, experaments/experiments; crechor/creature; and cinds/kinds. There is no paragraphing, yet the internal structure of the story works. If the dialogue were paragraphed correctly, there would be little need for the reader to slow down. However, because it is not (and because not all dialogue is in quotation marks), it is problematic at times to know who is speaking or when a speaker has changed.

Using the Education Northwest 6+1® Trait Rubric for 3–12, we score Emme's paper as follows: *Ideas (4); Organization (4); Voice (4); Word Choice (4+); Sentence Fluency (3.5); Conventions (2).* (See Table 5.6 Emme's Writing Sample Scores)

TABLE 5.6 Emme's Writing Sample Scores: Grade 3

Trait	Score	Rationale
Ideas, the main message	4	Paper attempts showing vs. telling details through active use of dialogue. The end is rushed, "Then some how we got the potal a we togst it in side!" I want to know how that happened! Ideas are fresh and original. The writer seems to be applying knowledge from reading, and is choosing significant events to form the basis of the story.
Organization, the internal structure of the piece	4	There is a clear beginning, middle, ending to the paper. Sequencing is logical and the pacing effectively entices the reader to read on. There is a clever conclusion, mimicking stories with sequels. While paragraphing is expected towards the end of Grade 3, it is easy to see where the breaks or transitions are in the story.
Voice, the personal tone and flavor of the author's message	4	The writer connects with the audience through dialogue and sequence of plot. The purpose of the writing is reflected in content and arrange of ideas. There is risk: the author is the hero of the story!
Word Choice, the vocabulary a writer chooses to convey meaning	4+	The writer's use of vocabulary is memorable, "experaments," "crechor," "demention," and "portal," reflect a fantasy reader and give the piece energy, enhancing the plot of the story. The writer is clearly thinking about vocabulary choices, creating new names for beings, a "flu fa"! She uses the colloquial phrase, "What in the world . . ."
Sentence Fluency, the rhythm and flow of the language	3.5	Sentences, while not quite musical, are moving in this direction. Varied sentencing is used. There are missing connectives in the dialogue that makes it somewhat confusing to know who has said what, yet the reader is not necessarily lost. There is a merging sense of cadence in this echo dialogue: "It is a culd a ful fall a flu fa?
Conventions, the mechanical correctness	2	Spelling errors are common but for the most part are phonetically correct and can be easily decoded. Incorrect paragraphing for dialogue can slow down the reader. Most end and beginning punctuation is correct, including correct use of exclamation and question marks. Moderate editing with teacher's guidance would correct the later and make the piece very readable.
Presentation, how the writing actually looks on the page	4-	Handwriting is consistent. White space is used well. Title is in larger handwriting. Name and date could be better placed. There is no experimentation with lettering or illustration.

Using the Scored Writing Sample for Targeted Writing Instruction

With minor revisions Emme's paper could score 5's in many categories. But raising scores isn't the point here: *this scored writing sample provides data necessary to revise Emme's individual writing goals.* It provides data about what Emme can do as a writer and directs the next steps of writing instruction for her. Emme can be taught how to paragraph and punctuate dialogue; this becomes an individualized writing goal for her. There are many lively words that can become spelling lessons and individualized goals for Emme. She can be shown how to present the work so a reader can enjoy it more fully; this, too, becomes an individualized writing goal. Following deliberate instruction and practice, we can expect that the next time Emme composes a piece of writing, no matter the context, we will see improvements in these targeted areas.

 Download and read through the 6+1® Trait Rubric for 3–12 writer's rubric from Education Northwest (2013a) website: http://educationnorthwest.org/traits/traits-rubrics. For additional guidance on scoring children's writing examine the scored examples on the Education Northwest (2014) website: http://educationnorthwest.org/traits/scored-examples.

 Find three additional Grade 3 papers composed by writers from Emme's class on the companion website. Practice scoring the writing using the 6+1® Trait Rubric for 3–12. Finally, practice writing individualized writing goals and writing instruction for each writer.

Doing the Work of Bricoleur: Piecing Together the Writer's Biography

Back away from this chapter for a moment and try to see the assessments and how they work as a whole. Pieced together, how do they tell the story of each individual writer? How do they document and assess writing practices, process, and craft?

 Take a moment to respond to the preceding questions. Visit with your colleagues. Create your own illustration of how the writing assessments work together to inform writers and teachers of writing.

Following the assessment plan described in this chapter, teachers like Mr. Mackie (Grade 5) and Ms. García Ramírez (Grade 1) are able to write thoughtful and informative summaries for parents/guardians and writers as part of permanent records.

By the end of the year Mr. Mackie writes the following about Yolanda:

Yolanda is a highly motivated fiction writer; her writing is strongly influenced by the amount of fictional novels she reads. Opinion writing is another strength of Yolanda as she is never unsure of what she believes. She is learning to develop more evidence and examples to back up her opinions. Yolanda's greatest challenge with writing personal narratives and informative texts was finding an idea of interest to her. Yolanda thrived when she was able to write collaboratively, especially when she had an opportunity to write with her friends Carmelita and Hallie. Together they were able to write three fictional stories this academic year, one was selected for the school's literary magazine.

Yolanda's conventions improved greatly throughout the year. She is able to correctly use dialogue, commas, and ellipses. Her spelling of unknown words is improving now that she knows how to access resources such as word processing programs on the computer and an electronic dictionary. Yolanda's written English grammar is developing alongside her oral English language skills. Her errors show evidence of her strength and knowledge of Spanish grammatical structures.

Ms. García Ramírez writes this about Gracie Lee:

Gracie Lee has really blossomed this year. She is focused on learning and works hard. She seems confident and appears to enjoy writing. She writes on meaningful topics and includes a lot of interesting details. She prefers to write personal narratives about adventures with her family and friends. Her nonfiction stories about frogs, sunflowers, and "All About Me" shows Gracie Lee's ability to write in multiple text types. Gracie Lee also enjoyed sending letters through the school mail system and was highly motivated to write when she received letters from her brother and friends. She uses many high-frequency words and sounds out unknown words, although she frequently misses some of the sounds in words (primarily medial sounds). Occasionally she leaves words out of her stories perhaps because she is writing so fast she assumes she has already written the words. This combined with leaving sounds out of words can cause her writing to be challenging to read. Her stories are organized with a clear beginning, middle and ending. She revises and edits her writing, especially when she is prompted with a self-assessment checklist. Rereading her own writing will continue to be a huge asset for Gracie Lee's development as a writer.

Grading and Writing Instruction

"Okay," you say, "these assessments sound good. I can see how they will be useful to me as a teacher of writing and to the writers in my classroom. But at some point, I am required to give a grade—an A, B, C, D, or F—or use a standards-based grading scale—Exceeding Standard, Meeting Standard, Developing, Emerging, or Beginning—or a proficiency-based grading scale—Highly Proficient, Proficient, Developing Proficiency, Beginning Proficiency, Not Proficient for writing. How do I do this?"

Honestly—we wish you did not have to do this. Grades are rarely productive (Kohn, 1993); they tend to reduce children's interest in learning and in taking risk. But at some point, teachers of writing are often asked to give a grade.

There are many ways teachers of writing give final grades. If you must do this, discuss with others about school and district policies, and, above all, find a system that honors the work of writers and aligns with what writers do and need to do. We suggest the following general guidelines for grading. Grade according to three categories:

- *Writing Practices.* Analyze data from Status of the Class; Teaching, Conferencing & Planning Notebook; Daily Writing Folder; self-assessments for how the writer is selecting for purpose and audience; writing for a range of purposes; alignment of time and writing tasks.
- *Writing Process.* Analyze data from Daily Writing Folder; Peer Conference data—specific forms and Status of the Class; self-assessments; Cumulative Writing Folder for how the writer is growing in his or her use of drafting, revising, conferencing, research, editing, and producing final work.
- *Writing Craft.* Risk—trying out something new; variety of text types or modes.

Data generated from Status of the Class; the Daily Writing Folder; the Teaching, Conferencing & Planning Notebook; writer self-assessment; and scored writing sample(s) work together to celebrate what a writer can do and to plan individualized instructional goals for future writing instruction. This is the role of quality, authentic assessment: to celebrate, to inform, and to move the writer forward in developing practices, process, and craft.

Problematizing Practice

The goals of Problematizing Practice are to deconstruct assumptions and beliefs and to consider multiple responses and implications of teaching decisions. It is best to do this in the company of colleagues and your instructor:

1. Read the scenario.
2. Quickly write down assumptions about the scenario. *Study your assumptions.*

3. Discuss and problematize assumptions with others and your instructor.
4. Discuss and write possible responses to the scenario.
5. Discuss the possible consequences (intended and unintended) of each response.

Scenario

Samantha, a third grader, takes school very seriously. She is a prolific writer. Her Daily Writing Folder includes attempts at multiple kinds of writing tasks: letters, lists, fantasy stories, opinions, poetry, and informative pieces. Many of these she has completed outside of the Writing Studio. Samantha takes great pride in her writing. Recently, Samantha along with her classmates, were required to complete a writing sample as a formal state writing exam. Samantha was very nervous about the exam. Her parent reported that she couldn't sleep the night before and refused to eat breakfast the day of the exam. Now, the official writing sample scores have been returned. Samantha received a "4" on her writing. While this is passing, Samantha is in tears! She overhead a classmate say that a "4 is barely passing." She is inconsolable.

References

Atwell, N. (1998). *In the middle: New understandings about writing, reading and learning* (2nd ed.). Portsmouth, NH: Heinemann.

Education Northwest. (2013a). 6+1° Trait definitions. Retrieved from Education Northwest: www.educationnorthwest.org/resource/503

Education Northwest. (2013b). 6+1° Trait Rubrics. Retrieved from Education Northwest: http://educationnorthwest.org/traits/traits-rubrics

Education Northwest. (2014). 6+1° Trait Writing Scoring Examples. Retrieved from Education Northwest http://educationnorthwest.org/traits/scored-examples

Kohn, A. (1993). *Punished by rewards: The trouble with gold stars, incentive plans, A's, praise and other bribes.* Boston, MA: Houghton Mifflin.

Owocki, G., & Goodman, Y. (2002). *Kidwatching: Documenting children's literacy development.* Portsmouth, NH: Heinemann.

Partnership for Assessment of Readiness for Career and College. (2014a). *PARCC Grade 2–3 Expanded Rubric for Analytic and Narrative Writing.* Retrieved February 14, 2014, from Partnership for Assessment of Readiness for Career and College: http://www.parcconline.org/sites/parcc/files/Grade%203%20ELA%20Expanded%20%20Rubric%20FOR%20ANALYTIC%20AND%20NARRATIVE%20WRITING_0.pdf

Partnership for Assessment of Readiness for Career and College. (2014b). *PARCC Grade 4–5 Expanded Rubric for Analytic and Narrative Writing.* Retrieved February 14, 2014, from Partnership for Assessment of Readiness for Career and College: http://www.parcconline.org/sites/parcc/files/Grade%204–5%20ELA%20Expanded%20Rubric%20FOR%20ANALYTIC%20AND%20NARRATIVE%20WRITING_0.pdf

Pinnell, G., & Fountas, I. C. (2011). *The continuum of literacy learning, grades PreK-8: A guide to teaching* (2nd ed.). Portsmouth, NH: Heinemann.

Routman, R. (2005). *Writing essentials: Raising expectations and results while simplifying teaching.* Portsmouth, NH: Heinemann.

Smarter Balanced Assessment Consortium. (2012, December 12). *Performance Tasks Writing Rubrics.* Retrieved February 14, 2014, from Smarter Balanced Assessment Consortium: http://www.smarterbalanced.org/wordpress/wp-content/uploads/2012/12/Performance-Tasks-Writing-Rubrics.pdf

part III
The Writing Studio Goes *Live*

Love the writing, love the writing, love the writing . . . the rest will follow.

—Jane Yolen

Figure PartIII.1 Mr. Johnson Selects Mentor Texts

Engaging in Struggle – Cycles of Revising and Conferring

Write your first draft with your heart. Re-write with your head.
—William Forrester, from the film *Finding Forrester*

How are you doing as a writer? When we last gathered, you were playing and experimenting with form and perspective, searching to find a topic for a personal narrative. We asked that by the time you finished reading Part II of *Becoming a Teacher of Writing in Elementary Classrooms*, you would have a draft, albeit a very rough draft, of a personal narrative in a form you most wanted to pursue. We also hinted that you might have more than one such draft, and we noted this would be absolutely okay.

If you have done this, you are at yet another decision point in your writing. You have one or more drafts of personal narrative: Can you commit to a draft? Do you need to change topics? (If so, return to earlier sections of *Becoming-Writer* and get started now.) If you have more than one draft, which one will you work with through the remainder of the time you are reading *Becoming a Teacher of Writing in Elementary Classrooms*?

Once you've committed to a draft, what's next? What will you next do as a writer with this piece to move it forward, to make it sound, look, *become* the story you want to tell?

Cycles of Revising and Conferring: Options

While reading Part III *Becoming a Teacher of Writing in Elementary Classrooms*, spend time as a writer working through cycles of revising and conferring with your personal narrative. This means engaging in any or all of the following:

- Self-conferencing
- Revising for content
- Revising for writing craft: word choice, format, beginning, endings, paragraphing, stanzas, imagery and any and all other parts of the personal narrative

- Conferring with peers
- Searching for inspiration (or finding the Muse)
- Taking a meaningful rest—aka taking a break from the writing

Self-Conferencing

On great days, reading draft writing can be an adrenaline rush: "Yes! This is it!" and as a writer, you find yourself scurrying to keep up with your thoughts, rearrange words, add details. On other days, a stream of doubting, critical voices fills our heads. When this happens, it's time to stretch, find resolve, turn on *other* music to play, and remind ourselves, "This is my story. No one gets to take this away from me!"

To have a conference with your self is to read your first draft without allowing yourself to make any changes in the text. Just mark up the margins: mark places you like, places you want to return to, add ideas for revisions, think about focus, and ask questions of yourself. We like using track changes on a word processor. Avoid falling in love with a first draft: it is always already a work in progress!

Donna Self-Confers

Donna has taken her four-page draft, completed a self-conference, deleted most of the draft, and now has a two-page narrative, along the lines of the Three-Minute Fiction model. Too bad the narrative has no ending. Donna is "stuck." Very soon, she is going to need a conference with Mindy. Without feedback, her personal narrative, now memoir, is going nowhere. As a writer, she is moving into the revising and conferring cycles, playing and experimenting with content and language, trying to "get it right."

Revising Content (Finding Focus)

Play with the content of the piece. Slow the action down. Replay it in your mind in s-l-o-w motion. Fill in missing pieces. Or, reread the piece and ask, "What is most necessary in this piece? What can I live without?" Delete—and save the deletion to another document, just in case you decide to return to them.

Confer With a Friend

At some point, a writer needs feedback. Once you've played with your draft, find a friend you believe will give you honest feedback. *Honest* feedback includes insightful questions, queries about purpose and motives, bluntness with kindness ("This is where the piece didn't work so well for me . . ."). In the world of writing instruction, we call this a "peer conference." But strip the title away and buy your friend a coffee or drink of choice and ask him/her to listen hard as you read your piece aloud. Better not to have him or her read it silently at this point; he or she may be distracted by typos or disjointed sentences. Have him or her listen for content, storyline, or dialogue—writing purpose. As the writer, you decide the areas of feedback you most need and focus on the listening ear of your friend. For example, "Does this part make you laugh?" or "I want the reader to feel panic—does it work?" or "What emotion do you sense as you hear this piece?" or "I have two different beginnings. Which one do you like best and why?"

Donna and Mindy's Conference

D: Okay, Mindy, I am stuck. I've deleted most of my original ramble and I now have a more concise draft. First question, I have the same beginning in past and present tense. Could you listen for which one you think works best? Is the narrative more focused now that I've deleted most of the draft? Can you tell what the focus is? And the big dilemma: I don't know how to end it. I am open to ideas!

M: Got it. Ready.

D: [Reads piece aloud.]

M: Wow. Well, definitely, if you want your reader to experience that opening with you, choose present tense. I like that line, what was it? "Play at adult." I get the sense of things moving on, of how important this moment was. This was a long time ago and here you are writing about it.

[Mindy and Donna continue talking about different aspects of the piece. The paper is now lying flat between them. Donna points at specific lines, words. Mindy notes that "salvage" yard might be good play on words; after all, "You are salvaging, or saving Morgan, from this environment when you first adopt him."]

D: But what about the ending?

M: Well, what is this piece about? I think you have to know that in order to write the ending—to make it memoir.

D: I don't know! That is the problem! What is it about?

M: Life works out? Are you writing to absolve yourself from guilt? For redemption? Is it "left, right foot, breathe"? Is it that nothing is left behind, that "behind" is always already our future?

D: Maybe something like the last . . . maybe it is a Barad (2007) thing about past, present, future, never a timeline, always intra-acting? I don't know.

M: I don't know either! Write to discover the meaning of your piece!

Other Rounds of Revisions

In the second, third, and fourth (and so on!) rounds of revision, you may want to focus on specific kinds of writing craft: language or word choice, beginnings, dialogue, action verbs, nouns, formatting, imagery; descriptive phrases, and endings. The list is long so take your time. Tackle just a few items each read through.

Content revisions take time. Try leaving your draft minimized on your computer and bringing it up throughout the day or night, or across days and nights. Print out a copy of your piece, or take your handwritten piece, and leave it near a place you pass often, like a kitchen table or a hallway entry. Stop for a few minutes now and then read, play, and fiddle with the story. Make a date with your draft: court it well during a specific period. Ask, "What is the story about? What gets to the heart of what I want to say?"

Other Rounds of Revision: Donna and Mindy Confer

After conferring with Mindy, Donna continued to revise her memoir. She printed it, left it on the dining room table, played with a word here and there, and finally returned to Mindy for another round of conferring.

D: I think I may know what my memoir is about. That's what I would like you to listen for today. I have an ending—I keep tweaking it so I really have three possibilities. I'll read the one I think works best.

M: Okay. Ready, friend. Let's hear it!

D: [Reads piece aloud.]

M: I am impressed with how much you have deleted and focused! Was that hard to do?

D: Not after we last talked and I set the piece aside—there were just too many stories there before—I needed to choose one.

M: I do think the imagery of "dust" works. You may be over doing it—may I look at your piece to make a few suggestions?

[Donna and Mindy look through piece together . . . talk. Donna makes changes in the draft . . .]

M: I think I like the third ending option but I wonder, is the dust refusing to bury or refusing to be buried? Aren't you the one that won't bury the dust—or are you saying the dust has its own agency and therefore can't be buried?

D: I am not sure. Maybe I don't want to be sure. Is it possible to let the reader decide?

M: Could be. See what you think in a day or two . . .

Other Rounds of Revision: Finding Inspiration

Sometimes we find that a first draft needs time to sit; other times we find we cannot stay away from a first draft—it draws us in and wants to play—and we cannot ignore it. Other times, we need to find inspiration.

If you are feeling the latter, here are some suggestions of short personal narratives we find inspiring: "Eleven" by Sandra Cisneros (1991), found in *Woman Hollering Creek and Other Stories*. Actually any short story by Cisneros illustrates the "one-inch picture frame" Anne Lamott (1994) writes about. Or check out *Kunckehead: Tall Tales and Mostly True Stories About Growing Up Scieszka* (Scieszka, 2008). Scieszka is particularly a good model if you are writing a humorous story. Barbara Kingsolver's (2002) *Small Wonder* is a beautiful example of short essays. We like her essay "Going to Japan." Do an Internet search for the poet William Carlos Williams. His poem "This Is Just to Say" (1938) may be good inspiration for those of you writing letters.

The preceding is not a step-by-step process. Revising and conferring cycles will not be the same for every writer, so "the process" is dependent on you. How this process looks is dependent upon several factors, including the following: How willing are you to engage beyond your comfort zone? How much time do you have and are you willing to devote to the process of seeing this draft personal narrative to a final product? How important is it to you that you have a final product you are proud of, one that you care about and are willing to share with others?

Your Writing Goal

Your writing goal is to move your personal narrative through cycles of revision and conferring until you believe the content is set, or you are satisfied with your personal narrative, by the time you finish reading Part III of *Becoming a Teacher of Writing in Elementary Classrooms*. This writing includes composing a title for your piece.

Metacognition Practice

Practice metacognition throughout the revising and conferring cycles. Ask yourself, "What makes this difficult, easy? Why do I want to stop, continue? How am I feeling as a writer at this moment?"

When you feel you have the content set and before you move on to Part IV of *Becoming a Teacher of Writing in Elementary Classrooms* and the last section of *Becoming-Writer* reflect on the following:

- What parts of revising and conferring were difficult, easy? Describe your response.
- How is your above response unique or different to this writing experience?
- Did you take any writing risks as you were revising and conferring? Why or why not? Is this typical of you as a writer? Please explain.
- What have you learned about yourself as a writer during the revising and conferring cycles? How might this influence who you are becoming as a teacher of writing?

If possible, talk about your responses with others who are reading and writing their way through *Becoming a Teacher of Writing in Elementary Classrooms*. Through sharing your experience, you will begin to gain perspective on how different writers process and engage in writing.

Donna Practices Metacognition

For me, the most difficult part is finding a focus for my memoir. I think that is why it rambled so much at the beginning—it was more than one story. Even after I deleted so much content, it still didn't have a focus! I had to keep writing, revising, reading to find that focus, to discover what the piece was about. I think I am mostly a writer who writes to make discoveries, so while it doesn't surprise me that this is what I did with this memoir, it does surprise me how much time and energy was required for such a short piece of writing! The risk to me is always sharing personal writing with others. Still makes my heart rate increase twofold, even when I am sharing with a good friend like Mindy. Every time I do this kind of writing and share it with students I am reminded of what teachers of writing are asking their students to risk—it just isn't something to take for granted.

References

Barad, K. (2007). *Meeting the universe halfway: Quantum physics and the entanglement of matter and meaning*. Durham, NC: Duke University Press.

Cisneros, S. (1991). *Woman hollering creek and other stories*. New York, NY: Vintage Books.

Connery, S., Mark, L. (Producers), Rich, M. (Writer), & Van Sant, G. (Director). (2000). *Finding Forrester* [Motion Picture].

Kingsolver, B. (2002). *Small wonder essays*. New York, NY: HarperCollins.

Lamott, A. (1994). *Bird by bird: Some instructions on writing and life*. New York, NY: Random House.

Scieszka, J. (2008). *Knucklehead: Tall tales and mostly true stories about growing up Scieszka*. NY, NY: Viking.

Williams, W. C. (1938). *The collected poems of William Carlos Williams: 1909–1939* (Vol. I; Eds. W. Litz & C. MacGowan). New York, NY: New Directions.

Chapter Six
Writing Strategies to Teach

Writers in the Studio are composing biographies of relatives or people they know and admire. Writers are conducting research and learning to organize common details together; they are collecting fun pictures and planning to publish small books they can give as gifts to the special person. But the stories are flat. They are not really stories but facts strung together, more often beginning with "So-and-So was born" and a lot of "and then" sentences. Writers seem uninspired and Ms. J is fearful this writing is starting to feel like an assignment. Ugh. Her writers love to write stories: stories of themselves, adventure and fantasy stories, and fairy tales, but these biographies . . . (sigh).

Stories. "They are not writing biography as story." Ms. J sat up in bed and said this aloud last night. What to do about this? What if writers learned the writing strategy of choosing one illustrative story from someone's life that captures the essence of who that person is? What if they understood that they didn't need to tell all the details of someone's life, just one really great story? What if they applied the "one-inch picture frame" writing strategy they already use in their fiction writing to their biographies?

After her last night revelation, Ms. J rises early, gets into her classroom, and searches the classroom library shelves for mentor-texts that might illustrate how a single story can be illuminating about a person's life and character. How about Jeanette Winter biographies? The Watcher: Jane Goodall's Life with the Chimps (Winter, 2011), focuses just on Jane cultivating friendship with the chimps. And, yes, The Librarian of Basra: A True Story from Iraq (Winter, 2005) tells just the story of how Alia Muhhammad Baker saves the precious books of the library from being destroyed. Ms. J laughs. "Scieszka (2008) to lighten things up!" Although autobiography, any single story from his collection illustrates something about himself.

Ms. J is feeling inspired (a good sign—writers find her inspirations motivational!) "Why not draft my own biography, illustrating this writing strategy?" she announces to the empty room. She can write about her mom. So many stories that illustrate what a remarkable women she was! "How about the time my Mom chartered a plane when there were no flights from her small college town to the Bahamas and she and her friends wanted a vacation?" she thinks. "It so defines my mom as a 'make it happen' kind of person! Besides the kids will love this story! Perfect!"

Ms. J feels her own energy rise as she piles picture books and jots down notes for her own biography writing. "This is going to be good," she says aloud. It is a sure combination to bring energy back to the Writing Studio: a "just write" writing strategy, great mentor texts, a teacher jazzed about her own writing—yes, this is the Writing Studio, live, and Ms. J can't wait for the show to start!

The classroom as Writing Studio is arranged with care, folders, and forms organized as a canvas of bright colors. Beginning-of-the-year assessment data have been analyzed and writing goals drafted; expectations and anticipation hangs in the air. We have a framework for staying accountable to our writers and their families. "Teaching is planned opportunism," writes Peter Johnston (2012, p. 2), and we are ready for opportunity, for possibilities: the Writing Studio is going *live*.

There's a lot of action in the Writing Studio as children work independently and collaboratively, explore possibilities, negotiate challenges, experience the ups and downs of *becoming-writer*. In Part III of *Becoming a Teacher of Writing in Elementary Classrooms*, we explore these dynamics by focusing more closely on illustrating what is taught in the Writing Studio and how it is taught through mini-lessons, individual teacher–student writing conferences, and guided writing. We also look more closely at how independent and collaborative writing is fostered and the role of sharing and celebrating in fostering an environment of collaboration, risk taking, and thus successful, authentic writing.

"But what do I teach in the Writing Studio?" is an honest question our teacher candidates ask us. In this chapter, we provide illustrative (but by no means exhaustive) examples of the kinds of writing strategies taught in the Writing Studio. Before diving into this topic, let's step back and review Johnston's (2004, 2012) dynamic-learning frame for teaching and his research on how teacher language is a strategy of influence when presenting mini-lessons, conferencing one-on-one, and facilitating guided writing instruction.

We do this now because how the Writing Studio goes live depends on how teachers of writing frame their role, their words, and thus the world where children will grow up and write. And this, in turn, will influence the happiness, well-being, and futures of these same children as writers and global citizens. A dynamic-learning frame stresses how learning takes time, is a process, which includes challenges, persistence, and embraces "failures" as positive risk taking; collaboration is critical to success (Johnston, 2012). This dynamic-learning frame alters life in the Writing Studio. For example, "modeling" as the expert *telling* the writer and the writer listening and receiving information (fixed-performance frame) is transformed as the *becoming-writer* as a teacher collaborates and learns *with* writers (dynamic-learning frame), sharing their own writing risks, failures, and ability to meet writing challenges. A dynamic-learning frame in our experience means there is a lot more wonder and joy in the Writing Studio!

How is this dynamic-learning frame communicated to writers? "As teachers, we choose our words and, in the process, construct the classroom worlds for our students and ourselves" (Johnston, 2012, p. 1). *Our words matter*: we can choose words that develop independence, identity, agency, and *becoming*; words that support writers as they transfer knowledges from one location to another (Johnston, 2004). Language that notices and names celebrates what children can do; it provokes thought probing questions, "Did anyone notice . . .?" (Johnston, 2004, p. 13) "I remember when getting started in the Writing Studio seemed like such a difficult task, but now you all do this automatically!" or "What other things are you noticing about mysteries as you read them? What surprises you or makes you wonder about these things we are noticing?" "I noticed today how you read your piece with emotion. You are really putting yourself as the character into the piece you have written." "Did anyone try one of the leads we experimented with earlier today? Johnston (2004) writes, "Through our noticing and naming language, children learn the significant features of the world, themselves, and others" (p. 20).

Teachers scaffold identity and independence by asking sincere "how" questions (Johnston, 2004): "How did you come up with this idea for writing? Tell me your thought process," and "Last week you used a two-column dialogue chart to plan the talk between your characters. How did that work? How else might you use the two-column chart to help your thinking about characters?" "Why" questions can help children become independent problem solvers: "Why do you think you are stuck here?" just as "What else" questions invite play and experimentation: "What else might you try or have you tried?"

Johnston (2012) notes that our talk as teachers reflects our own histories, our own parents and teachers. We need to consciously think about our talk and how we are framing writers and writing throughout talk; we may need to change our belief system frame and how we communicate to children. Children have opinions, interests, fears, dreams, and ideas. The Writing Studio is designed to honor these. Be conscious of your belief system frame as you read through Part III, "The Writing Studio Goes *Live*." If, for example, you hear a voice saying, "This will never work," practice saying, "Why am I questioning this? What histories influence my response? What might happen if this did work? How might it work? What else might be possible if it does work?" Imagine possibilities—create opportunities for children *becoming-writers*.

The Writing Studio is going *live*—be organized; be prepared; may your belief system of possibilities and opportunities be reflected in your actions and words as you begin to teach writing strategies through mini-lessons, teacher–student writing conferences, and guided writing.

What We Teach in the Writing Studio

Teacher candidates with whom we work raise the question of what to teach in the Writing Studio most often after their first round of conducting teacher-student writing conferences. Face-to-face with a writer during a one-on-one conference, the teacher candidate later confesses, "I didn't know what to say. I couldn't think of a way to help the writer. I finally just looked for misspelled words." In part, as fluent writers, it is easy for teacher candidates to take for granted what they do as writers: slow down and study your own process for writing; analyze what you do; name it; pass on the writing advice to others! (Note: The *Becoming-Writer* sections of this book provide you opportunities to do this.)

Sometimes, it is a feeling that one is not "expert enough." Frank Smith (1998) has wise advice:

> try to be more than an observer in these learning situations, and become a participant. Don't attempt to teach anyone how to do art, science, read, or writing, or how to behave collaboratively, respectfully, democratically, and so on, *but engage in these things yourself* [emphasis added], demonstrating how they are important to you. (p. 86)

"All very inspiring," you say, "But I still don't know what to teach as a teacher of writing!"

Fair enough—let us jump start your thinking, exploring, and discovering strategies writers use—and we can teach—as practices, process, and craft. Here's the caveat: whole books are written on these topics! (Some of our favorites are listed in Appendix O.) Our goal here is to describe a few illustrative strategies; the following does not pretend to be anywhere near a comprehensive list. These are served as appetizers—as you are an engaged participant, expand the menu and keep it interesting over time for yourself as a writer and as a teacher of writing. These illustrative strategies can be, should be, tweaked, and adjusted, for the context and writers of the Writing Studio—and they are best served up with a dynamic-learning frame (Johnston, 2012)!

We have arranged these illustrative strategies according to writing practices, process, and craft. The boundaries of these categories are blurred so many of the strategies can be used across the spectrum of practices, process, and craft.

Teaching About Writing Practices

"When you get stuck writing, what do you do to get unstuck?" This is the question Mr. Mackie posed to writers in his classroom several days prior to the discussion he is leading today. Writers have been collecting data on how they deal with being "stuck as writers." Writers generate a list of ideas including "doodling, wandering in the library, talking with a friend, re-reading what I've written." After the list is generated, Mr. Mackie and the writers will categorize their findings, name them, and then problematize the categories by asking, "How are these strategies useful? When can these same strategies be distracting? During what kinds of writing conditions are these strategies most helpful to me?"

Discussing "How do writers get unstuck?" is an example of teaching about writing practices through talk. Thoughtful discussions about writing are a critical teaching strategy for writing instruction. These are not onetime discussions, but discussions that surface again and again during mini-lessons, guided writing, and teacher–student conferences.

Here is a partial list of questions that will guide discussions about writing practices:

- *What is writing risk, and why is it important?* Discuss what it looks like, feels like, what it can produce, and how it is different for everyone. Have writers compose "writing risk goals" for themselves. "If you were going to take a writing risk, what would it look like?"
- *Why do people write?* Inquire and collect data on the many purposes, possibilities, and reasons for writing.
- *Is the Writing Studio working?* Deconstruct the taken-for-granted routines; practice problematizing and finding alternative processes and procedures as necessary.
- *How do writers sustain their writing?* Inquire and collect data on how favorite authors sustain their writing lives.
- *Do writers always need to be inspired?* Inquire and collect data to find out if favorite authors always feel inspired when they write. Ask, "What does it mean to be inspired anyway?"

Author web pages, essays, student writing, and teacher writing can all be useful in these discussions.

Teach Metacognition: The Study of One's Own Writing Process

Metacognition is to think about thinking. Metacognition is particularly important in teaching writing practices (Cremin & Myhill, 2012; Fu & Hansen, 2012). Writing is a uniquely individual act and each writer benefits from analyzing their own process. While we can generalize about writing process, the fact is writers all approach writing differently based on the writing task, purpose, audience, context, need, and physical/emotional/spiritual/intellectual state-of-being.

For example, Cremin and Myhill (2012) discuss research dividing writers into two groups: discovery writers who write to find out what they want/need to write about and planners who need to outline and plan prior to composing sentences. Although staging binaries can be dangerous, the research can also be useful to writers in discovering what they need as writers. Support writers in determining where they are on the continuum of "discovery writers" to "planners." Have writers consider when they are more likely to write to discover the purpose of their writing through writing and when they are more likely to need to plan for their writing. Have them practice both—what seems to work best, when?

Some additional questions to spur metacognition thinking are as follows:

- What makes writing hard? What makes writing easy?
- How does the setting matter when you are writing? Does the setting always matter? For example, do you always need a quiet space or only for certain kinds of writing?
- What makes you nervous about writing?
- What makes you excited about writing?
- How do you think past experiences with writing may be influencing your writing today?
- What do you know about yourself as a writer now that you didn't know last year?

Teaching writers to practice metacognition and learn about their writing practices and process is a step in developing independence as a writer. When we know our trigger points, understand how we work best, know where our challenges lie, we can better gauge the kinds of time, support, and structure we will need to face a variety of writing tasks. Likewise, the more teachers of writing know this about the writers in their classroom and their process, the more they are able to adapt and create the most beneficial learning environment for all children.

Teach Organization and Routines

Five-year-old Rhoda is giving several adults a tour of her kindergarten classroom. "These are our writing supplies," she says with authority. "We keep them neat and we put 'em back carefully 'cause when we want to say something important, we want to have the right tool."

Rhoda is mimicking what she has heard her teacher say repeatedly. She knows the purpose for the routine of storing writing supplies. Managing the Writing Studio (as we have said before) is about teaching routines and expectations and the purpose behind those routines and expectations.

"Every day at this time we are going to write. You can count on this. It is important that we write daily. This is the way we develop our writing practices, build writing stamina, and become better writers. Let's begin to explore what this looks like so we all know how working in our Writing Studio will look."

This kind of opening statement begins the Writing Studio. Explaining, modeling, discussing, and revisiting and examining routines and schedules keep the purpose lively and worthwhile. During the first month of school, teach, model, and practice schedules and routines that are critical to a well-organized Writing Studio. Make this engaging; for example, practice and then time how efficiently Status of the Class can be completed.

Revisit schedules and routines as necessary. Deconstruct them with writers. Collect observational data and use these data to problematize with writers: "Several of you mentioned how distracting it is for you as writers when other writers are coming and going from the computer area. Why is this causing a distraction? How might we resolve this?" Consider video recording individual and collaborative writing time. View the recording with writers, ask, "What do you notice in this video recording? Are there any places where we might change what we are doing?" During mini-lessons, model how to organize, review, and use Daily Writing Folders. Reinforce this during sharing at the end of the Writing Studio by having writers highlight elements of their Folders.

Teaching, reinforcing, and problematizing schedules and routines support independence and ownership—two critical components in managing the Writing Studio. Do this well at the beginning of the year, and many "management issues" will be avoided throughout the year.

 What are additional strategies for teaching writing practices that you have observed being taught in classrooms or used, yourself, as a writer? Write them into the margins of this text for future reference.

Teaching About Writing Process

Writing process—the processes of finding a topic, getting the first words on paper and composing a complete draft, doing the work of content revisions (usually more than once), seeking and giving feedback, deciding if the content is set, completing editing process, making design decisions, and publishing and broadcasting a piece of writing—must be modeled, individualized, adapted, and developed in different ways based upon the writing task, purpose, and audience. Illustrative teaching and writing strategies for these writing processes are described in the following sections.

Finding a Topic

"So what have you discovered?" Mr. Mackie inquires of the small group of children gathered with him at the conference table.

"The New York Public Library website says that Gary Paulson gets his ideas for writing from his life or from history," reports Joaquin.

"Cynthia Rylant's website says that she gets her ideas from favorite things she does in her life. For example, she likes animals and lots of her books have animal characters," Bella adds.

"I found out on Kate DiCamillo's website that she wrote *Because of Winn-Dixie* during a bad winter when she was lonely and was missing her dog," chimes in Suelita.

Because the writers in this guided writing group have struggled finding writing topics, Mr. Mackie sent them off to inquire how the writers they read find ideas. Individuals are now reporting the information they gleaned from author pages on the Internet. Mr. Mackie will guide them in using this information and applying it to their own lives as writers.

Create a Common Experience

Creating a common experience that children can write about is a useful way to grow writing ideas. For example, in early grades, observing, recording, and writing about eggs hatching; collecting and categorizing fall leaves; acting out a story with multiple endings; or playing "pretend" can generate writing ideas. Older writers might engage in a service project, visit a watershed, participate in a simulation; or enact a role-playing scenario.

Plan common experiences carefully. Create opportunities for lots of interactive talk, observations, lists, graphic organizers, and categories as the experience unfolds. Model and engage in shared writing and allow for individual opinions and perspectives.

Tap Into Questions

Questions drive writers. Sometimes, these are wonder-questions ("I wonder if ants ever stop moving?"); sometimes, they are self-questions ("Why are my eyes blue and my brother's eyes brown? Could I travel to Mars for real?"); or, maybe they are big universal "Why" questions ("Why do people die?").

Sometimes, these are "what if" questions. Reading Rylant's (2013) poetry collection *God Got a Dog* inspires "what-if" questions: "What if God got a dog? What if God went to the doctor?" Read Rylant's poems; write a class poem; and continue making a class list of "what-if" questions.

Create opportunity for writers to ask questions. Create categories of questions (*fun, crazy, serious, scary* questions). Have writers brainstorm specific questions under these categories. Suggest a writer carry a notebook and write down questions for a day. Allow a writer to interview another writer about a topic or their life and see what kinds of questions and topics emerge. Keep a "wonder-box" and invite children to write questions for this box and share them often as writing possibilities. As a teacher, wonder aloud. Make talk about questions a common practice in the Writing Studio.

Timelines and Graphic Organizers

Timelines are an effective way to find an idea. Writers can create timelines of their lives, of the last weekend, or a specific event. Graphic organizers can be used in all kinds of ways to generate ideas. Writers play with ideas by placing any topic in the center of the organizer and brainstorming possibilities. Note: there are premade graphic organizers, and these are useful with some writers who need specific scaffolds, but overusing these promotes dependence, not independence. Work toward the goal of independence and having writers devise their own graphic organizer from several common formats. We find Gabriel Rico's (2000) work to be useful to us as teachers of writing. Check out her website, www.gabrielerico.com/, and reconnect with graphic organizers.

Start With Emotions

Tap into writers' emotions by placing an emotion in the center of a graphic organizer like "scared," "happy," or "angry." Allow time for writers to talk and think about different times when they experienced these emotions or allow them to play with literary devices and consider how such emotions sound, look, and what they are like.

Readers Who Write

A dynamic way to find writing ideas is through reading. A writer can consult their reading log, browse the shelves of the library, or check out an area of interest on the Internet. This may be a reader/writer researching facts, or it may be a reader/writer saying, "I'd like to write a story like *Scaredy Squirrel*" (Watts, 2011).

Teach About Drafting

When asked, Ezra will tell you that what is hard about writing is getting the first words on the page. He has ideas—that is not his challenge. It is that first line, sometimes the first word. If he can get the first three lines down, he is on his way. The blank page syndrome is a common conundrum for writers. While getting those first words onto paper can be difficult, it is also creative and exciting to see the words come together into sentences that entice a reader! Following are some strategies that may be useful to writers in your Writing Studio.

Talk First

It is one thing to have an idea in your head. The idea is often fuzzy at the edges, perhaps in isolated frames, or maybe just a seed waiting for germination. Telling another person the story as it happened to us, talking through an idea, showing someone a messy kind of graphic organizer that loosely outlines a possible report act as a springboard to actually writing those first lines. Plan for, and encourage, talk in the Writing Studio! Model this kind of talk. "I have an idea. I'd like to write about a necklace my grandmother gave me when I was a child. Could you help me think about this necklace?" Now let the writers ask you, even as you tell them about, that necklace. Teach writers to turn to one another, find a peer, and talk about an idea prior to writing. Teach writers to say, "I really liked how you just told me about your brother leaping from under the bed and scaring you while you were falling asleep! I think we should break now so you can write down what you just said!" Talking prior to drafting is particularly important for English learners; be deliberate in planning talk time for them (Cloud, Genesee, & Hamayan, 2009).

Sketch First

Young writers draw to write but illustrations and sketches can support our writing long after we learn to spell words and string them together into sentences. Teach storyboarding as a way to think about writing ideas and to provide a framework from which a writer can work. Model this through shared writing and teacher demonstration. Sketching first is another strategy English learners can find particularly useful.

Titles First!

As young readers discover chapter books as readers, they often begin to write chapter books. The best part may be writing the title at the top of the page. It is after the title that the writer often becomes stuck. Encourage such a writer to not only write the title of the book but also the title of the chapters. This works like outlining but is much more fun. Combine title writing with illustrations and the writer has a scaffold that will carry him or her to the end of his or her story.

How About a Letter?

There is always someone or something to which one can write! Write a letter to a famous person, a relative, animal, school personnel (e.g., media specialist, principal, crossing guard), or anyone else or even a thing. Express gratefulness, admiration, remorse, or share a great memory. Receiving a response can be very gratifying and motivational to a writer—plan accordingly.

Teaching Revisions

"Never fall in love with a first draft!" First drafts are not sacred; they are canvases on which to play with this art form. Frame revision as a creative challenge, not as a "next step," a "requirement," or a "necessary evil." Revision is what writers do—it is the rethinking and the reworking of content. Revision is *not* editing. It is not that writers do not revise and edit simultaneously—they do, but revision is content and editing is spelling, punctuation, and grammar (more on this later). The process may comingle, but the definitions and the intent of each should not. Model often how as a writer, you scrape entire drafts and start over again. Avoid lockstep approaches to teaching writing: Day 1: draft; Day 2: revise; Day 3: edit; Day 4: publish.

Avoid making revision unduly hard. Above all, avoid having writers recopy work and call this revision! We repeat, avoid having writers recopy work! There is nothing productive about simply recopying to include a couple of extra words; besides, it can be painful if doing this by hand. Teach writers to literally cut and paste: cut apart writing and paste or tape in revisions into the main paper. Teach writers to write every other line so there is room to cut and paste or to write in and around the original writing. Teach them to use the caret (^) to insert additions or a number system, placing a "1" at the first place where there is a revision and then using a "1" below the text to add in revision or rewrite a line. Teach older writers to use a word processor, not just for "final copies" but also for drafting and revising. Many teachers have writers use composition notebooks for their writing. Such notebooks are fine for collecting data, for research, and for note taking or for specific, assigned response writing, but composition notebooks can be difficult for writers who are learning to revise and need space to do so.

Altered Text

Altered text is a good way to teach the process of revision. Take a piece of photocopied published text and model revision by cutting it apart and adding in additional text, comments, and responses. Illustrations and dialogue or anything else can be used to create an "altered text." This is fun play with picture books that perhaps have good pictures but not so great stories or stories with distinct points at which characters could do something to change the course of the story. Altered text can work with nonfiction text as well. Selected portions of rather boring textbooks are prime material for altered text. Writers can practice inserting additional facts and details as needed. Altered text, as a form of mixed-media artwork, can become pieces of art in and of themselves.

Slowing Down the Details

The Evil Pancakes

In a holtel it was 9:30 am when a few evil panckes broke in the hotel. The few evil panckaes were stealing a lot of money. this looks like a job for super boy. Super boy was fighting the evil panckaes . . .

Jon's is breathless kind of writing and if only the reader could have heard how this story was told with gestures, animated voice, and pretend dialogue! Writers like Jon need to learn to slow down the pace, take a breath, and zoom in on an area to revise and make the story sound on paper the way it does when told aloud or in their head. A useful writing strategy is to frame with your hands a select portion of the text, for example, in the earlier text "*In a holtel it was 9:30 am when a few evil panckes broke in the hotel.*" Have the writer read it aloud and encourage them to slow down the story and tell it as if they were a movie director filming each frame (Calkins & Oxenhorn, 2003). Draw out the animation from the writer. Sometimes, it can even be helpful to take notes for a writer so they have an outline to write from later.

Perspective Taking

Wallace Steven's (1982) "13 Ways of Looking at a Blackbird" is an excellent reminder of how a poet or writer can view anything from multiple perspectives. Learning to see a topic another way is an effective strategy for revision. *The True Story of the Three Little Pigs* (Scieszka & Smith, 1996) is another classic mentor-text for perspective taking.

Too often, once ideas are formed as words on a page, it is difficult for a writer to seemingly destroy that work by cutting and pasting and drawing and writing all over that text that took so much effort to get on the paper. Another approach, then, is for a writer to attempt to write a piece using a different form or from another perspective. If the narrative is told from a third-person perspective, choose one character and try a few lines as a first-person narrative. If the piece is an essay, turn it into a letter poem. Then, just for fun, illustrate it and write only one line under each illustration. Choose a different point of view: tell the story from an inanimate object's side of the story! If the story has been a telling, suggest the writer revises using dialogue only. Teach writers to play with ideas, language, and form. Writing a piece using different forms and perspectives can teach this kind of play and revision.

Finding a Focus

Anne Lamott (1994) advises writers to begin by writing only what will fit into a one-inch picture frame. Use this concept to support writers in finding focus in a piece that rambles. Literally cut out a one-inch picture frame in the shape of a heart. Have the writer use it to scroll across the piece and find the "heart" of the piece. "Now start writing here, at the heart of the piece." As with any strategy, model it, practice it—more than once.

Give It a Rest

Writers know the value of giving a piece a rest. Sometimes, we have stared at the page too long. We need a walk, a run, recess, or to talk with friends. When elementary writers feel a need for a rest, they often rush through a piece, trying to finish it, so they can finally leave it alone. Teach writers to gauge themselves as writers and to know when they need to give a piece a rest. Encourage them to work on something different, create art, or take a break and read. There is value in leaving a piece of writing for a day or so. Teachers of writing often get nervous about this: what if the writer will not return to his work? What if she never finishes a draft? But it is artificial of teachers to expect writers to never pause and give their writing a break. Elementary writers need to learn to walk away from a piece and to return to that same piece. In upper grades, use a calendar and plot out a revision strategy for a writer who is stuck or doesn't want to revise at a certain moment. Use Status of the Class as a "calendar alert" ("Joanie, today is your day to return to your draft 'Summer Dream'")

 What are additional strategies for teaching writing process that you have observed being taught in classrooms or used, yourself, as a writer? Write them into the margins of this text for future reference.

Teaching About the Craft of Editing

Editing gets a bad rap. And it gets too much attention too early in most cases. Set the stage with editing: it is nuanced writing. It is why writing is powerful, persuasive, and makes a reader laugh (or cry): a paper edited well is easy for a reader to enjoy without distracting errors. That said, there is ample research showing how proficient readers overlook errors all the time—the brain is wired to make sense of text (Goodman, 1996). Too often, a well-edited paper seems to be the only or most significant signal of "success" for many adults. For this reason, teach parents, guardians, administrators, and other caring adults the role of editing and how to interact with young writers about editing.

Editing and Revision: Two Different Skills and Craft

Editing is a technical process, but it can be applied in creative and interesting ways (think about the poet ee cummings). It is critically important. But its importance is toward the end of a piece, when a writer is fairly sure the content is set (e.g., revisions are complete). That said, proficient readers/writers often find that while revising a piece, they need to edit, and while editing a piece, they need to revise. While writers often revise and edit at the same time, teach revision as working with content and editing as working with conventions—spelling, capitalization, punctuation, and grammar. They are not the same skill or craft. Model how writers generally revise content first and then edit, but avoid preaching a "must-do" process of steps. Most importantly, teach that writers should care about editing so that their final work will be masterful in communicating its meaning to readers.

Use mentor texts (see later discussion) to teach conventions so that writers can see how authors use conventions to communicate with readers. Provide access to shared and interactive practice and make sure writers include examples and rules as part of their individual writing goals (see Chapter 3 for a review of individual writing goal sheets).

A solid strategy for teaching writers to edit is to read their work aloud. Reading aloud slows down the reading process and allows a writer to see errors that might otherwise go unnoticed. Model this strategy repeatedly for writers.

 View a video of Yesica, Grade 4 writer, using the dictation feature on an iPad to edit her writing for spelling.

Common Editing Lessons

That said, writers have to be able to recognize errors when they see them whether in slow motion or not. Common lessons necessary to primary elementary writers include capitalization, end-of-sentence punctuation, and spelling sight words accurately. Common lessons necessary for upper elementary writers include comma use in a series, sentence combining, capitalization, paragraphing, noun–verb agreement, and how to punctuate and paragraph dialogue.

Teaching Spelling

We support a constructivist view in teaching spelling, punctuation, and grammar (Wilde, 2013). This means basing instruction upon writing development and need, teaching interactively with developmentally appropriate text; and, teaching and reinforcing specific strategies. For example, teach, "Commonly misspelled words" (lists for grade levels abound on the Internet) interactively as you model writing or conduct shared writing. Post a word wall that provides a resource for writers, reflecting their writing development and need. Giving all children a common list of words to memorize is "rooted in misconceptions about how children become conventional spellers. Such practices segregate spelling as a distinct act, when spelling should be learned in its natural context—as children compose" (Manning & Ransom, 2013, p. 87). Individualize spelling lists for writers and have them create these lists as a resource and the words on the lists as a writing goal.

Editing and English Learners

Teachers of writing must be deliberate and intentional in teaching conventions and editing skills. English learners in particular will need direct instruction (Goldenberg, 2013). Learning to write in a second language writing system is a challenging task and may require learning new skills or adapting writing skills from a first language (Fu, 2009). Work closely with English language specialists to individualize instruction for English language writers, who will have specific needs based on their home language.

Individualize convention and editing instruction through teacher–student conferences and guided writing (see next chapters). Reinforce lessons, celebrate writers' accomplishments, and hold writers accountable through individual editing goals.

 What are additional strategies for teaching conventions and editing that you have observed being taught in classrooms or used, yourself, as a writer? Write them into the margins of this text for future reference.

Teaching to Develop Writing Craft

Writing craft—the ability to take our thoughts, find the words, and place them on paper in such a way to make a reader yearn for more. (Sigh). Anne Lamott (1994) says of writing, "You are going to have to give and give and give, or there's no reason for you to be writing. You have to give from the deepest part of yourself, and you are going to have to go on giving, and the giving is going to have to be its own reward" (pp. 202–203). We find that part of the reward of such giving is learning different strategies of writer's craft. The excitement, for example, of learning to use personification and exclamation mark or of learning how to create cartoons can be such a reward for elementary writers. Teaching writer's craft is also a reward for teachers of writing—the energy from learning is infectious.

Mentors and Mentor Texts

Mentor texts are central to instruction in mini-lessons, teacher–student conferences, guided writing. As writers see mentor text used and modeled, they begin to seek this resource independently. A mentor text is any text (billboards, menus, newspapers, web pages, to published books) that can be used to illustrate, or mentor, the writer in specific genres and writing craft. Begin the quest for mentor texts with any text you hold in your hands, see on your computer screen, view from peripheral vision while on a daily commute: mentor texts lurk everywhere, often in plain sight. Read with the question, "What does this text illustrate to me as a writer?" And when a text pulls you in, perks you up, makes you sad—be particularly alert: you are probably reading an amazing mentor text!

You don't embark on this quest alone—teach children, their parents and guardians, to read in this same way. Honor the quest; celebrate the find. Grow your mentor text resource list in the company of others. View each book in your classroom library as a mentor text. And—*be organized* (have you heard this before?). Your organizational efforts will be rewarded when you are searching for the perfect mentor text, for a particular writer, with a particular need, and you can find it quickly using any number of applications, interactive online book review sites, or a word-processing or spreadsheet document.

Mentor texts are not necessarily published texts. Two equally rich sources for mentor text are student-writers and their teachers. Collect children's work from across grade levels to inspire and mentor. As teachers, write with children. Collect models of your own writing to use as demonstrations in the Writing Studio. Write along with this book using the *Becoming-Writer* sections to craft perhaps the first of many in your growing personal collection of mentor texts.

With mentor texts in hand, we are ready to further pursue the question, "What do I teach as a teacher of writing?" by examining strategies for writing craft.

Opening Line and Leads

My grandfather, Billy, hears the talk of birds. (MacLachlan, 2012)

It was a funeral in every way but one: The body was missing. (Korman, 2002)

The day I decided to steal a dog was the same day my best friend, Luanne Godfrey, found out I lived in a car. (O'Connor, 2007)

"Our land is alive, Esperanza," said Papa, taking her small hand as they walked through the gentle slopes of the vineyard. (Ryan, 2000)

An unmistakable hoot in the night lets you know that there is a tawny owl in the woods. (Taylor, 1998)

Each of the preceding first lines elicits an immediate response from the reader, raises a question, sets a mood. They also demonstrate how mentor text can be used to teach different ways to begin any genre of writing. An effective way to teach opening lines and leads is to use a combination of mentor text and inquiry. Invite readers to collect and post examples of opening lines, leads, and endings. As the teacher, have a good collection to begin the process. Next, categorize and name the categories of examples. Allow writers to name according to their own descriptions, meaning you may end up with titles such as "Stories that start with something happening." Post these categories on walls or have writers write down examples in their Daily Writing Folder. During shared or interactive writing, practice writing opening lines. Provide time for writers to experiment with the various approaches by applying more than one to their own writing. Share these experimentations!

This process can also be used to teach endings, topic sentences for nonfiction, the art of writing a great title, and a plethora of other writing craft. The pattern is the same: collect examples, notice and name categories, practice together, play and experiment, and then apply to one's own writing.

Developing Character

Many times teachers of writing encourage writers to include adjectives to describe a character. The results may not be what the teacher intended: "Super Donut was an awesome, really weird, amazingly green donut after he ate the enormous supersized bacon burger!" While teaching adjectives can be useful, focusing on verbs and better nouns develops character and voice: "Super Donut gagged, then gulped three times. His eyes bulged as he forced the supersized bacon burger down his throat. Slowly the pink donut morphed green."

Encourage this kind of character development by modeling with a two-column paper. On one side of the paper, write a general sentence: "Rabbit Ears was mad!" Now, on the opposite side, ask writers to show the character through careful word choice: "Rabbit Ears stomped the ground, and his long ears hissed red." Introduce and teach writers how to use a thesaurus. During teacher–student conferences and guided writing, have writers underline sentences that can be revised with careful word selection to develop character, guiding them through this process.

Developing Plot

Plot is the heart of a story, but how to teach this complex piece of writing? Begin by studying and analyzing mentor text. Plot diagrams can be useful as well. And perhaps the best strategy for beginning fiction writers is to write a plot collaboratively with the teacher. Interactive writing can be a powerful tool for teaching plot. While doing this, be sure to teach, use, and insist that writers use the language of plot: suspense, exposition, rising action, climax, resolution, point of view, internal and external conflict, and protagonist and antagonist.

Developing Dialogue

"What is in that box?" Cocoa asked.
"A surprise," said Cowgirl Kate.
"Sugar cookies?" he asked.
"A surprise," she said.
"Apple pie?" he asked.
"A surprise," she said.

The preceding excerpt from *Cowgirl Kate and Cocoa* (Silverman, 2005, p. 7) illustrates how dialogue works and is an effective mentor text for those readers/writers beginning to read chapter books. This excerpt can be studied more carefully by placing the dialogue in a two-column chart, showing how the characters talk back and forth. Next, use the same two-column format to interactively write with children, composing dialogue between two characters or even children in the classroom.

Informative Writing

Informative writing involves doing research and gathering facts. Several strategies are useful in teaching writers to gather facts for informative writing:

- *Study illustrations or photographs (we like books published by DK Publishing).* Create a list of facts you see in the illustration or photograph. Teach individual or small groups of children to use sticky notes and place the notes directly on the illustration or photograph. These can be used later to organize writing.
- *Provide index cards or sticky notes for writers.* As they read and find interesting facts about their topic, they jot down the fact on an index card. Later, the index cards or sticky notes can be sorted and categorized to organize writing.
- *Fold a paper into quarters.* Write a question about the topic being explored in each quadrant. For example, if the topic is "Rabbits," then the questions may be "What do rabbits eat?" "Where do rabbits live?" "How are rabbits different?" and "Do rabbits make good pets?"

For English learners, add picture cues for added support.

Informative Writing Strategies That Spark

Children love writing narrative and find their voice in doing so, but writing informative text can often become a list of facts. There are many ways to approach writing informative text. Study the following example from *Shark Life: True Stories About Sharks and the Sea* (Benchley, 2005):

Each of the following statements about sharks has been printed, preprinted, and guaranteed to be the absolute truth. Of the three, which one would you say is true?

1. Of the 380 species of sharks known to science, fewer than a dozen pose any threat whatever to human beings.

2. Of the more than 400 species of sharks in the world, only 11 have ever been known to attack a human being.
3. Of the 450 species of sharks on record, only 3 qualify as man-eaters. (pp. 44–45)

Engaging the reader by using a quiz-type format is an effective informative writing strategy.

Likewise, storytelling can be effective. A writer can write about the gray squirrel and about how it can move quickly up and down a tree, or the writer can write these facts as narrative: "The gray squirrel seemed to freeze against the trunk of the tree, hoping his mottled gray color would look like the tree trunk. As the great hawk swooped over head, the squirrel darted like an acrobat, hurling himself to a higher tree limb for safety." Demonstrate by showing writers "flat" and "active" writing. Experiment and play with writing active informative text.

Developing an Opinion

Effective opinion writing needs solid supporting evidence. Look no further than the "Letters to the Editor" or blogs to find examples of opinion writing. Tease out the difference with writers: what is a rant, what is a rave, what is an argument? How do these differ? Find, collect, and display results of the inquiry.

Magazines for children provide examples of opinion writing that can also be analyzed and used for writing instruction. For example, have writers read the following letters submitted by readers to *New Moon* (2013). Readers were invited to express their opinions regarding the "no-kill" policy of many animal shelters:

> I believe in putting down an animal, and here's why. It isn't painful. Stray animals roaming the streets without food would be much happier not suffering anymore. Also, the world has too many animals and they can't get the care they need.
> Sarai, 12
> Connecticut
>
> *(New Moon, 2013, p. 8)*

> When a human gets sick or has a disability, do we put them down? No! We actually ARE animals, but when we are sick, we are sent to doctors to get better. With an animal, you have to adopt it within a short period of time or it gets put down. That's wrong!
> Roxianne, 10
> Idaho
>
> *(New Moon, 2013, p. 8)*

These particular letters represent a specific genre of opinion writing; writers must be very concise in presenting their opinions. With writers, explore what makes these opinion pieces work.

For younger writers, consider using the very popular Pigeon picture-book series by Mo Willems. In each book, the main character, a pigeon, is making an argument for being able to do something like stay up late or own a pet. In *Don't Let the Pigeon Drive the Bus* (Willems, 2003), the pigeon uses a number of persuasive tactics to argue for being allowed to drive the bus:

- "I'll be your best friend!" (p. 19).
- "I bet your mom would let me" (p. 19).
- "I have dreams, you know!" (p. 20).

These are fun arguments to categorize, name, and rate for effectiveness and then use in developing opinions.

Teaching Organization

We can teach beginning, middle, and end through strategies already mentioned: storyboards, graphic organizers, book title and chapter title writing, or using paper folded into four boxes.

Additionally, teach writers about transitional words and phrases; this can enhance organization and develop non-fiction writing craft. These "sign posts" are useful for English learners in particular, as they act as cues to a reader of what is coming next in the text. Here is a short list of transitional words to teach: *furthermore; finally; next; after; meanwhile; sometimes, subsequently; wherever, nearby, below; to illustrate; for instance; for example; yet; however; therefore; consequently.* With writers, study the function of each word. Collect examples, categorize, name, and practice their use.

Teach Literary Devices: All the Time

Listen to this line from "Grandpa's Shoes" (Chandra, 1993, p. 3), "Grandpa's shoes / speak in a husky / whisper." What a delightful line to introduce writers to the beauty of literacy devices. But literary devices are not just for poetry—play and experiment with them all the time. Ask writers to visualize similes and metaphors. Draw illustrations of literacy devices and then have writers guess their meanings or write captions for one another's pictures. Encourage talk bubbles that use onomatopoeia. Collect literacy devices used by authors and study them. But mostly, have fun with literacy devices. Writers of all ages need to have literary devices in their toolbox. Key literacy devices to teach include imagery, simile, metaphor, hyperbole, personification, alliteration, and irony.

 What are additional strategies for teaching writing craft that you have observed being taught in classrooms or used, yourself, as a writer? Write them into the margins of this text for future reference.

These are the kinds of writing strategies we teach and model during mini-lessons, teacher–student conferences, and guided writing in the Writing Studio. A handful of reliable writing strategies can fill a teacher of writing's toolbox. From this, teachers of writing can tweak and modify for a wide range of writing abilities and developmental levels. Even so, as teachers of writing, we continue to explore and expand our repertoires. We do this as engaged participants, eager to risk and to continually discover and rediscover what writing can do for ourselves as writers and for the writers of our classrooms.

Problematizing Practice

The goals of Problematizing Practice are to deconstruct assumptions and beliefs and to consider multiple responses and implications of teaching decisions. It is best to do this in the company of colleagues and your instructor:

1. Read the scenario.
2. Quickly write down assumptions about the scenario. *Study your assumptions.*

3. Discuss and problematize assumptions with others and your instructor.
4. Discuss and write possible responses to the scenario.
5. Discuss the possible consequences (intended and unintended) of each response.

Scenario

Grant, a first grader, has difficulties with classroom transitions, or moving from one scheduled event to another in the classroom. He benefits when the teacher cues him in advance about upcoming transitions; he also benefits from practiced routines. As his teacher, you want to develop a cueing system to support Grant through the transitions of the Writing Studio:

- Writing Studio is about to begin
- Status of the Class (Specifically, how to check the Daily Writing Folder and choose a writing goal)
- Individual and collaborative writing time
- Upcoming share time

How many ways might you do this? What would the benefits of each be?

References

Benchley, P. (2005). *Shark life: True stories about sharks and the sea.* New York, NY: Yearling.

Calkins, L., & Oxenhorn, A. (2003). *Small moments: Personal narrative writing.* Portsmouth, NH: firsthand.

Chandra, D. (1993). *Rich lizard and other poems.* New York, NY: Farrar, Straus, and Giroux.

Cloud, N., Genesee, F., & Hamayan, E. (2009). *Literacy instruction for English language learners: A teacher's guide to research-based practices.* Portsmouth, NH: Heinemann.

Cremin, T., & Myhill, D. (2012). *Writing voices: Creating communities of writers.* London, England: Routledge.

Fu, D. (2009). *Writing between langauges: How English language learners make the transition to fluency, grades 4–12.* Portsmouth, NH: Heinemann.

Fu, D., & Hansen, J. (2012, July). *Writing: A mode of thinking.* Retrieved from Language Arts Podcasts Conversation Currents website: http://www.ncte.org/journals/la/podcasts/july-2012

Goldenberg, C. (2013, Summer). Unlocking the research on English learners: What we know—and don't yet know. *American Educator,* 4–11.

Goodman, K. (1996). *On reading: A common-sense look at the nature of language and the science of reading.* Portsmouth, NH: Heinemann.

Johnston, P. H. (2004). *Choice words: How our language affects children's learning.* Portland, ME: Stenhouse.

Johnston, P. H. (2012). *Opening minds using language to change lives.* Portland, ME: Stenhouse.

Korman, G. (2002). *Everest book one: The contest.* New York, NY: Scholastic.

Lamott, A. (1994). *Bird by bird: Some instructions on writing and life.* New York, NY: Anchor.

MacLachlan, P. (2012). *Kindred souls.* New York, NY: HarperCollins.

Manning, M., & Ransom, M. (2013). Supporting writers as they learn to spell: A holistic approach. In R. J. Meyer, & K. F. Whitmore (Eds.), *Reclaiming writing: Composing spaces for identities, relationships and action* (pp. 87–97). New York, NY: Routledge.

New Moon. (2013, May/June). Voice box. *New Moon,* pp. 8.

O'Connor, B. (2007). *How to steal a dog.* New York, NY: Macmillan.

Rico, G. (2000). *Writing the natural way: Using right-brain techniques to release your expressive powers.* New York, NY: Penguin.

Ryan, P. (2000). *Esperanza rising.* New York, NY: Scholastic.

Rylant, C. (2013). *God got a dog.* New York, NY: Beach Lane.

Scieszka, J. (2008). *Knucklehead: Tall tales and mostly true stories about growing up Scieszka.* New York, NY: Viking.

Scieszka, J., & Smith, L. (1996). *The true story of the three little pigs.* London, England: Puffin.

Silverman, E. (2005). *Cowgirl Kate and Cocoa.* New York, NY: Harcourt.

Smith, F. (1998). *The book of learning and forgetting.* New York, NY: Teachers College Press.

Stevens, W. (1982). *The collected poems of Wallace Stevens.* New York, NY: Vintage Books.

Taylor, B. (1998). *Forest life.* New York, NY: DK Publishing.

Watts, M. (2011). *Scaredy Squirrel.* Tonawanda, NY: Kids Can Press.

Wilde, S. (2013). Constructivist spelling, yes! Constructivist grammar, too! In R. J. Meyer, & K. F. Whitmore (Eds.), *Reclaiming writing: Composing spaces for identities, relationships, and actions* (pp. 98–101). New York, NY: Routledge.

Willems, M. (2003). *Don't let the pigeon drive the bus.* New York, NY: Hyperion.

Winter, J. (2005). *The librarian of Basra: A true story from Iraq.* New York, NY: HMH.

Winter, J. (2011). *The watcher: Jane Goodall's life with the chimps.* New York, NY: Schwartz & Wade Books.

Chapter Seven
The Writing Mini-Lesson

"Writers of Room 23," Ms. J smiles as bodies are settling into their chairs, readying for Writing Studio, "are you ready to write?"

"Yes." The reply comes as a chorus from the students.

"Excellent!" Ms. J responds. "Today I want to demonstrate a way to revise a poem. Last night I was remembering my recent trip to the Everglades in Florida. You already know how excited I was to see so many new kinds of birds! One of the photos I took was of these Anhinga chicks."

Ms. J places a photo on the document camera. Children giggle and respond.

"Oh, they are cute!"

"He looks funny!"

"It looks like a fuzz ball"

"It is hard to imagine these little white and yellowish chicks ever turning black and growing to a little over 2.5 feet high, but they do," Ms. J. exclaims and places another photo of a mature Anhinga on the document camera. There is a brief discussion among the children and Ms. J. about this.

"Well," says Ms. J, "I composed a poem about these Anhinga chicks last night. This is my first draft. I haven't read it since last night. I expect it will need some revision."

Ms. J places the following poem on the document camera and reads it aloud:

"Anhinga Chick

You are naked and helpless without any feathers

Yellow and white fluff—a blur of softness

You are waiting for your mom and dad:

'Feed me! Feed me!' you seem to say

Very soon you will climb out of this nest and be on your way!"

Ms. J continues. "Now I've learned this advice from poets, a way to begin revising a poem is to put the poem on a diet. Too often, we use too many words in a poem. We have poems overweight with words! Poems are small snapshots, packed with imagery. That's the beauty of a poem: you can say so much in such a little space! I think my poem has too many words—it needs a word diet! I am going to read it again and think about what words are not really necessary."

Ms. J reads and thinks aloud, working through the poem. "'You are naked and helpless without any feathers.' Mmm . . . . I don't think I need all those words. How about if I cross out 'You are' and 'without any feathers'" She draws a line through these words before she continues reading. "'Yellow and white fluff—a blur of softness.' I think I like this line for now. I think I will keep it. 'You are waiting for your mom and dad.' That doesn't sound very poetic to me. I wonder if I could show . . ."

"Instead of tell," a writer cries out!

"Yes." Ms. J smiles. "Show rather than tell. Mmm . . .what do these chicks do when they are hungry?" With animation, Ms. J imitates a chick stretching its neck, and with her hands she forms long beaks opening and closing. The children laugh.

She continues to revise, "I am going to cross out the line, 'You are waiting for your mom and dad' and write, 'Long beaks open wide, clicking, Feed me! Feed me!' and I don't think I need this line, 'you seem to say.'" This next line seems very wordy. 'Very soon you will climb out of this nest and be on your way!' I'd like to end in a different way. Mmm . . . maybe this would be a good place for wonder lines. Remember, we talked about wonder lines when we were writing our Big Questions books?'"

Ms. J pauses, then thinks aloud. "These chicks are sitting on this nest high in the tree, what a view! And I know that Anhingas sun themselves to dry out their plumage. . .these chicks have yet to fly, but in several weeks . . .mmm . . ." Then she writes, "I wonder how the clouds look to you? I wonder how the sun feels upon your wings? I wonder when you will fly?"" "Okay," Ms. J says, "I am going to read this poem again aloud to myself:

"Anhinga Chick

Naked and helpless

Yellow and white fluff—a blur of softness

Long beaks open wide, clicking

'Feed me! Feed me!'

I wonder how the clouds look to you?

I wonder how the sun feels upon your wings?

I wonder when you will fly?"

"I think I like this better now. I think I am going to put this aside now and let it rest. Maybe I will play with it a bit more this evening. Yes, it needs more work, and I know some of you have ideas, but I am not quite ready for a peer conference. I think I want to sit on this poem for a bit more, okay?"

Ms. J continues, "'Putting your poem on a diet,' or deleting words that are not absolutely necessary, is a good revision strategy when writing poetry. I am going to challenge those of you who have a poem completed to try this strategy today. Be prepared to share your 'before and after' lines during our closure to the Writing Studio.

"Now, take a minute to open your Daily Writing Folder and make a decision about what you will be working on in the studio today. I'll start Status of the Class in about one minute."

The mini-lesson begins the Writing Studio—writers can depend on this. They anticipate the mini-lesson as a time of exploring writing practices, process, and craft. The mini-lesson is most often a teacher demonstration. It can also be a shared or interactive writing experience (see Figure 7.1, "Ms. Coy Teaching a Writing Mini-Lesson").

Margret Mooney (1990) uses the language of *to, with, by* to talk about authentic literacy learning. We can apply this to the Writing Studio: the teacher models, demonstrates, presents *to* writers (mini-lesson); *with* writers (interactive or shared writing with the teacher; guided writing; one-on-one teacher conferences); and following a handover by the teacher to writers, *by* writers (writers writing independently or collaboratively with peers).

Using this framework, the mini-lesson is, then, an example of *to* or the teacher modeling and demonstrating writing practices, process, or craft or it can be *with* writers when the teacher composes interactively with children.

Figure 7.1 Ms. Coy Teaching a Writing Mini-Lesson

Managing the Mini-Lesson

This teaching and learning structure is called "mini-lesson" for a reason—it should be a short, focused time of demonstration: "*mini.*" A danger of implementation is when the "mini-lesson" is too long! The mini-lesson should be 10 to 20 minutes in length. It should be proportionate to the entire Writing Studio time slot. If there are 60 minutes allotted to the entire studio, than an occasional 20-minute mini-lesson is more acceptable. There will still be 35 minutes for writing time, teacher–student conferences, and guided writing, followed by a shortened 5-minute sharing time for closure. However, as the Writing Studio time decreases, so should the mini-lesson time. Kindergarten and Grade 1 mini-lessons rarely need to be longer than 5 to 10 minutes, unless it is a shared or an interactive writing experience. It comes down to this: the mini-lesson supports and scaffolds independent and collaborative writing—*it does not distract from it!* When we reflect on our own teaching and visit with teachers who find it difficult to have time for teacher–student conferences or guided writing, we often find it is because the not-so-mini mini-lessons at the beginning of the Writing Studio are absorbing too much time.

Another critical point: the mini-lesson is *not* a teacher lecture but a demonstration. The teacher as writer, as curious questioner and inquirer, models writing practices, process, and craft. The mini-lesson is intentional and focused on no more than two goals. This means that the topics of mini-lessons are often repeated and cycled throughout the Writing Studio.

For example, in Chapter 6, we illustrated how writing a lead may take an inquiry approach with a teacher beginning by sharing three leads found in published writing. This 10-minute lesson ends with an invitation for writers to find their own examples during Reading Studio. Teachers and writers begin collecting examples of leads during the next week. The sharing of these examples may be another mini-lesson (or lessons), or they may be shared during Reading Studio or Writing Studio closing share time. During a follow-up mini-lesson, the teacher facilitates a writing experience during which the teacher and the writers experiment and play with writing the model lead during an interactive lesson.

Because mini-lessons are for whole-class instruction, they reflect general writing lessons related to the writing unit at hand. Choice units may include more general mini-lessons about practices, processes, and the craft of editing, whereas genre-specific units may include more craft lessons focused on the said genre. Mini-lessons may be planned ahead because the teacher of writing anticipates the needs of writers, the models they will require, and the necessary support from which most everyone will benefit. (Instruction is tailored to meet individual needs during the teacher–student conference and guided writing—see Chapter 8.)

Mini-lessons, as with everything in the Writing Studio, are based upon the needs of writers. Therefore, there are occasions when a mini-lesson needs to become a *lesson*. (Name it as such!) Longer lessons may be necessary, for example, during the beginning inquiry phase of a genre unit or during interactive writing sessions, where teacher and writers compose together. These occasions are far and few between—check yourself—put some barriers around the mini-lesson in order to honor and preserve the writing, conferencing, and guided writing of the Writing Studio.

Choosing the Mentor Text

Central to meaningful and intentional mini-lessons is choosing an appropriate mentor text. In Chapter 6, we noted that a mentor text could be any published writing, children's writing, and teacher writing samples. What makes a mentor text appropriate? Besides the fact that a mentor text demonstrates writing practices, process, and/or craft, the best mentor texts also reflect the interests and abilities of the writers in the Writing Studio. Choose mentor texts that will resonate with the writers in your class. Be more than willing to write your own mentor text as necessary! Know the authors the writers in your class are reading. Learn to integrate your Reading and Writing Studios. When you share a book as a read aloud in the Reading Studio, plan to use the same book as a mentor text connected with your Writing Studio mini-lesson. (See Chapters 10 and 11.)

Mini-Lessons Illustrated

We can very generally divide mini-lessons into three categories: *demonstrations*, *inquiries*, and *interactive or shared writing experiences*. Read the introductory lines of the following mini-lessons for a sense of these categories:

- Writers, today I want to demonstrate for you a strategy for developing plot.
- Writers, I have a question today, how do the authors you read introduce characters that are going to speak or engage in dialogue?
- Yesterday, writers, we studied verb models from authors. We looked at how vivid verbs gave two different pieces voice and excitement. Today—let's give verbs a try together. I have a paragraph here. Let's work on the verbs.

These categories are fluid and most often overlap; however, they are useful in planning purposeful mini-lessons for the Studio.

The Demonstration Mini-Lesson

A demonstration mini-lesson generally follows the order shown in Figure 7.2

Figure 7.2   Demonstration Mini-Lesson Template

Mini-lesson: Demonstration

Date:

Writing Unit:

Grade:

Standards; Goal(s); or Objective(s) – no more than two:

Focus Statement(s) or Invitation:

Body of Lesson:

     Example(s) from a mentor text

     How it works - demonstration

Connection & application to individual or collaborative student writing

The Demonstration Mini-Lesson: Kindergarten Sample Lesson Plan

Standard Addressed in the Lesson

CCSS L.K.2. Demonstrate command of the conventions of standard English capitalization, punctuation, and spelling when writing.

a.   Spell simple words phonetically, drawing on knowledge of sound-letter relationships.

Content and Language Objectives

- Writers will be able to write the sounds they hear in words.
- Writers will be able to insert spaces between words in their story.

Focus Statement or Invitation

"Yesterday I drew a picture about a time I got in trouble as a kid. My picture was of the first thing that happened in the story. Writers need to think about what they are going to say before they write it down on paper. Today I am going to write a sentence to go with my picture from yesterday. I'm going to write the sounds I hear in the words and use spaces between words."

Body of Lesson

How It Works—Demonstration

- "My first sentence in my story is 'I went to the campground with my family.' How many words are going to be in my sentence? Let's count the words together." As modeled in previous lessons the teacher will say each word of her sentence slowly as she puts up a finger from her hands for each word. "'I—went—to—the—campground—with—my—family.' Eight words."
- Teacher will ask children to point where she should start writing on her paper. Anticipated responses will be to point to the top, left of the paper.
- Teacher will write down the first word of her sentence, "I" then ask children, "What do we need next?" Anticipated response: "Space girl" ("Space girl" is a wooden clothespin painted like an astronaut for writers to place on their writing paper after each word to create a space between words).
- Teacher will reread her writing "I . . .," then say the next word in her sentence, "went." "Let's sound out the beginning of *went*: w-w-w." Children will respond with the letter "w" that makes the sound /w/. The teacher will finish writing the word *went* spelling it conventionally.
- Teacher will ask, "Now what do I need?" Anticipated response: "Space girl."
- Teacher will reread her writing: "'I went . . .,' then say the next word in her sentence, "to." Let's sound out the word *to* together, 't-t-o-o.'" Teacher will write down the word *to*.
- Teacher will say, "Here comes a new word; now what am I going to need?" Anticipated response: "Space girl."
- Teacher will reread her writing: "I went to . . ." Writers respond with the next word in the sentence, "the." Teacher will ask, "How do we spell *the*?" Anticipated response: "t-h-e" chant they have been practicing daily in their guided writing groups.
- Teacher will ask, "Now what do I need to do if I don't have room to write another word on this line?" Anticipated response: "Swoop back down," which the teacher has been modeling in her daily writing demonstrations. Teacher will ask, "Will I need 'Space girl' at the beginning of my new line?" Anticipated response: "No."
- Teacher will reread her writing using "call and response": "I went to the . . ." Anticipated response: "campground."
- Teacher will provide a quick model of why writers use "Space girl" between words versus between the letters of words by showing writers how the word *the* looks if there is a space between each letter "t h e" to reinforce the print concept of letter versus a word.
- Teacher will reread her sentence and write the word "*campground*," pointing out that there are a lot of letters in the word *campground* even though it is only one word. Teacher will ask writers, "Are we done writing our sentence? Let's count the words. One, two, three, four, five. That is only five words.

My sentence has eight words. Let's say my sentence again. 'I went to the campground with my family.' We need three more words."

- Teacher will reread her writing "I went to the campground . . ." Writers will respond with the next word in the sentence, "with."
- Teacher will model moving the "Space girl" after the word *with*. Teacher will reread her sentence: "I went to the campground with . . ." Writers respond with the next word, "my." Teacher with writers will spell out *my*, one of the high-frequency words writers have been learning in their phonics stations.
- Teacher will show how she needs to return sweep to write the next word of her sentence because it won't fit on the line.
- Teacher will reread her writing: "I went to the campground with my . . ." Writers will respond with the next word, "family." Teacher will ask, "Let's listen for the sounds we hear in family." Teacher will model pulling every sound of *family* by using a hand motion of her hand reaching from her lips out into the air while saying the word slowly, "Fff—aa—mm—iii—lll—yy."
- Teacher will reread her writing with the writers: "'I went to the campground with my family.' What do I need now?" Anticipated writer response singing the class song they have been learning, "Per-i-od, at the end of the sentence."
- Teacher will remind writers, "This is just the beginning of my story. It is going to take me a lot of days to work on this story. I am going to need to keep this story on the green side of my writing folder so I can work on it every day until I write the whole story." [Teacher has taught writers to keep current work on the "green side" of the folder; completed work stays on the "red side" of the folder.]

Connection and Application to Individual or Collaborative Student Writing

- Teacher's transition writers to independent writing by stating, "Today, when you head to a comfortable place to write, the floor or your table, you will want to think about your story from yesterday, look at the picture you drew and think what you want to write. Write down the sounds you hear and use a 'Space girl' or 'Space guy' to help you put spaces between your words."
- Excuse writers to independent writing.

 Watch Ms. Coy teach her demonstration mini-lesson.

Inquiry mini-lesson

An inquiry mini-lesson generally follows the order shown in Figure 7.3.

Figure 7.3 Inquiry Mini-Lesson Template

Mini-lesson: Inquiry
Date:
Writing Unit:
Grade:
Standards; Goal(s); or Objective(s) – no more than two:
Inquiry Question
Body of Lesson:
The inquiry
What have we learned? Synthesizing the Inquiry and Connecting and Applying to Individual or Collaborative writing

Inquiry Mini-Lesson: Grade 3 Sample Lesson Plan

Standard Addressed in the Lesson

CCSS ELA 3.SL.1 Engage effectively in a range of collaborative discussions (one-on-one, in groups, and teacher-led) with diverse partners on Grade 3 topics and texts, building on others' ideas and expressing their own clearly.

a. Come to discussions prepared, having read or studied required material; explicitly draw on that preparation and other information known about the topic to explore ideas under discussion

Content and Language Objectives

- Writers will read like writers—looking for common elements in a variety of narrative picture books.
- Writers will share with peers and the whole class what they are noticing in narrative picture books.

Inquiry Question

What do you notice about the picture books at your table? What do the picture books have in common?

Body of Lesson

The Inquiry

- "As you can see, there is a stack of picture books in the center of your table. Some of the picture books are books we have read previously; others are new. Read the books by yourself or with a partner. As you read, think about what you are noticing in the picture books. What do the picture books have in common?"
- Writers begin reading picture books individually or with a partner as the teacher goes around the room checking in with writers—sometimes asking writers about what they are noticing and other times modeling what she is noticing: "I am noticing that both of the books I read have a problem that needs to be solved," or "I am noticing that the author uses dialogue to have the characters express how they are feeling."

What Have We Learned?

- Teacher will gain class' attention by stating, "One, two, three, eyes on me" and writers will respond "One, two, eyes on you." Teacher will state, "Take a few minutes to share what you were noticing about the picture books with your table group. Start your sentence with 'I noticed . . .'" while the teacher points to the same sentence stem on the board. The teacher will check in with table groups listening in and writing down notes in her Teaching, Conferencing & Planning Notebook. She will note how writers are noticing, how writers are able to piggyback their noticing to another writer's idea, and groups that worked well together. Occasionally the teacher will model how to build on a person's idea by joining the discussion.
- Teacher will gather the class for a whole-group discussion. The teacher will type two headings up on the SMART Board document: What are you noticing? What do these picture books have in common? "Today you read a variety of picture books. I enjoyed hearing all of the great conversations you were having with your partners. I'd like to have you share what you or your table group members

were noticing. I will pull names out of the jar." Teacher will call on a variety of writers and type their responses on the computer that is projected on the SMART Board to record what writers were noticing about the picture books.

- Writers will share responses. (Anticipated responses: I noticed the books all tell a story. I noticed the books all have characters. I noticed the characters have strong feelings. I noticed the books all have illustrations that help tell the story. I noticed some of the books are funny. I noticed some of the books are sad. I noticed the author gives a lot of details to describe where the story takes place. I noticed the books all have a problem that needs to be solved. I noticed the problem gets solved. I noticed sometimes the solutions are obvious other times they were a surprise.)

What Have We Learned? Synthesizing the Inquiry and Connecting and Applying to Individual or Collaborative Writing

- "Wow, we worked together to create this long list of what we are noticing about the picture books at our table and the commonalities they have. We are going to continue to 'read like writers' over the next 2 days as we prepare for a new narrative writing unit. We will continue to notice what authors of narrative stories do when they write. We will use what we are learning and experiment trying to include some of these same elements in our own narrative stories."

Interactive mini-lesson

An interactive mini-lesson generally follows the order shown in Figure 7.4.

Figure 7.4   Interactive Mini-Lesson Template

Mini-lesson: Interactive
Date:
Writing Unit:
Grade:
Standards; Goal(s); or Objective(s) – no more than two: The Invitation (setting the context): Body of Lesson: Interactive or shared writing Connection & Application to Individual or Collaborative Student Writing

Interactive Mini-Lesson: Grade 5 Sample Lesson Plan

The lesson is adapted from Georgia Heard's (1999, pp. 82–83) *Awakening the Heart: Exploring Poetry in Elementary and Middle School.*

Standards Addressed in the Lesson

CCSS ELA 5.L.5 Demonstrate understanding of figurative language, word relationships, and nuances in word meanings.
a.   Interpret figurative language, including similes and metaphors, in context.

Content and Language Objectives

- Writers will be able to work with a partner to determine poetic words to place in a cloze version of Langston Hughes' poem "April Rain Song" (Rampersad & Roessel, 1994).

The Invitation

"Now that we have warmed up by reading some poetry together, I am going to pass out a piece of paper with a poem titled 'April Rain Song' by Langston Hughes. I have taken some of Langston Hughes' words out of the poem and replaced them with blank lines. Listen as I read the poem one time to you with a pause for each of the blank lines."

Teacher reads the poem with the missing words: "You and your writing partner will work together to fill-in-the-blank lines with your own poetic words to create your own version of 'April Rain Song.' If you can't agree on a single word or phrase, then write both of your ideas down. Turn to your writing partner and repeat the directions."

Body of Lesson

Writing partners will work together to determine poetic words to fill in a cloze version of "April Rain Song" while the teacher checks in with partners, beginning with partners that are arguing or appear to be uncertain what to do.

Interactive or Shared Writing

- Teacher will bring the class together by turning off the classroom lights once the cloze version of "April Rain Song" is projected from the document camera to the screen. The teacher will read the poem stopping once she comes to a blank line. She will call on writers to share the poetic words either they or their partner selected. The teacher will call on multiple writers for each blank line recording multiple ideas for poetic words for each blank line.
- As writers' poetic words are written on the blank lines, the teacher will ask writers questions to show the metacognitive thinking behind their choices. Questions include:
  "Why did you select this word?"
  "What mood does this word convey?"
  "Why did you put this particular group of words together?"
  "How does your word tie in with the words earlier?"
- The teacher and the writers will continue to work together to fill in the entire "April Rain Song" poem.
- The teacher will call on one to three writing partners to come forward and share their "April Rain Song" poem with the class.
- "It is clear as poets you understand the value each word a poet uses in his or her poem. Let's read Langston Hughes' version of 'April Rain Song' together and notice the poetic words he selected."
- Shared reading of Langston Hughes's "April Rain Song."

Connection and Application to Individual or Collaborative Student Writing

- "Today as you head to independent and collaborative writing, imagine you are Langston Hughes. You can revise one of your poems in your poetry folder or start a new poem. As a poet, think about each word you select, the mood and feeling it conveys, and how your words work together throughout your entire poem."
- Writers head off to independent and collaborative writing.

Return to the beginning of this chapter and the Ms. J. vignette. Given the preceding descriptions and illustrations, what kind of mini-lesson was Ms. J presenting? What is the goal of Ms. J's mini-lesson?

 Visit the companion website to view writing mini-lesson videos.

 Give it a try: draft a mini-lesson of your choosing to teach writers a specific writing craft. For a challenge, revise the mini-lesson for two other grade levels. Share your work with your colleagues.

Planning Mini-Lessons Ahead

Mini-lesson can be planned ahead. As you embark upon planning for a unit of writing, ask, "Given the writers in my class, what writing practices, process, and/or craft may be new or require reinforcement in this writing unit? What mentor texts will best model the end-goals of this unit?" Analyze the end goals and then create the mini-lessons that will be necessary for most all writers in the classroom (see Part IV for more on unit planning).

Planning for Mini-Lessons Illustrated

For example, Mr. Mackie planned a framework for the integrated science, mathematics, reading, and writing unit he planned to teach. As an integrated unit, he planned to teach across these disciplinary areas and connect them through the theme of "Songbirds, Threatened!" Mr. Mackie envisioned this unit as an opportunity for children to practice research skills in finding out why songbirds existence are threatened; reading nonfiction reports on songbirds; math skills to interpret graphs, charts, and percentages shown in the research; and, as a writing unit, to teach writers how to craft opinions or pieces that might incite others to action. Mr. Mackie knew this integrated unit would interest his writers, in part, because he anticipated some of his writers finding it difficult to believe that the primary predator of songbirds is the family cat. He also knew the children would be concerned about songbirds and their declining numbers in their state. He believed the dissonance between a family cat as pet and predator would pose a strong learning possibility as children toggled between reading the research and reconciling this with their own lovable kitties.

In planning this integrated unit, Mr. Mackie considered what writing practices, process, and craft writers would need to learn in order to be successful in expressing their opinions about the plight of songbirds.

Under writing practices, he listed: children will need to (1) learn how to read research and find information, particularly from Internet sources (reading lessons); (2) have experience collecting field data through bird watching experiences, tallying, graphing, and charting this data, interpreting data (science and mathematics lessons); (3) inquire about the different genres of scientific writing met to express an opinion or persuade the reader to action (reading and writing lessons); and (4) learn how to read graphs, charts, and percentages (mathematics lessons).

In planning for genres that express an opinion, Mr. Mackie reviewed his Teaching, Conferencing & Planning Notebook and analyzed the varying abilities of writers. He was fairly certain that a collaborative process resulting in a web page was perfect for some of his writers. Other writers would be more inclined to use story to express an opinion. Because many children were already reading graphic novels, he was confident the opportunity to use elements of graphic novels would spark interest. Finally, he knew some of his writers resisted writing anything non-fiction. These writers needed to be lured into this circle. Poetry would be perfect, he determined. Designing and creating posters, web pages, and chapter books as end products would ensure an audience greater than the classroom—and a response. For all these writing possibilities, Mr. Mackie knew he would need to demonstrate and teach the need for a piece to be focused, include clear and persuasive facts, and how to apply voice in such a way as to hook a reader. He planned mini-lessons in these areas.

Mr. Mackie regularly teaches revision during the Writing Studio, and he anticipated the need to cycle back to this skill again. In particular, he anticipated writers needing mini-lessons on focusing the content, using related facts, and then revising for both factual information and clarity in presenting opinions. More than likely, Mr. Mackie mused, he would also need some mini-lessons on the craft of paragraphing. Most of the writing being done would include several subtopics, and he knew that paragraphing was not a strong suit for many of his writers.

Next, Mr. Mackie planned for specific mini-lessons focused on design, or how illustrations support text (and text supports illustrations). He envisioned writers designing web pages, posters, and stories as a way to publish their work, so choosing or creating illustrations that supported text was important. He planned mini-lessons to address these anticipated design needs.

This is the kind of planning Mr. Mackie did prior to his unit "Songbirds, Threatened!" Even as Mr. Mackie planned these mini-lessons, he also left open the possibility that along the way, writers might need mini-lessons he had not yet imagined to support them in their opinion writing.

As his "Songbirds, Threatened!" unit went live, he discovered through the use of Status of the Class and the Teaching, Conferencing & Planning Notebook that many writers were rushing through their writing in order to continue with publishing. The anticipation of using illustrations, colors, and very cool effects on web pages seduced writers into sacrificing the writing, becoming sloppy in the selection of facts. When Mr. Mackie saw this, he paused and adapted mini-lessons to address this current need. Other more specific needs for smaller groups of writers, for example, how to storyboard, he addressed through guided writing.

Part IV of *Becoming a Teacher of Writing in Elementary Classrooms* details unit planning more vividly. For now, the illustration of Mr. Mackie and his songbird unit demonstrates how mini-lessons are planned in advance by anticipating the needs of writers and then adjusting the mini-lessons plans as the unit goes live and the needs of writers surface.

Mini-lessons can often be adapted for new groups of writers who arrive yearly to your classroom. Save and organize mini-lessons so they can easily be retrieved from year to year.

Intentional and well-planned mini-lessons are integral to the Writing Studio. "Nothing just happens" in the studio. The primary learning structure for making sure all writing practices, process, and craft are taught is through mini-lessons. Make them count!

Problematizing Practice

The goals of Problematizing Practice are to deconstruct assumptions and beliefs and to consider multiple responses and implications of teaching decisions. It is best to do this in the company of colleagues and your instructor:

1. Read the scenario.
2. Quickly write down assumptions about the scenario. *Study your assumptions.*

3. Discuss and problematize assumptions with others and your instructor.
4. Discuss and write possible responses to the scenario.
5. Discuss the possible consequences (intended and unintended) of each response.

Scenario

The writers in your Grade 2 class love anything graphic! They so want to write graphic narratives of their own. But honestly, while you read the graphic novels children love, you have never written anything graphic, and you are not in love with the genre. You need to develop a series of mini-lessons to support writers. How do you know where to begin? How do you educate yourself to teach the craft and language of graphic narratives?

References

Heard, G. (1999). *Awakening the heart: Exploring poetry in elementary and middle school.* Portsmouth, NH: Heinemann.

Mooney, M. E. (1990). *Reading to, with and by children.* Katonah, NY: Richard C. Owens Publisher.

Rampersad, A., & Roessel, D. (Eds.). (1994). *The collected poems of Langston Hughes.* New York, NY: Vintage Classics.

Chapter Eight
Individualizing Writing Instruction: The Teacher–Student Writing Conference and Guided Writing

Ms. J studies her Status of the Class chart and simultaneously observes children moving into their "writing poses," as she likes to call them. They search through their Daily Writing Folder, rummage to find a pencil, set up an iPad, or move in close with a peer. She notices Tommy already has a book opened most likely looking for more space facts and Jade has snuggled into a corner with his earbuds, writing on a clipboard. It is satisfying to see children settle in, comfortable in the routine of the Writing Studio.

Today Ms. J plans to conference with two writers and one group of children writing a story together. Tommy has asked for a "fact check" as he writes a piece about living in space and has asked Eliza for help with revision. A group of writers is working on a mystery and since it is their first collaborative effort, they more than likely need some direction. In addition, she will do quick check-ins with Sophia, Belinda, and Samir, who are developing English skills, and Colton, who is on an Individual Education Plan for writing, to make sure he is focused and clear on his writing plan for the day. This will not take the entire time and so Ms. J plans to do "drop-in" conferences with writers as she circles the room. She will use the drop-in visits to adjust tomorrow's lesson plans for guided writing, focused teaching in small groups based on writers' needs.

Ms. J grins. She can't help herself. Ms. J loves days like these in the Writing Studio. "There is no telling what third graders will say and write." She loves hearing their passionate stories, even their deep sighs of despair as well as their triumphant "Ta-Dah!" moments. Ms. J became a teacher because she loves kids—she wanted to spend time with children, make the world a little better place one child at a time. During individual teacher–student conferencing and guided writing she gets to know children through their stories and illustrations, learning what motivates them, how and why they "shut down," and how and why they laugh. This one-on-one time is "teaching with a capital T" (Atwell, 1998, p. 330). Scaffolding learning for a specific writer, at this time, and at this place. Seeing writing goals met and new goals set. Watching children grow up right in front of her through the words and sentences and paragraphs that become the autobiographies of their lives.

Tommy is holding up the space book for Ms. J to see, pointing to a picture of an orange swirling planet somewhere in the galaxy—it is time to get to work . . . Teaching.

Mini-lessons are whole class lessons from which most all writers will benefit. They represent the teacher of writing teaching *to* students through demonstration (Mooney, 1990). Writing instruction is individualized and differentiated through individual teacher–student writing conferences and guided writing instruction. These structures of teaching and learning represent the teacher *with* writer, providing targeted instruction and specific feedback (Mooney, 1990). "Informative feedback to learners" is both a general principle of effective instruction and necessary to promote English language learning (Goldenberg, 2013). Teacher–student conferences and guided writing represents intentional and focused feedback and can be tailored for writers with Individual Educational and 504 Plans, English learners, Talented and Gifted writers, and every other unique and wonderful need, challenge, and possibility present in the Writing Studio. These teaching and learning structures exemplify how the Writing Studio is truly *all-inclusive*.

The Teacher–Student Writing Conference

During a teacher–student writing conference, a teacher sits one-on-one with a writer, listening and observing to determine the kind of writing support, instruction, and feedback is necessary (see Figure 8.1, "Ms. Coy and Maddie Having a Conference").

Figure 8.1 Ms. Coy and Maddie Having a Conference

A conference lasts between 2 and 6 minutes. When we query teachers of writing who say they do not have time for individual conferences, we most often find such teachers are spending too much time with the mini-lesson or each individual conference. There are several time and management tips that can make writing conferences meaningful and doable even in overcrowded classrooms.

Guard Writing Time

We emphasized this in Chapter 7, and it is worth repeating: guard writing time in the studio. Hold it sacred. If mini-lessons take up the largest percentage of writing time, there will not be sufficient time for teacher–student conference. Writers need a minimum of 30 to 40 minutes a day to actually write. Likewise, teachers need at least 30 minutes to conduct individual conferences and guided writing. Protect writing time!

Teach Expectations for the Teacher–Student Writing Conference

Teach writers the purpose of the teacher–student conference and about what to expect from a teacher–student conference:

- Teacher–student conferences will on average be about 4 minutes in length. This is important so that all writers can receive individual instruction and feedback from the teacher.
- The conference is focused support for a writer.
- Remember peer conferencing also supports writers. (It doesn't always need to be the teacher!)
- Writers may request a conference during Status of the Class.
- If a writer discovers a need for a teacher conference during the writing time, he or she may check with the teacher but not while the teacher is conferencing or conducting a guided writing group.

Teaching writers to be prepared for a teacher-student writing conference is teaching writers to practice metacognition by being able to notice and name how and where they need help as a writer:

- "I would like to conference about my lead."
- "I would like feedback about how to include more details."
- "I think I might be finished with my piece but I am not sure."
- "I am having trouble getting started with my writing."
- "I am wondering if my piece is really persuasive."
- "I am ready for an editing conference."

Early-grade writers (K–2) can also learn to notice and name the kind of feedback they might receive from the teacher:

- "I'm done."
- "I don't know what to write about."
- "Can I publish this?"
- "How do I spell . . .?"

Learning to specify a purpose for a conference with the teacher or a peer is to practice using the academic language of a writer. This increases writer's agency as they become proficient in applying this language to their own writing; it places writers in the "writing club." Be mindful not to assume writers know this language, particularly English learners. Practice defining terms while using them: "Today let's explore strategies for revision, or adding and deleting details and words that make up the content of our stories."

Not all teacher–student writing conferences are by writer request. The teacher initiates an equal number or more (depending on the context and the writing unit).

The Structure of the Teacher–Student Writing Conference

The work of Graves (1994) and Calkins (1994) has been instrumental in developing teacher–student conference protocol—we draw from their work here. Both Graves and Calkins note the importance of a writing conference following a predictable pattern. Teaching writers this pattern allows the writer to know what to expect and to work with the structure to make sure his or her needs are met. An organization schema for teacher–student writing conferences is described in this section.

Inquire—Listen Hard/Observe

The writer reads the piece aloud. It is read aloud so that if there are editing errors, they do not distract the teacher. Likewise, reading writing aloud is useful to a writer; we often hear places where revisions are needed or editing needs to be done. The teacher practices *engagement*, listening hard, perhaps taking notes, and observing the writer's behavior. For example, "fidgeting" could mean nervousness, excitement, lack of confidence, or an uncomfortable chair—all are important to note. The question driving this phase of the writing conference is, "What is the meaning work of this writer?" (Ray, 2004). If the teacher is initiating the conference, she will often ask, "Where are you as a writer today?" If the writer has initiated the conference, the teacher may ask, "Okay, you've requested to conference about your opening line, or lead. What have you tried and what would you like me to listen for as you read aloud?"

Give Back

Having listened hard, the teacher of writing now summarizes back to the writer what he has heard. "This is what I heard as I listened to your piece. This is about a birthday present you received. You were disappointed when you opened it, but then you received the real gift, and you were surprised when your mom let a kitty into the room! Is this correct? Am I missing anything?" Allow the writer to give more information as necessary or correct the summary. Follow the summary by asking clarifying questions. If there are places where you are confused or need more information as the listener, ask, "What was the gift you opened? How did you react to that? How was that different than your reaction to the kitty?" Make a point of noticing what the writer is doing and naming what the writer can do (Johnston, 2004), "I noticed here how you added a phrase to describe your mom talking, 'Mom winked and said, . . .' That is an effective strategy when you add a descriptive word or phrase to describe the speaker of dialogue."

Teach With Intention

Having gathered the data from listening, observing, summarizing, clarifying, and asking questions, the teacher is ready to move into teaching. If the writer has initiated the conference, teach in the area of the writer's stated request. Otherwise, focus on an area that will support the writer's individual writing goals or develop specific skills as specified by the genre, "In hearing your action adventure, it seems that as a writer you might be able to use onomatopoeia. Do you know this term? It is a really fun word! Say it with me, *onomatopoeia*! These are sound words, or words that represent a sound or noise like *bam* and *pow*. You have already used these two, *bam* and *pow*. Let's brainstorm some other kinds of sound words that could spice up your writing!"

Next Step

Before the teacher leaves the writing conference, she makes certain the writer has a next step. Sometimes, this next step is directed by the teacher, "We have brainstormed some possible onomatopoeias you can use in your writing. Your next step is to return to your adventure story and insert these where they make the most sense and where they will add the most value to the story you are telling." Other times, this is a question to the writer, "What will you do next as a writer now that we are coming to the end of our conference?" Much depends on the writer and the context of the writing. The goal is always already writer independence: choose a response that will best support this goal. The teacher steps aside and hands over the writing to the writer.

This same process is followed when writers are working collaboratively. An additional piece is to confirm that each member of the collaborative team knows what he or she will be doing next.

Determining Who Needs a Teacher–Student Writing Conference

All teacher–student writing conferences are documented both on the Status of the Class and in the Teaching, Conferencing & Planning Notebook. Recording conferencing makes sure all writers are receiving conferences and provides data for how writers are moving towards their writing goals (review Chapter 5). These same tools are used to determine who needs a conference (review Chapter 5). A quick check of Status of the Class informs the teacher with whom he or she has or has not most recently visited. Knowledge of each writer also informs the need and frequency for conferencing. For example, one writer may struggle more with informative writing than another writer will. Or English learners and writers with identified challenges in writing may need more frequent quick checks. Data from the Teaching, Conferencing & Planning Notebook inform a teacher when a writer may need a goal conference, to revisit or revise individualized writing goals. The teacher–student writing conference is a critical tool for differentiation.

Teacher–Student Writing Conference Illustrated

A transcript of a teacher–student writing conference is included in this section. This conference was held in a Grade 4 classroom. Children were writing descriptive essays based on photographs. The teacher issued a challenge: when writers completed their essays, the essays would be posted on one side of the bulletin board and the photos on the other. The challenge was to see if readers could correctly match the descriptive essay to the photograph.

Read the transcript noting how the teacher moves through the conference; the language she uses; and how the writer responds.

Javier:	Then, this—then—
Ms. Lawrence:	Okay, hang on. Tell me where you are as a writer with this piece today? We conferenced recently, didn't we? [She flips through Teaching, Conferencing & Planning Notebook.]
Javier:	Yesterday, I think.
Ms. Lawrence:	Yes, got it. Here are my notes. Looks like we were discussing how to add more description to your essay. So, what's the purpose of this conference today?
Javier:	To see if I got—I made it better.
Ms. Lawrence:	What would make it better in your opinion? What did we last discuss?
Javier:	Better details. To talk about the green spots in the water. And I did some stuff and I think it is better. [He points to specific place in writing.]
Ms. Lawrence:	Great! Let's hear what you've done. Read just the parts you revised.
Javier:	Oh, "back in the water, I noticed the lake spots that look like giant lily pads." Oh, and here: "There are also shadows in the water making it look like a darker green. And when I touched the water, it makes me shiver and I breathe and I smell all the trees and water."

Ms. Lawrence:	Ah—you have used a comparison to make the description more vivid, "the lake spots look like giant lily pads." How did you think of that?
Javier:	Elena helped me!
Ms. Lawrence:	Elena helped you think of that? I love it when another writer helps me in that way.
Javier:	And, oh, this is the part I just fixed today [points to paper].
Ms. Lawrence:	What do you mean you fixed that part? What did you do?
Javier:	I moved this down and I wrote this.
Ms. Lawrence:	So you practiced revision. Will you read it for me?
Javier:	Yeah. "The bushes around the lake seem to be trying to hide behind the trees."
Ms. Lawrence:	That's personification right there: "the bushes are hiding." . . . That's giving the bushes human characteristics! What an effective writing strategy to use when trying to describe something. How did you think to use this?
Javier:	I wrote it down from the mini-lesson. And I just thought, what do those bushes look like they are doing? And I thought they looked like they were hiding, see [points to photograph] under these bigger trees.
Ms. Lawrence:	Wow—I am going to write that here in my notebook. That you applied what you learned from a mini-lesson to your revisions and used personification. What are you doing now? [Javier is drawing an arrow and writing a new sentence.]
Javier:	Um, I am going to add more . . . "like an elephant trying to hide behind a pencil" [Javier writes as he says the words.]
Ms. Lawrence:	[Laughs] Well that is an image! How do you feel about your writing now after you've added in that part and revised a little bit?
Javier:	It seems like I made it better.
Ms. Lawrence:	How did you make it better? What word do we use as writers to describe what you have done? [She waits.]
Javier:	Uh . . . I did revision?
Ms. Lawrence:	Yes, you did revision and as your reader, I can tell you this is much more descriptive! What are you thinking you will do next?
Javier:	Yeah, now I need to edit.
Ms. Lawrence:	I wonder if I might make a suggestion before you begin editing.
Javier:	Okay, what?
Ms. Lawrence:	You have made quite a few revisions to your paper, adding in more descriptive details and even personification. Writers find it useful at this point to pause and read the entire paper through one more time to make sure all the revisions make sense and the paper flows. A good way to do this is to read the whole paper aloud from start to finish. What if you give this a try?
Javier:	Okay. Do I just read it to myself?
Ms. Lawrence:	You could read it to a peer writer. Are you thinking that would be more useful?
Javier:	Yeah. [He begins looking around the room.]
Ms. Lawrence:	I just finished a conference with Ashkir. He is at a similar place in his writing. Why don't you check with him about a peer conference?
Javier:	Okay. I'll go find him!

In the conference, Ms. Lawrence begins by inquiring of Javier the purpose of the conference; she also checks her Teaching, Conferencing & Planning Notebook. Note how Ms. Lawrence does not have Javier read the entire piece; just the parts he has revised. This decision focuses the conference, narrows the purpose, and allows the conference to be completed in 4 minutes. Javier reads his revision and Ms. Lawrence gives back a summary of what she hears. Notice how she names what he has done: "you have used a comparison" and "that is personification!" She queries Javier, asking how he thought to use the personification, thus teaching him the practice of metacognition, and increasing his own agency by later asking him, "How?" These kinds of comments develop writer identity as Javier acknowledges his learning. Notice that Ms. Lawrence does more than offer verbal praise; she writes down Javier's accomplishment, celebrating this moment, and documenting how he has applied the mini-lesson to his own writing. Over time, Ms. Lawrence's notes will be the data demonstrating his developing skills as a writer.

Ms. Lawrence also gives back Javier the academic language of writing, repeatedly using the word *revision* and then insisting that he use the term toward the end of the conference. She does not settle for Javier continuing to say, "I made it better." Likewise, she reinforces the definition of personification by not only naming what Javier has done but also by restating the definition.

Finally, analyze how the teaching point evolves. Javier announces he is ready to edit the paper, but Ms. Lawrence with a quick glance of the writing, can tell there are a lot of scribbles, erasures, and add-ins. She can be fairly certain that there are missing words or places where Javier may need to add transitions in order for the piece to make sense and flow. Javier needs to slow down his process. The teaching point becomes a revision strategy of reading one's writing aloud. "What if," Ms. Lawrence challenges Javier, "you give this a try?" Javier is willing to do this, in part, because Ms. Lawrence in this short conference has named what he can do and how he has learned. He is ready to take a risk.

In the next transcript, Ms. Lawrence returns to Javier for another conference on the same paper. Javier has read his paper aloud, revised places that didn't flow, using the feedback of a peer. Now, he has edited the piece and he is asking Ms. Lawrence for a last check prior to typing the final on a word processor. Read the transcript and identify the flow of the conference, the language Ms. Lawrence uses, and how this conference develops Javier's identity and skills as a writer.

Ms. Lawrence:	Javier, you requested an editing conference?
Javier:	Yeah, I need to fix the spelling.
Ms. Lawrence:	Okay—we can work on that. What have you done in preparation for work on spelling?
Javier:	What?
Ms. Lawrence:	Did you read your piece aloud? How did that revision strategy work for you that we discussed yesterday?
Javier:	Yeah—I read it to Ashkir and I fixed some more stuff. Now I need help with the spelling.
Ms. Lawrence:	Okay—happy to hear you tried reading your paper aloud for a final revision check and you feel it was successful. What are the spelling questions you have?
Javier:	Ashkir says I spelled *forth* wrong.
Ms. Lawrence:	Okay. *Fourth* and *forth*. These two words are a little tricky because they sound the same but are spelled differently. [Ms. Lawrence is writing]. They are homonyms. *Fourth* refers to a number, like fourth grade. [She writes the number 4 next to *fourth*.]
Javier:	Okay.
Ms. Lawrence:	There is a different type of *forth* for when we say back and forth. [She sketches two boys tossing a ball back and forth; she labels the drawing, "forth."]
Javier:	Okay.
Ms. Lawrence:	I'd like you to write these two words and their definitions on your personal spelling list. Do you have that?
Javier:	[He finds list in Daily Writing Folder.] Yep. Right here.

Ms. Lawrence:	Great. So write down those words on you spelling list, add the drawings, and then correct them in your paper. And, Javier, be proud of yourself for trying out the read aloud revision strategy and for seeking help in spelling these words. They are tricky ones—you've got them now!
Javier:	[He grins.] Yep, I am almost ready to type up my paper!
Ms. Lawrence:	Yes, you are! What are you doing first?
Javier:	Spelling list, fix spelling!

Ms. Lawrence illustrates the teacher of writing as bricoleur, piecing together information about the writers of her classroom through the teacher–student writing conference. She practices engagement; she is a participant in the process. During the teacher–student conference, the teacher of writing is also a visionary, seeing ahead of the writer and imagining the writer's potential and next steps as a writer.

Visit the companion website to watch both individual and group teacher–student writing conferences across grade levels.

If you are teaching in a classroom now, during the next opportunity you have to hold a teacher–student writing conference, audio record the conference. Later, listen and analyze the conference flow and your use of language. Notice and name what you do well and set goals for the next writing conference.

Guided Writing Instruction

Guided writing is small-group, focused instruction based on writers' interests and needs. Like individual writing conferences, guided writing is a teaching and learning structure that meets writers where they are and moves them towards independence by providing "just right" instruction and feedback. It follows, then, that guided writing facilitates differentiation, not just by modifying an assignment but also by teaching writing strategies and skills unique to a small group of writers' needs and interests.

Guided writing instruction fills the space between whole-class mini-lessons (demonstrations) and individual teacher–student writing conferences (guided independence). Guided writing groups are small (rarely more than five students; in early grades, usually two to three writers), flexible and changing. Guided writing is *not* ability grouping. Instruction can be in any area of writing practices, process, and craft. Most guided writing group instruction is between 10 to 20 minutes. Guided writing is a predictable part of the Writing Studio; teaches writers expectations for guided writing (see Figure 8.2, "Guided Writing With Ms. Lomas").

Determining Who and When for Guided Writing Groups

Determine who needs guided writing group instruction based upon data gathered from the Status of the Class and Teaching, Conferencing & Planning Notebook. A review of Daily Writing Folders and/or samples of children's writing can also be used to determine guided writing groups. For the most part, guided writing groups emerge after several days or a week of individual teacher–student writing conferences.

For example, during the first week of a unit on writing memoirs, most teacher–student writing conferences will focus on finding a topic and narrowing that topic. These will also be the objectives of

Figure 8.2 Guided Writing With Ms. Lomas

the mini-lessons. After 2 days, if there are any writers without a topic, it makes sense to group them and to focus on finding a topic in a guided writing group. After 3 to 5 days of teacher–student writing conferences, the teacher can analyze Status of the Class and Teaching, Conferencing & Planning Notebook data and determine how writers may be grouped according to needs. Writers struggling to narrow their topic could be one group; for another group, a lesson on leads; and for a final group, a lesson on transition words.

Recall Mr. Mackie's "Songbird, Threatened!" project (Chapter 5, Status of the Class, and Chapter 7, mini-lesson planning). At the end of a week of individual conferencing, Mr. Mackie analyzes his Status of the Class and plans guided writing groups. Four writers, Alannah, Yolanda, Carmelita, and Ada, are working on storyboards, planning to do a chapter book. The writers are writing independently, yet all need support in organizing the facts they are collecting for the songbird covered in different chapters. Three partnerships (Joaquim and Enzo; Maddie and Gabby; Austin and Esteban) have lots of ideas, but all need to find a focus for their writing. Lilly and Suelita are both using poetry writing to express their concern for the dwindling numbers of songbirds. Both writers will benefit from a focused lesson on how to show rather than tell scientific facts in poems. Grouping writers will make the most of Mr. Mackie's time. He will still have time to meet individually in teacher–student writing conferences with writers he has not placed in guided writing groups during the week. By the following week, it is highly likely that the needs of writers will change and so will the members of the various guided writing groups.

Choice units necessitate different kinds of guided writing groups. During a choice unit, writers may write about any topic and in any genre they choose. Mini-lessons tend to be more general to writing practices, process, and craft: how to gauge and use time, review of revision strategies, and how to slow down to check spelling. Guided writing most often groups writers choosing the same genre. There may be a mystery, adventure, fantasy, and poetry guided writing group. These groups may stay the same throughout the choice unit, allowing the teacher to specifically support writers according to genre need.

Toward the end of a writing unit, a quick review of writing in Daily Writing Folders allows the teacher to group writers according to editing needs. Some writers may need extra support with paragraphing; others with slowing down and reading aloud to edit; others with using end punctuation; some hearing more sounds in each word; and still another few, with noun-verb agreement. This may be a time to group English learners with similar language backgrounds and/or needs together for specific instruction (Laman, 2013).

Specific writing goals may also be a reason to convene a guided writing group. Each writer has individual writing goals; however, usually more than one writer has the same goal. There may be several writers, for example, who have as a writing goal "I will try a new genre of writing." It would not necessarily be wise to group together all the children who have this goal if they do not share a common interest. But using data from the Reading Studio, a teacher could group writers who are all reading graphic novels, for example, and introduce them to the genre of informative graphic novels. They could discuss informative topics of interest and then think about how they might be presented in graphic genre.

Planning a Guided Writing Lesson

A guided writing lesson plan is different from a mini-lesson since the goal is to provide intentional guidance, or scaffolding, for specific writers. Guided writing is *with* writers, the teacher alongside the writers. This means there should be plenty of opportunity for guided practice. Here is one of the guided writing lessons Mr. Mackie planned for Alannah, Yolanda, Carmelita, and Ada, who needed additional instruction in organizing facts.

Guided Writing Instruction: Alannah, Yolanda, Carmelita, and Ada

Standard:

- CCSS.ELA-Literacy.W.5.2 Write informative/explanatory texts to examine a topic and convey ideas and information clearly.
- CCSS.ELA-Literacy.W.5.2b Develop the topic with facts, definitions, concrete details, quotations, or other information and examples related to the topic.

Objective: Writers will practice organizing facts in a way that makes sense to the reader.

Materials: Flowers (Burnie, 1992); a copy of one chapter from each writer's draft work; example of cut apart sentences about a Junko.

Introduction: "Writers, we are meeting today to learn more about how to organize facts in a way that makes sense to the reader. All of you are writing chapter books about songbirds. Each chapter is about a different songbird. It is helpful to a reader, if a book like the ones you are writing, are organized in the same way, using a predictable pattern, so that the content makes sense to your reader. I think this book, *Flowers* by David Burnie (1992), will be helpful in illustrating this to you. Let's look at how this book is organized."

Inquiry With Mentor Text:
- Read and study pages 36–37; 46–47; 50–51 with writers.
- Note how the facts are organized (introductory paragraph, followed by illustrations and short captions or sentences).
- Analyze the introductory paragraph closely: topic sentence as a statement or a question followed by key supporting facts and a closure sentence.
- Discuss how the writing and layout work together.

Model: "Here are some sentences that might go in a chapter about a Junko. I've cut the sentences apart. Experiment with me to put these in an order that will make sense to the reader. Let's try and use the same pattern as Burnie did."

- Work with writers to arrange sentences.
- There is missing information in the example—if writers do not notice this, ask, "Do you think this paragraph needs any additional information or fact?"
- Write a sentence strip together that will fill in the missing information (what Junkos eat). Add it to the paragraph.
- Glue all sentence strips onto a new piece of paper once the paragraph is organized in a way that makes sense.

Practice: "What if you each try this strategy with your own writing? I've made copies of one chapter from each of your books. I've even cut apart the sentences for you! Don't worry—this is a copy! I didn't cut apart your original! Right now, go ahead and play with different ways you might arrange the sentences. Collaborate as needed. Try to use the pattern that Burnie did in *Flowers* (1992). If you find a place where you need more information, leave a little extra space, write a new sentence strip, and place it where you think it belongs. When you think your paragraph is better organized with all necessary facts, let me know, and we'll check your work together."

Guide: Guide each writer as needed with this task.

Closure: "Look what you have done with your writing! You have organized facts in a way that will make sense to your readers. You can glue your new paragraph together and then you can try this strategy with your other chapter book pages. Would some of you consider sharing before and after paragraphs during share time today?"

Mr. Mackie's guided writing lesson illustrates how this teaching and learning structure supports specific needs of writers. Not everyone in the class required this lesson. Conversely, if Mr. Mackie were to do this lesson with each individual during a teacher–student conference, it would require too much time. By grouping these writers together he is able to provide focused instruction and feedback that is "just right" for Alannah, Yolanda, Carmelita, and Ada at this time in their writing.

The beauty of the Writing Studio is really how a teacher of writing can teach so many children with different abilities, needs, and interests through teacher–student conferences and guided writing. Children are challenged and taught based upon where they are as writers. Each writer is accountable to individual goals that are monitored through carefully documented data. In this way, the teacher of writing *can* teach *all* children well.

Problematizing Practice

The goals of Problematizing Practice are to deconstruct assumptions and beliefs and to consider multiple responses and implications of teaching decisions. It is best to do this in the company of colleagues and your instructor:

1. Read the scenario.
2. Quickly write down assumptions about the scenario. *Study your assumptions.*
3. Discuss and problematize assumptions with others and your instructor.
4. Discuss and write possible responses to the scenario.
5. Discuss the possible consequences (intended and unintended) of each response.

Scenario

You are not satisfied with the way your teacher–student writing conferences are going. They seem to take way too long, and the writers often are not able to continue without you. You audio record your teacher–student writing conferences during two Writing Studios. On your commute home, you listen to the audio recordings. You are a bit unnerved to hear how much your voice dominates the recording: You realize you simply talk too much and don't listen enough. How can you train yourself to listen more and talk less?

References

Atwell, N. (1998). *In the middle: New understandings about writing, reading and learning* (2nd ed.). Portsmouth, NH: Heinemann.

Burnie, D. (1992). *Flowers.* New York, NY: Dorling Kindersley.

Calkins, L. (1994). *The art of teaching writing.* Portsmouth, NH: Heinemann.

Goldenberg, C. (2013). Unlocking the research on English learners: What we know—and don't yet know. *American Educator, 37*(2), 4–11.

Graves, D. (1994). *A fresh look at writing.* Portsmouth, NH: Heinemann.

Johnston, P. H. (2004). *Choice words: How our language affects children's learning.* Portland, ME: Stenhouse.

Laman, T. T. (2013). *From ideas to words: Writing strategies for English language learners.* Portsmouth, NH: Heinemann.

Mooney, M. E. (1990). *Reading to, with and by children.* Katonah, NY: Richard C. Owens.

Ray, K. W. (2004). *About the authors: Writing workshop with our youngest writers.* Portsmouth, NH: Heinemann.

Chapter Nine
Individual and Collaborative Writers: Sharing, Celebrating, and Broadcasting Together

Aisha and Sayo are working on the computer, doing research on butterflies. Oliver is reading in the classroom library while Lucas has found his place in the quiet corner where he is less likely to be distracted. Four pairs of writers are engaged in peer writing conferences; all have moved their chairs alongside desks so they can be knee to knee to listen and focus more effectively to provide peer feedback. Hasina is drawing; markers are strewn across his table. Children sit in clusters of desks and there is a lot of talk coming from two of these clusters. Hands are waving, someone dips to the floor to recover a pencil, and chairs scrape the floor. There is laughter. Most children are writing independently, occasionally pausing to visit with a peer or ask a question, or move from their desks to find supplies. Ms. J is meeting with a guided writing group of four writers, teaching a lesson on showing rather than telling.

Ms. J is focused on the writers surrounding her, and she is also monitoring the rest of the class. She deliberately positions the guided writing table so she sits with her back to the wall. This means she can glance up and look across the heads of the writers in front of her to see the entire classroom in action.

There is a hum in the Writing Studio. It is a productive hum, sometimes a little louder, sometimes strangely hushed. When Ms. J first started teaching with the Writing Studio, it took awhile for her to distinguish the sounds of desks, keyboards, pencils scratching, voices rising (was that anger, frustration, excitement, success?) and to know which kinds of sounds required attention. She finds with each new school year and new mix of children, there is always a period of relearning to listen, to find the particular song of the Writing Studio that is productive and useful.

Now, her quick observant glance across the classroom informs her that all is well. More than likely, one of the table clusters is a bit off task, but they will find their way back to writing. Perhaps Ashia and Sayo could be more productive on the computer—she will need to check their work later and, if needed, follow up with this tomorrow. She is loving the peer conferencing she observes—writers are intent in listening and giving feedback. She refocuses on the guided writing group surrounding her . . . "Could you read your example one more time, Mara?"

The Writing Studio, happily, Live.

Ultimately, the goal of the Writing Studio is for children to write independently with confidence. This is the final stage in Mooney's (1990) description of authentic literacy learning, when writing is composed *by* children, without the help of a teacher. Because writing is not a solitary act, independence includes the ability to collaborate with others as writers to provide feedback. The Writing Studio is based on the premise that children can and do engage in writing and writing practice while the teacher of writing moves about the classroom, either facilitating individual conferences or guided writing. Sometimes, teachers feel like this is surely an impossibility: children will not behave without sitting in well-planned groupings without a teacher monitoring movement and carefully dictating their next steps. Yet, is it ever really a possibility that 27 children will all sit quietly, all doing the exact thing, at the exact speed, all learning the same material? If they are learning, what *are* they learning? Writing Studio is based on the fact that human beings want to learn, do learn, want to communicate and collaborate: that children are, in fact, eager to write, if given the environment and opportunities to do so, and that they do this in different and unique ways.

Becoming-Independent

Teach independence and how to make decisions and handle choices in the Writing Studio by reinforcing expectations for writing, especially at the beginning of the year. Begin by teaching the schedule: mini-lesson, Status of the Class, independent and collaborative writing time with teacher–student writing conferences and guided writing, followed by sharing. Demonstrate and discuss the decisions for each phase of the Writing Studio. For example, immediately prior to Status of the Class, each writer examines his or her writing folder and determines what they will work on for the day. This is goal setting. During the first of the year in particular, share at the end of the Writing Studio how writers accomplished these goals. Right after Status of the Class, is a second important transition. Writers have choices. They may reread a piece to determine next steps, have a peer conference, complete research, perhaps find a quiet space to think about their writing, or begin writing immediately. These choices can be made into a wall chart as a reminder to writers.

Teaching about decision making and about why and when different decisions are made is to teach independence.

Notice and name when writers are making good decisions and fulfilling expectations: "Did you notice today that during writing time, it started kind of noisy, then, everyone seemed to get so quiet, and then again, it seemed to get noisy. Why do you think sound ebbs and flows like this during writing time? How might we describe and name this phenomenon?" Donald Graves (2001) writes these wise words: "What you pay attention to, you reinforce" (p. 45). Pay attention to the good decisions!

Problematize management challenges with writers and individualize as necessary. "Some children just need structure," we often hear. And we answer, "Then give them structure." The Writing Studio is predictable and structured—maintain the schedule. For those writers who need additional structure, set very specific tasks and time goals: "Andrew, your goal for the next 15 minutes is to write five sentences, all related to your camping trip." Use more templates and graphic organizers and even time sheets to help focus writers. Create cueing systems for transitions. While necessary for some writers, other writers would find these kinds of scaffolds a barrier to writing and they will teach dependence, not independence. Know the different support needed by each writer by collecting and analyzing data (see Chapter 5).

Embrace and explore the motivational aspects of choice. Do not shy away from it. This seems to be a common response when teachers feel they are "losing control." They will assign everyone the same prompt as if having all children write on a topic they do not care about will keep them on task. Rather, embrace choice and teach children about writing decisions: how to choose any topic from their writing topics list, or even another writer's list. Then extend the challenge: "What if you could stick with this topic just for 10 minutes, walk around the room, and go for another ten? What if you give this a try? Let's work on this together." Celebrate small steps as needed for those individual writers that need to develop writing stamina.

Stay focused on the writer and their potential. Do this by keeping individual writing goals lively, achievable, and up-to-date. Visit and revisit these goals often. When writing goals are monitored, children know they matter. As reviewed in Chapter 6, support metacognition, so writers become aware of their needs and learn to state them: "I am being distracted. I need a place where I can focus. Can you help me find a place where I could work today?" "I don't really like what I am writing. Is it too late to change topics?" "I just feel restless and I don't really want to write. What do I do?"

If you are new to the Writing Studio, it takes some time to learn to listen and observe for the many productive sounds and actions of writers. Sometimes, from across the room, two writers can appear to be off-task. Scout out the situation first: it may just be an animated conversation about how to spell a word! If you feel like the Writing Studio is edging "out of control," stop and observe. Learn from children: gather a small group of writers and listen to them talk about the studio. Collect data. Analyze results: Ask, "What if?" and "What else?" Ask, "Do changes need to happen for everyone or just for a few writers?"

Children learn independence when they are given opportunity to practice choice making and receive feedback on how to make real decisions. It means they will sometimes make mistakes. This is part of growing up—it is an opportunity for learning.

Becoming-Collaborative

Gracie Lee and Marta are bent over a table, drawing a mural together about fall leaves on the white butcher paper spread out in front of them. "It is a story about all the things you can do with leaves," Marta announces. "We are working together so we can have a really big picture with lots of ideas!" Together the two first graders illustrate and help one another write sentences to match the many pictures they draw. They are animated and excited about their work!

Collaboration among writers creates synergy. Promote collaboration; avoid mandating it. As adults we choose to write with others when we have common interests or goals or simply because we like the other person. Although there is a time and a place for a teacher to create collaborative writing groups, such groups usually work better when they are formed organically, and not when everyone is required to write in a group. Save teacher-created collaborative writing groups for special projects and occasions when it seems necessary to arrange the class in this way.

For example, Keith and Benjamin, two fourth-grade boys, wrote collaboratively because both are fans of the St. Louis Rams football team. Their teacher noticed that they could talk on and on about the Rams and suggested that they write an informative piece together. Both boys were "psyched." Benjamin is labeled "special education" with specific challenges that might have isolated him or set him apart, but finding a common interest with Keith, he created a successful partnership that might not have otherwise happened. Both writers challenged one another, and they both grew as writers as a result of this collaboration.

Choosing to write with another is a decision writers need to learn how to make and negotiate. Turn collaboration challenges into possibilities for learning about negotiating and conflict resolution skills. Observe for collaborators who may become too dependent on one another or unevenly matched collaborations where one writer may be doing most of the work and cannot seem to renegotiate roles. As with all things in the Writing Studio, listen, observe, collect data; then, teach and intervene as necessary.

Collaborative Writing Strategies

There are a number of ways to write collaboratively. Here are three ways to begin:

- Writers may brainstorm and support one another but write individual pieces.
- Writers may take turns holding the pencil, writing alternative lines, paragraphs, or even pages.
- Writers can each take a different chapter of a longer fiction or nonfiction work.

Check in with collaborators: "How is this collaboration working? What else might you try as collaborators?"

Collaboration and English Learners

Research demonstrates the importance of social interaction for English learners (Krashen, 1982; Rigg & Allen, 1989; Rigg & Hudelson, 1986). "Language develops when the language learner focuses on accomplishing something together with others rather than focusing on language itself" (Rigg & Hudelson, 1986, p. 117). Collaborative writing offers a rich opportunity to develop English learning as writers focus on a topic of interest, finding ways to write and present their work to others.

Collaboration and Technology

Teach and use technologies to foster collaboration beyond the classroom. Upper grade elementary writers can use Google documents (google.com), for example, to compose together, each from their own home! Google Draw (google.com) can be a useful tool for planning writing projects and then dividing writing tasks between collaborators. Mixed Ink (www.mixedink.com) is another online writing website that encourages writing as a social and collaborative writing experience. Wikis hold potential for collaborators. Applications for tablets can be used for all kinds of genres, as collaborators take photos, edit, and create cartoons. Even young writers can use applications such as "Story Kit" (International Children's Digital Library, 2012) to create delightful stories easily uploaded to the Internet so that parents, guardians, friends, and family can enjoy them.

 Watch a video of three Grade 5 boys collaboratively writing a fantasy story.

Supporting Independence and Collaboration Through Peer Conferencing

Gabby and Maddie sit knee to knee in a corner of the Writing Studio. Gabby leans into Maddie and says,

Gabby: I like how you say that the Junko doesn't really stand a chance. I wonder if you could show that more?

Maddie: Like what do you mean?

Gabby: Well, you know, Junkos eat on the ground, right? So cats just sneak up on them so you . . .

Maddie: Oh, I could write that scene!

Gabby: Yeah, like a movie script!

Gabby and Maddie are peer conferencing, collaborating to support one another as writers. They illustrate the importance of peer conferencing to the Writing Studio. If all writers are dependent on the teacher alone for feedback and writing support, then not only will the teacher be overwhelmed, the studio will also not function. Writers must learn to support one another. For this reason, peer conferencing is central to the Writing Studio.

There are three general questions that drive a writer to seek help: Does this piece make sense? (Content feedback), "I am stuck and I don't know what to do next. Can you help me?" (Process advice), and "Would you be a second pair of editing eyes for me?" (Editing advice). Brainstorm questions for each category with writers. Teach children the language writers use to seek and receive writing assistance. Publish and create a wall chart of the categories and questions.

These kinds of questions reflect the guiding principles behind all peer conferences: (a) the writer has a piece he or she feels committed toward and is seeking feedback with the goal of improved writing, (b) the writer is prepared to accept feedback in the form of critique and suggestions, and (c) the writer makes the final decision about what feedback to incorporate into his/her writing. It is necessary to teach, model, and practice how these principles look in action in the Writing Studio.

Conversely, teach writers how to respond in a peer conference, first as the peer and then as the writer. As a peer supporting a writer, model and practice how to summarize what is heard, how to give a specific compliment and how to frame a suggestion. These are excellent mini-lesson and guided-writing objectives as well as individual writing goals. Lessons in peer conferencing are worth repeating throughout the year, making them specific to genre and choice units. Likewise, teach writers appropriate ways to respond. Writers need to know how to accept advice, discuss writing without being defensive, and how to tactfully say, "Thanks for the suggestion. Let me think about what you are telling me." (See Table 9.1 Possible Responses in a Peer Conference.)

TABLE 9.1 Possible Responses for Peer Conferences

Peer to Writer	Writer to Peer
Could you tell me a little more about your thinking when you write. . . *(Seeking clarification)*	"Let me think about that suggestion." *(Honors peer's suggestion; provides time for writer to consider the suggestion)*
I think what I am hearing is . . . is this correct? *(Seeking clarification)*	Are you suggesting that I . . . *(Asking for clarification)*
I like this place in your writing [select specific place]. It makes me [think of, react in this way] *(Giving specific praise)*	Oh, I like that idea! *(Specific thanks for writing support)*
I wonder how it might work if you . . . *(Giving suggestions)*	How would you write this section? OR Could you help me write this? *(Seeking additional help)*
How did you think to . . . *(Inquiry into writer's process and/or craft)*	Have you ever used this strategy? Could I see how you did this? *(Seeking additional help)*

Model and practice peer conferencing often, particularly at the beginning of the year. Reinforce and teach nuanced peer conferencing as the year progresses. As a teacher, ask a writer to peer conference with you in front of the class. (Consider the writer; it may be wise to prep the writer prior to the mini-lesson.) Using a "fishbowl" approach can also be effective. Ask for two volunteers prior to the mini-lesson, a writer and a peer. Have them sit knee to knee in the center of the other writers and hold their peer conference. When they have finished, the other writers can name and notice what the writer and peer were doing in the conference that was effective.

Protocol for Peer Conferencing

A simple protocol for peer conferencing is as follows:

- The writer identifies need. The writer states specifically what he or she would like the peer to listen for. For example, "Could you listen to see if my writing makes sense?"
- The writer reads piece aloud—peer listens hard. The writing is read aloud because it has not yet been edited and editing errors could distract the peer from the content of the writing.
- The peer summarizes what he or she heard and shares this with the writer. If the peer summarizes differently than what the writer has intended, it is a good indicator for the writer that the writing may need further focusing and development.
- The peer gives writer a compliment. "I like how you write, 'Mad Cat shrieked!'"
- The writer and the peer discuss piece. The peer may ask questions such as "I wonder if you could tell me more about this part of your writing?" Or the peer might offer suggestions or further develop the compliment and say, "I wonder if there are other places you could use words like *shrieked*."
- Writer decides on how to follow-up on the peer conference. The writer considers the discussion and suggestions she has with her peers. Then, she makes writing decisions about what to do next to her writing (see Figure 9.1, "James and Morgan Peer Conferencing").

Figure 9.1 James and Morgan Peer Conferencing

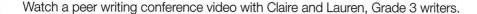 Watch a peer writing conference video with Claire and Lauren, Grade 3 writers.

In early grades, narrow the purpose and direct peer conferences by providing a focus for peer conferencing: "We have been working on making sure our writing has a beginning, a middle, and an end. Today, when you read your piece with a writing buddy, see if they can hear the beginning, middle, and end of your piece."

Some teachers of writing effectively use peer-response groups, strategically placing writers in a group of three to four to regularly provide feedback. Writers may also form their own peer response groups; teachers can guide this choice (and teach about making the choice) so that a response group brings together writers with different kinds of strengths. Peer-response groups can meet on a regular basis. Provide peer-response groups with specific feedback and instruction to maximize their effectiveness.

Some teachers of writing like to use a peer conference form or a peer conference log. Other teachers asks writers to note at the top of a draft any dates of a peer conference. The Status of the Class or My Writing World also provides a record of peer conferencing. Any of these alternatives are ways of tracking writers' development as writing peers.

Learning to peer conference is a powerful way to support children's mastery of Common Core State Standards in Speaking and Listening (NGA Center for Best Practices & CCSSO, 2010). "Comprehension and Collaboration" describes the ability to engage with grade-level peers in collaborative discussions, follow discussion protocols, and asking clarifying, summarizing and confirming what has been heard, and asking and answering questions. Any assessment forms used, and notes in the Teaching, Conferencing & Planning Notebook can be aligned with these standards.

Collaborative writing nurtures independence in the Writing Studio. Writers learn to advise and listen to one another, make choices, negotiate, and ultimately appreciate one another's strengths. It is common for certain writers to develop status as "expert" spellers, idea people, page designers, or "lead-ers of opening lines." Cultivated collaboration develops community, not only in the Writing Studio but also across the elementary school day and in all disciplines. Sharing, celebrating, and broadcasting writers' work is yet another way independence, collaboration, and community are developed.

Developing Independence, Collaboration, and Community Through Sharing, Celebrating, and Broadcasting

Kiara cannot wait to share at the end of Writing Studio today. She is writing an essay about how she wants to be a police officer when she grows up. She has revised her opening paragraph several times, and she is proud of her revisions. Kiara is learning English as a second language. Collaborating with writers at her table group supports her English-language learning and her confidence as a writer. Her table group helped her with this opening paragraph, and she is proud to share her work.

Formal Sharing in the Writing Studio

Sharing, as collaboration, happens throughout a writer's process of a piece. Formal sharing occurs at the end of every Writing Studio. Sharing time is 5 to 10 minutes in length. Teachers cue writers several minutes prior to share time so they can organize Daily Writing Folders and think about what they might share. To keep sharing meaningful, practice it daily, teach writers how to share, and how to compliment one another. Writers might end the studio by reading an entire piece to the whole class, a small group, or a partner. But they might also share revision triumphs "before" and "after" sentences or paragraphs great verbs or amazing nouns they have discovered a simile or metaphor they have written or small parts of writing that may have been the focus of the mini-lesson, such as "using transition words."

Writers might share "failures" or "struggles" and how they have overcome these. "I had a really hard time coming up with an idea. I was pretty discouraged, and then I talked with Javier and we decided to collaborate and write a soccer play book!" Writers may share about their writing practices: how a writer was able to write for a longer period of time or finished a "really long piece." Or a writer may share about what he or she can now do: "I used to write a lot of sentences without periods, but now I use them all the time."

 Watch an example of daily sharing in the Writing Studio in a Grade 3 classroom.

Teach and prompt writers to share and celebrate one another: how to listen to one another, to encourage each other to share, and to give specific compliments. Expect nothing less; teach nothing less.

Sharing at the end of the Writing Studio doesn't need to be limited to those in the classroom. Kindergarten teacher, Ms. Coy, invites all parents, guardians, and caring adults to celebrate at the end of each writing unit by attending share time. Sharing and celebrating takes on new meaning when additional ears are present to listen!

It is easy to see how sharing and celebrating in the Writing Studio encourages collaboration and ultimately, a sense of community. We risk more as writers when we are in the midst of friends and mentors. And "Risk allows children to outgrow themselves" (Fletcher, 1993, p. 17), moving children toward the goal of being independent writers.

Developing Independence and Collaboration by Broadcasting Writers' Work

While sharing happens throughout writing practices, broadcasting speaks to publishing the final work of a writer. Broadcasting a writer's work is a celebration of taking risks, reaching goals, and enjoying a reward of writing: having an appreciative audience!

Broadcasting writing marks a milestone a moment of individual and collaborative triumph for the writer. There are many ways to publish children's writing. A guiding principle is that final writing is broadcast to, and celebrated by, an audience greater than the teacher.

When writers are ready to publish their work, they will need to make a series of *what, how, where,* and *when* decisions. How much latitude a writer in a Writing Studio has about publishing decisions is dependent on how much choice a teacher allows.

The following are some questions to consider about broadcasting writers and their work.

What

What pieces should be published?

How

How should a piece be published? How should it look? This is a design decision and includes how illustrations and text are arranged on a page. Should text write around the illustrations, be under the illustration, be separated by pages? If the writing is to be published on a web page or blog, additional design decisions must be made. Perhaps the piece might be recorded and become part of the classroom's podcast collection? Or maybe it will be formally presented orally. A variety of tablet applications make it easy for a writer to post his or her work and to read it aloud so that the reader can both read the text and hear the writer reading the piece.

Design decisions encourage writers to think about their readers and/or listeners. See Figure 9.2, "Claire's Toe Gym Commercial," as an example: Claire, after examining her own feet, decided what she needed was a toe gym. Notice the design decisions she is drafting and will need to consider prior to her piece being published.

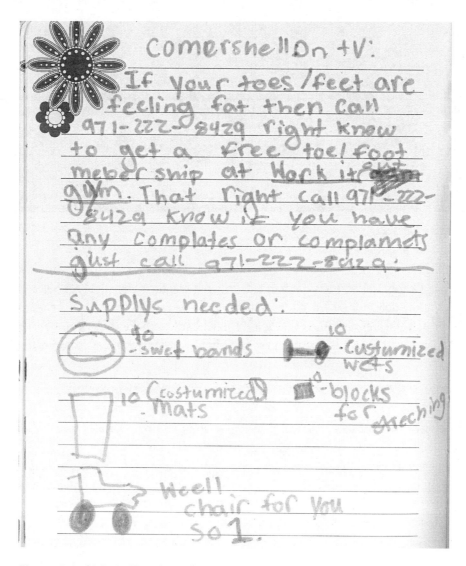

Figure 9.2 Claire's Toe Gym Commercial

Where

Where should a piece of writing be published? Poems are good on a bulletin board, longer pieces may need a space on a class-publishing website, some pieces can be read aloud to the class or a small group as a read aloud, and still others may require the function of a book with a hard cover and become part of a classroom library collection.

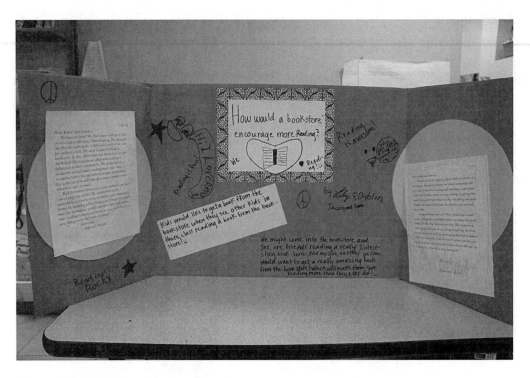

Figure 9.3 Bookstore Display Board

Writers in one Grade 3 classroom deliberated on what might make their school a better learning and living space. They determined a used bookstore would be perfect so they wrote letters to the principal and vice principal, carefully constructing a display board to make their argument (see Figure 9.3, "Bookstore Display Board"). And, yes, the parent council worked with the children to set up a used bookstore!

When

When should a piece be published? Not all pieces of writing will be read at a parent/guardian writing night, but some will. Is this *the* piece for this occasion?

Writing can be published on blogs, classroom or school websites, online publishing magazines, walls, bulletin boards, in podcasts, as books shared with others, read-alouds, through tablet applications, and even on bulletin boards at local businesses. As writers have options in your classroom, teach them about the choices and the decisions authors make when publishing their work.

Learning to Read Writing Aloud

Writers need to learn to read their work aloud. This is scary stuff—writing, no matter the subject, is always personal. Helen Keller said, "But if I write what my soul thinks, then it will be visible, and the words will be its body" (Anagnos, 1982, p. 229). Asking children to read their work publicly requires us as teachers of writing to ensure a safe environment for doing so. Again, teach children how to listen and to respond. Set expectations for listening to one another's work by acknowledging that reading our writing can be both frightening and exciting.

Teach writers to read their work aloud with confidence. Teach about eye contact, reading with fluency and expression, and speaking clearly. This can be reinforced during daily share time. Practice

Figure 9.4 Nickolas Reads His Writing Aloud

formally before ceremonial presentations. Many teachers use an "Author's chair" (Graves & Hansen, 1983) a special place for a writer to sit and command the attention of others when reading their writing aloud. Other teachers "lay out the red carpet," literally a section of purchased remnant of red carpet or a large piece of red butcher paper on which writer's stand when presenting their work. Some construct or purchase a small platform for the same purpose. Consider purchasing an inexpensive microphone, then model and allow writers to practice using the microphone to read their work aloud (see Figure 9.4, "Nickolas Reads His Writing Aloud").

Note that broadcasting one's work supports the CCSS for Speaking and Listening. The anchor Standard, "Presentation of Knowledge and Ideas," includes the skills of using multimedia for presentation of work and oral presentation. Consider these standards, as well as the writing anchor standard, "Production and Distribution of Writing," for each grade level when planning how to broadcast the work of writers.

Although reading one's writing aloud can be a cause for anxiety, when a writer has time to practice, reads his or her work well, and receives genuine praise from peers and adults, it is a rewarding experience that motivates and serves to further develop writer's identity and confidence. Plan such experiences thoughtfully, mindful of the teaching and learning context and the children in your classroom. Above all, celebrate and broadcast the good work of writers!

 How do you feel about reading your own writing aloud? Recall several occasions where you have read your work aloud. (If you are following along the parallel *Becoming-Writer* section, you will have an opportunity to share the work you are now writing!) What conditions made this a rewarding or not so rewarding experience? Discuss this with your colleagues. What are ideas you have for creating a safe environment for children to share their work and teaching them how to read their work aloud?

The companion website includes videos of writers from multiple grade levels broadcasting their writing.

Creating Possibilities From Writing Studio Challenges

The Writing Studio *Live* is a place of movement and motion. Challenges arise as a result of children learning, growing up, taking risks, and their changing needs. See these challenges as possibilities for learning. Context and the individual child always matter in factoring possibilities and solutions that may arise so there are no "magic bullets" or fixes. We can address some common challenges and possible ways for strategically thinking about them, but each situation is always unique and requires the teacher of writing to collect data, listen hard, often seek the wisdom of a professional colleague, and, then, make a strategic intervention.

Writer Is Not Responsive

It happens. Sometimes a writer just doesn't respond, doesn't want to talk or engage. And sometimes, this is fine. We all have moments likes these. Know when to allow a writer space and time. If, however, a writer has a pattern of non-responsiveness, it is worth collecting additional data. Does the child respond the same in other discipline areas? Is he/she only "shutting down" during writing? Find out more about the child's writing history. If a writer has little confidence in his/her writing, revision can be threatening. Start small.

Resistant Writer

Sometimes we know the exact teaching point a writer needs; we have a great suggestion that will so improve a writer's paper. And—the writer isn't interested. He or she resists our teaching and our suggestions, insisting the paper is fine the way it is. Writers are entitled to have opinions about their pieces. Know when to walk away from a teacher–student writing conference and allow the writer to exercise their individual decision. Again, if this becomes a pattern, then a different approach will be needed. But on the occasion a writer just doesn't see it the way we do as teachers, give way to the writer's preference: they are learning independence.

Writer Is Way Below Grade Level

Start where the writer is. Design scaffolds such as graphic organizers for success. Find areas where the child does excel, for example, in art or web design or oral storytelling and use this as a starting point. Start small. Set obtainable goals, positioning the writer for immediate success. Focus on the writer's interests—the possibility for learning is greatly increased when we are interested in the topic! Most important, meet with the parents or guardians, the special educator, the English-language teacher, and/or the counselor. Work together as a team to develop a plan for success. Collaborate! You are not alone!

The Reluctant Writer

Begin your inquiry: why is this writer reluctant to write? There are so many possible reasons: the physical act of writing may be difficult; the writer is a perfectionist; the writer is already convinced he or she "can't do it." Reluctant writers need success. Tap into their interests. If the writer speaks a language other than English, encourage him or her to write in his or her first language. Consider technology: what technologies might support and motivate the writer?

When Children Write Things That Make You Shutter

Writers may include violence or profanity in their work or seem to write too many stories about death or even about forms of abuse. This is where the individual and the context are absolutely critical. Boys often choose to write about violence (Newkirk, 2000); war may be a standard topic. Writers find inspiration from movies, video games, and graphic novels. So topics found in movies, video games, and graphic novels are "normal" and motivational. For most elementary children, use of profanity is not acceptable by school standards. If writing is particularly graphic, however, about any of these topics, it can be a writer's call for help. Consult and collaborate with counselors and specialists when you have concerns.

When Writers Fly Through Work: "I Am Done!"

Sometimes, as writers we are inspired, and we do fly through work! This becomes problematic when it is a habit. Writers develop revision abilities over time; by the end of Grade 3, children are growing in this area. Inquire more about a writer who regularly flies through his or her work: is he or she a perfectionist? Does he or she not know how to revise? Is it his or her personality to like to "get things done"? Maybe the writer will do well with a checklist of "things to do"? Sometimes, writers, known as "above-grade-level writers" have never been required to rethink and revise their writing; they need new challenges and focus as a writer. Other writers need a direct challenge or intervention: "On this piece, I need you to revise in three different places to meet phase one of your writing goal. How can you make this happen?"

When the Writing Studio Seems Stuck

Time to mix it up! What have you been doing in the Writing Studio? Maybe it is time to write shorter pieces or poetry, to create a shared experience from which to write, to tap into a new genre that reflect writers' reading interests, to write a class play together, to create a "challenge" write, to go on a real or virtual field trip, or how about inviting in a local writer or illustrator or doing an author study?

When You as a Teacher Feel Disengaged

Take yourself on a reading/writing retreat! If you have been reading lots of children's books, try an adult novel. Writing too many "examples" for use in the Writing Studio? Write something heartfelt for yourself—don't imagine writers in your class as the audience. Join a writing and/or book group. Take a teaching risk—try out something entirely new. Go on a hike, run—party with friends. Better yet, do any of the previous while attending a professional conference (in a great location). Can't afford this? Invite your friends over and watch a webinar together—or a great, unrelated movie. Pull in close and conference with a writer who you know will inspire you. Check children's individual goal sheets and tally up all the successes. Teaching in the Writing Studio is rewarding and it can be exhausting. Mix it up for yourself as well.

And Now—One More Thing—Because It Matters

In Part III, "The Writing Studio Goes *Live*," we have reviewed the importance of viewing learning through a dynamic frame (Johnston, 2012), described (in part) what is taught in the Writing Studio, illustrated the role of mentor texts, focused on primary teacher actions (mini-lessons, teacher–student writing conferences, guided writing), and zeroed in on developing writer independence and collaboration and broadcasting writers' work. We have even looked at some common challenges of the Writing Studio. We have steadily repeated the mantra: be organized, collect informative data, analyze data, and, then, *act*. All of this may dangerously imply that a dynamic-learning frame, an insightful and well-organized teacher using language of empowerment, the just-right mentor text, and well-crafted mini-lessons, and teaching routines and expectations are the *only* factors that *matter* in a successful Writing Studio. We use physicist Karen Barad's (2008) work to demonstrate the complexity of *becoming* in the Writing Studio. Barad gives us language like: "reconfigurings/entanglements/relationalities/(re)articulations" (2008, p. 135) to describe what she refers to as the *intra-activity* between all the beings (human and nonhuman) in the classroom. We can use Barad's language and ideas for an enticing description of how each writer, teacher, desk, clock, notebook, genre, and physical classroom is a meeting of histories and futures, all wrapped in motion, in *becoming*, in changing, in real time, *live*. She gives us language, theory, and ideas for what we as teachers of writing often know or find puzzling or think but find hard to put into words:

> *Maribel is restless today; she can't sit doesn't listen keeps bouncing in her chair and thumping her pencil and as the teacher, I am restless, too, and I can't find a rhythm, and why does the office call on the intercom right in the middle of the studio and disrupt learning? And why am I thinking about dinner tonight and the discussion I really need to have with my partner, and I really need a different chair to move around the classroom with, and Maribel isn't telling me something, or I am not hearing her, or why does it sometimes feel the document camera's bright lights make Ritchie go a little crazy, and, oh, only 6 minutes left and we haven't started share time, and the bouncing ball Jack is sitting on does seem to be lulling him almost to sleep but is making Linda spiral into another sphere—she does remind me of myself . . .*

Entanglements—live bodies living together, relationalities, and the constant evolution of all that is *matter* means the classroom and its contents are never the same, always changing, and constantly in motion. It means teaching and learning is unpredictable, always already possibility, impossibility, surprise, shock, and/or wonder; it means teaching and learning cannot be orchestrated precisely: we just can't know for certain the outcomes. Even if there is a script, the script itself is not static, not as it intra-acts with other beings of the classroom.

You can read these last paragraphs and feel a bit of panic, or you can embrace this and get ready for the ride. As a matter of physics, these entanglements and (re)configurations happen whether we acknowledge them or not. Learning to recognize and accept these entanglements, we have found, is what opens our teaching up to possibilities, keeps us engaged and on our toes, and cultivates anticipation, "Just what will happen next?" and "What if it is . . ." The perspective honors the complexity of our humanness, our histories and futures and intra-actions with all *things*. It "explains" a lot of what is not "explainable" in the classroom, all those "variables" of which educational research cannot account.

Yes, there is no substitution for being well organized and intentional, for careful planning of mini-lessons and guided writing based on informative and analyzed data, for cultivating a dynamic-learning frame and being mindful of our language as we listen and teach writers, for focused teaching of independence and collaboration as writing and life skills. And—in the midst of all that is well planned, there are entanglements, relationalities, (re)configurations—and, yes, this signals transformation, learning, and why we are all *becoming*.

Problematizing Practice

The goals of Problematizing Practice are to deconstruct assumptions and beliefs and to consider multiple responses and implications of teaching decisions. It is best to do this in the company of colleagues and your instructor:

1. Read the scenario.
2. Quickly write down assumptions about the scenario. *Study your assumptions.*
3. Discuss and problematize assumptions with others and your instructor.
4. Discuss and write possible responses to the scenario.
5. Discuss the possible consequences (intended and unintended) of each response.

Scenario

You have a group of five Grade 6 boys who like one another, play well together, and want to write collaboratively. Normally, you are hesitant to have five writers in one collaborative group but the boys were insistent: they wanted to compose a "really cool" adventure story with "lots of pictures and stuff." But now, one week into the collaboration, the group is falling apart. They want to compose on the computer, but having five boys sharing one computer isn't going well, and although there are more computers in the classroom, they are trying to compose as a group. Rarely do all five boys seem to be doing writing work; at least two or three of them are "off" in the name of "research" or just playing. You have noticed that on occasion this play has been acting out the adventure they are supposed to be writing. The real problem appears to be disagreement about the story plot. They have a hero, but they can't decide what the exact adventure is.

What are some options?

References

Anagnos, M. (1982). *Helen Keller.* Boston, MA: Wright & Potter Printing.

Barad, K. (2008). Posthumanist performativity: Toward an understanding of how matter comes to matter. In S. Alaimo, & S. J. Hekman (Eds.), *Material feminisms* (pp. 120–154). Bloomington: Indiana University Press.

Fletcher, R. (1993). *What a writer needs.* Portsmouth, NH: Heinemann.

Graves, D. (2001). *The energy to teach.* Portsmouth, NH: Heinemann.

Graves, D., & Hansen, J. (1983). The author's chair. *Language Arts, 60*(2), 176–183.

International Children's Digital Library. (2012, January 10). StoryKit 1.1 [Mobile application]. College Park, MD: The University of Maryland.

Johnston, P. H. (2012). *Opening minds using language to change lives.* Portland, ME: Stenhouse.

Krashen, S. (1982). *Principles and practice in second language acquisiton.* New York, NY: Pergamon Press.

Mooney, M. E. (1990). *Reading to, with and by children.* Katonah, NY: Richard C. Owens.

National Governors Association (NGA) Center for Best Practices & Council of Chief State School Officers (CCSSO). (2010). Common Core State Standards for English language arts and literacy in history/social studies, science, and technical subjects. Washington, DC: Authors.

Newkirk, T. (2000). Misreading masculinity: Speculations on the great gender gap in writing. *Language Arts, 77*(4), 294–300.

Rigg, P., & Allen, V. (1989). *When they don't all speak English.* Urbana, IL: National Council of Teachers of English.

Rigg, P., & Hudelson, S. (1986). One child doesn't speak English. *Australian Journal of Reading, 9*(3), 116–125.

part IV
Bringing It All Together
Writing Curriculum

When you choose curriculum, it is a political act. When you make a decision about who will learn what and how, you are taking political action. And even if you choose not to act, your passivity is also a political action.

—Joan Wink

Figure PartIV.1 Teachers Collaborating

Sharing, Celebrating, and Broadcasting Your Work as Author

I am writing for myself and strangers.

—Gertrude Stein

How are you doing as a writer? Have you completed your personal narrative? Are you satisfied with the content, the flow? Have you found the meaning and purpose of your personal narrative? If so, now is the time for the final work of editing and preparing your manuscript to broadcast to others.

Focus on Editing

More than likely, you have been editing as you have been revising. This is often the case. But once content is set, then the writer turns her or his attention to careful editing, making sure the manuscript is ready to share with others. We recommend the same kind of processes as we wrote about in Chapter 6 of *Becoming a Teacher of Writing in Elementary Classrooms*:

- Read your piece aloud, deliberately reading each word. If you have composed on a word processor or tablet, is now the time to print a hard copy for editing? As you read, listen for sentence fluency: does your piece flow?
- Pay attention to conventions (spelling, punctuation, grammar, capitalization). You can play with conventions—but do so intentionally and because the play adds to the overall meaning. For example, incomplete sentences can create tension, action, or a sense of incompleteness.
- Make corrections as needed in the manuscript. Anything you are unsure of, mark and bring to a peer-editing conference.
- Share your paper with a friend. Ask him or her to give it an editing read. Have them mark your paper using standard editing symbols (www.merriam-webster.com/mw/table/proofrea.htm).
- Go ahead—make those corrections (note: "corrections" refers to editing, "revision" to content).

- Set the paper aside. Let it rest. Come back to the paper later (at least 24 hours is our experience) and check it again: Content set? Editing correct? You are ready to make broadcasting decisions!

Celebrating, Sharing, and Broadcasting Your Work as an Author

How will you share your final manuscript? We hope you will read aloud and broadcast your work with the colleagues with whom you are presumably reading *Becoming a Teacher of Writing in Elementary Classrooms*.

We encourage you to (a) experience reading your personal narrative aloud, (b) publish your work in some form of digital or print version for others to read, and (c) make certain there is a way for readers to provide you with feedback, either verbal or written. This is what we routinely ask writers to do in elementary classrooms; it is important that as a teacher of writing you experience what you will ask of children.

If you are reading *Becoming a Teacher of Writing in Elementary Classrooms* as part of a university course or a writing group, here are some options:

- Create a paper literacy magazine of everyone's work. Include artwork or photography. Organize an "open mic" so authors can read their work aloud. (This can be done in small groups as well.)
- Create an online literacy magazine using technology such as Google Documents (docs.google.com) or Edublog (edublog.org). Make sure everyone in your course is invited to read and comment!
- Create a podcast of your work. Post the podcast either on personal web pages, Facebook pages, or on a course-designed webpage so everyone can listen and leave comments.
- Try a tablet application like Story Kit (International Children's Digital Library, 2012) and, again, make your work available to everyone in your course via the Internet.

Chapter 9 of *Becoming a Teacher of Writing in Elementary Classrooms* includes information about design decisions writers must make. Review these and consider them in designing how your final product will look as a published piece.

 Donna finished "Dust," her memoir about Morgan! To read her memoir and hear a podcast of Donna reading "Dust," go to the companion website.

We hope you find sharing and broadcasting your work and celebrating the writing of peers energizing. When you have finished this final act of broadcasting your work, take time to practice metacognition one more time.

Practicing Metacognition

Consider the following questions and after doing so independently, discuss your responses with others who have been writing along this same journey:

- What do you like best about your final piece?
- Describe the experience of reading your piece aloud to others.
- Describe seeing your piece published.

- What have you learned about yourself as a writer from the process of sharing, celebrating, and broadcasting your personal narrative?
- What have you learned about who you are becoming, might become, as a teacher of writing?
- The *Getting Started Becoming-Writer* section asked you to respond to this quote:

The first priority is for *teachers to be writers* themselves. Only in this way do they learn empathy with their pupils, which enables them to give more space to pupils when they are writing and respond more appropriately to their work. They are also then able to model writing 'live' rather than repeat what has been rehearsed. (Horner, 2010, p. 30)

What do you think of this quotation now?

The following is Donna's final practice of metacognition:
I like the imagery of dust and the line, "As if you can ever leave, behind." I think the piece speaks to how life evolves, and twists, and turns, and how, even if we think we have "left," we haven't entirely; we still carry with us certain memories and emotions that frame who we become, who we are becoming. Honestly, when I first read the piece aloud to John, my spouse, there were tears. So—making the podcast was actually quite difficult. I practiced reading the piece several different ways and it took more time than I care to admit to finally say, "good enough." I publish academic work, but each semester when I teach the language arts methods course at my university and I write personal pieces with the teacher candidates in my course, I find myself nervous about drafting and sharing my writing all over again. We all publish together, read our pieces aloud together, and it is a practice I will continue. Each semester I become a writer and a teacher of writing in varied and rich ways, all over again, through this experience. I am grateful to be a writer, I am grateful for what writing can do for me.

Thanks for joining us in writing while reading *Becoming a Teacher of Writing in Elementary Classrooms*. Keep writing—keep growing your identity as a writer. See what writing can do for you as a teacher of writing!

References

Horner, S. (2010). *Magic dust that lasts: Writers in schools—sustain the momentum.* London: Arts Council England.
International Children's Digital Library. (2012, January 10). StoryKit 1.1 [Mobile application]. College Park, MD: Author.
Stein, G. (1995). *The making of Americans: Being a history of a familiy's progress.* Normal, IL: Dalkey Archive Press.

Chapter Ten
Yearlong Themes to Integrate Writing

It is June, and Ms. J and grade-level colleagues are headed to the teacher inservice day to map out writing curriculum for the following school year. Ms. J keeps the big picture in the forefront of her mind as she approaches this work. Her goal is to create conditions so children can become responsible, literate, democratic citizens in our global world. Ms. J knows every group of children is different—different lives, families, interests, and strengths. And because of these differences, she goes into the yearlong writing curriculum mapping with a more general outlook, bringing her knowledge about writing, writing process, her personal value of the power of writing, and her dynamic beliefs about who writers are and what they can do to think about curriculum possibilities, purposes, and goals. In preparation for their writing curriculum mapping, Ms. J and her colleagues gather their curriculum resources, reread their grade-level standards, their current yearlong curriculum map, as well as their current weekly lesson plans and their Teaching, Conferencing & Planning Notebooks. They also bring with them hours of informal and formal processing of teaching highs and lows completed over lunch, during recess duty, and at their monthly grade-level meetings and staff meetings. This is energizing work. Ms. J loves the thought of new beginnings, of her continual becoming, and children becoming-writers

---

The scope of this book is on writing, but writing doesn't fit into a single tidy square box in a lesson plan book. Writing is both a stand-alone discipline and a discipline within the language arts. Language arts encompass reading, writing, speaking, listening, and language. Additionally, language arts, in general, and writing, in particular, are inherent in all disciplines such as science, mathematics, and social studies. There are specific disciplinary ways in which scientists, mathematicians and social scientists read, write, speak, listen, and use language (Shanahan & Shanahan, 2008).

When planning a yearlong writing curriculum, it is helpful to balance planning for teaching specific writing practices, process, and craft within the Writing Studio with plans for integrating writing across the discipline areas of language arts, mathematics, social studies, and science. The intent of this chapter is to work alongside Ms. J and her colleagues and illustrate how yearlong writing curriculum is designed.

Yearlong Themes to Integrate Learning

Creating a cohesive yearlong curriculum can be challenging. One way to connect children's learning is to create one to three yearlong themes. The key is to select broad, overarching themes that integrate children's lives and learning and create opportunities for inquiry. Examples of themes are interdependence, equity, change, problem solving, relationships, issues, citizenship, and community.

"Change" as a Yearlong Theme

As Ms. J and her grade-level colleagues share around a large table, Ms. J reflects, "This year we incorporated three themes: community, change, and big questions. I love how children made connections between the themes and how they synthesized concepts from the disciplines to our themes. Yet often it just felt like too much—as if we were part of the pervasive problem in education of trying to do too much in too little time. I'm wondering if you would be willing to try one yearlong theme? I think we can develop and expand the theme of 'Change.' This theme will provide continuity for our year, will connect to the lives of children, and hopefully will guide them to think about big questions."

Her colleagues nod in agreement, willing to try something new together. This is one of the many joys of teaching—having colleagues to collaborate, process, plan and take risks together in developing meaningful learning experiences for children.

Planning With Standards

Standards describe what children should know and be able to do by the end of designated grade levels in specific disciplines. Standards do not define how teachers should teach nor do they describe all that can or should be taught (National Governors Association [NGA] Center for Best Practices & Council of Chief State School Officers [CCSSO], 2010a). In the U.S. over the past 30 years, discipline standards have been written, revised, and adopted by individual states. More recently there has been a shift to a single set of mathematics and language arts standards—the CCSS (review Chapter 2). The CCSS were adopted by 45 states that received waivers for the No Child Left Behind Act. In 2013, both the New Generation Science Standards (NGSS Lead States, 2013) and the C3 Framework for Social Studies Standards (National Council for the Social Studies, 2013) were published. There is significant shift in the U.S. from state-created standards to common standards adopted by the majority of states.

For the purposes of this book, we use the following discipline standards to guide our curriculum mapping as a means to show how teachers align, integrate, and spiral discipline standards into yearlong and unit curriculum maps:

- Common Core State Standards for English Language Arts & Literacy in History/Social Studies, Science, and Technical Subjects (NGA Center for Best Practices & CCSSO, 2010a)
- Common Core State Standards for Mathematics (NGA Center for Best Practices & CCSSO, 2010b)
- New Generation Science Standards (NGSS Lead States, 2013)
- C3 Framework for Social Studies Standards (National Council for the Social Studies, 2013)

Regardless of the discipline standards you are required to teach toward, the purpose of this chapter is to illustrate how writing can be taught all day long. Elementary teachers rarely teach a single, isolated discipline; rather, elementary teachers are immersed in the planning, teaching, and assessing of all disciplines. When one reads through all of the standards for each discipline, it is clear that there aren't enough hours in the day, days in a week, weeks in a school year to teach all of the disciplines in isolation. The key is integration.

"Change": Yearlong Integrated Units for Grade 3

As Ms. J and her grade-level colleagues examine the language arts, science, social studies, and mathematics standards, they think about how they fit together, what has worked in the past and what they want to teach in the upcoming year. Ms. J knows that teaching an inch deep and a mile wide leaves her and the children in her class exhausted without much opportunity to process, think deeply, and make connections. This is especially true for children that are English learners or those with IEPs and 504 plans. Because of this, Ms. J and her colleagues create integrated units that vary in length from 3 to 6 weeks to provide time and space to dive deeply into integrated social studies, science, mathematics, and language arts learning. Ms. J knows that teaching topics that interests her as well as children is key to everyone's sense of well-being and contributes to the energy of learning.

Ms. J and her colleagues begin by listing integrated units that have engaged children as well as themselves in past years. They consider new ideas and how these new ideas support the yearlong theme of Change. They discuss how some units will be integrated language arts and others integrated language arts with one or more additional disciplines (mathematics, science, social studies).

Their brainstorming results in eleven integrated units, each with an inquiry question connecting back to the yearlong theme of "Change." Their initial planning is in Table 10.1 Grade 3 Integrated Units.

TABLE 10.1 Grade 3 Integrated Units

Month	Integrated Curriculum Unit	Integrated Curriculum Inquiry Question	Disciplines Addressed
September	Choice Reading & Writing	How have I changed as a reader and writer over the summer?	English Language Arts (ELA)
	Classroom Citizenship	How has the role of citizen in the classroom changed since Grade 2? What do these changes mean for the citizens of our current classroom?	Social Studies, ELA
October	Climate Change	How is climate change affecting our lives?	ELA, Social Studies, Science, Math
November	Memoir Reading & Writing	How does narrative reading and writing change for authors depending on purpose and audience?	ELA
December	Interdependence	How are living beings connected, and how do we affect change on one another?	ELA, Social Studies, Science
January	Author Study	How can an author study change my writing practice, process, and craft?	ELA
February & March	Investigations	How do investigations change society?	ELA, Social Studies, Science, Math
April	Our Community Over Time	How has our community changed over time?	ELA, Social Studies
May	Decision Making	How does decision making change depending on context?	ELA, Social Studies, Science, Math
June	Choice Reading & Writing	How have I changed as a reader and writer this year?	ELA
	Life Cycles	How do life cycles change?	Science, ELA

Next, Ms. J and her colleagues identify the discipline standards that will be integrated into their units. They cut and paste the various discipline standards addressed in each unit, ensuring children will have access to discover and learn all the Grade 3 standards.

 For a complete yearlong curriculum map with all discipline standards, please see the companion website.

Ms. J and her colleagues use this yearlong curriculum map as an outline to further develop their writing curriculum. Together they go back through the units that integrate writing and identify the writing modes (text types) and genres for each integrated unit. Their thinking and planning are outlined in Table 10.2 Grade 3 Integrated Units with Writing Modes, Genres, and Standards.

 To better understand the curriculum map, take a break and review the English Language Arts CCSS now. You can find them at http://www.corestandards.org/ela-literacy. Compare the yearlong curriculum map in Table 10.1 with the Integrated Units with Writing Modes, Genres, and Standards in Table 10.2. What do you notice, and what can you name about this strategy for integrating writing across the disciplines?

Writing All Day Long, All Yearlong

Based on this initial planning, Ms. J and her colleagues continue to plan writing instruction, using the yearlong theme "Change." This kind of planning requires conceptual thinking with attention to specific standards. Their thinking is outlined in the unit descriptions that follow.

TABLE 10.2 Grade 3 Integrated Units With Writing Modes, Genres, and Standards

Month	Integrated Unit	Writing Mode	Writing Genres	Common Core Grade 3 Writing Standards Addressed
September	Choice Reading & Writing	Choice	All	1, 2, 3, 4, 5, 10
	Classroom Citizenship	Informative	Classroom contract	1, 2, 4, 5, 6, 10
October	Climate Change	Opinion	Persuasive letters Informative text responses	1, 4, 5, 6, 7, 8, 10
November	Memoir Reading & Writing	Narrative	Memoir: poetry and picture book	3, 4, 5, 10
December	Interdependence	Informative	Informative poetry	2, 4, 5, 6, 7, 8, 10
January	Author Study	Choice Author	All	1, 2, 3, 4, 5, 10
February & March	Investigations	Informative	Science tri-fold display of an inquiry project	2, 4, 5, 6, 7, 8, 10
April	Our Community Over Time	Narrative	Historical fiction picture book or short story or photo essay	3, 4, 5, 6, 7, 8, 10
May	Decision Making	Opinion	Graphic novel or essay	1, 4, 5, 6, 7, 8, 10
June	Choice Reading & Writing	Choice	All	1, 2, 3, 4, 5, 10
	Life Cycles Science	Informative	Diagrams with captions	2, 4, 5, 6, 10

September: Classroom Citizenship and Choice Reading and Writing

The "Classroom Citizenship" unit facilitates children getting to know each other and focuses on developing a cohesive classroom community. Theme-related questions include "How has the role of citizen in the classroom changed since Grade 2?" and "What do these changes mean for the citizens of our current classroom?"

The choice reading and writing unit provides children time to explore their reading and writing identities through free choice of reading texts and writing modes and genres. It also allows teachers time to conduct beginning-of-the-year assessments and to notice specific writing interests, strengths, and challenges. A theme-related question includes "How have I changed as a reader and writer over the summer?"

Writing in the Writing Studio

During the Writing Studio children complete the beginning-of-the-year writing assessments while exploring their writing identities through writing in any mode and genre of their choice. The sharing time of the Writing Studio provides an important opportunity for children to learn more about each other, take risks, and develop trust.

Writing in the Disciplines: Reading, Mathematics, Social Studies, and Science

Children write during the social studies block—brainstorming, writing, revising, and editing their Classroom Bill of Rights and Constitution. They also write short opinions in the Reading Studio, describing which books and authors they enjoy and why.

Discipline Learning That Supports the Writing Studio

During Reading Studio children are provided opportunity to read in a variety of genres as they explore their reading identities. The Reading Studio supports the work of the Writing Studio through mini-lessons on "Reading Like a Writer" and finding mentor authors.

October: Climate Change

"Climate Change" is an integrated language arts, social studies, science, and mathematics unit focusing on the interaction of population, agriculture, industry, geography, weather, and climate. A theme-related question is, "How is climate change affecting our lives?"

Writing in the Writing Studio

In the Writing Studio, children explore the mode of opinion writing. Children write persuasive letters related to climate change.

Writing in the Disciplines

Children write responses to text readings during the Reading Studio.

Discipline Learning That Supports the Writing Studio

In the Reading Workshop, the teacher models and provides guided instruction on the author's craft of informative and opinion writing with science and social studies texts such as weather and climate change essays, reports, newscasts, charts, and graphs. In mathematics, children learn how to read charts and graphs.

November: Narrative Reading and Writing

"Narrative Reading and Writing" is an integrated language arts unit investigating the practices, processes, and craft of narrative writing, specifically memoirs. A theme-related question is, "How does narrative reading and writing change for authors depending on the purpose and the audience?"

Writing in the Writing Studio
In the Writing Studio, children dive into the mode of narrative writing through writing memoirs in multiple genres: poetry and picture books. The focus is developing writing practices, process, and craft as memoir writers.

Discipline Learning That Supports the Writing Studio
The Reading Studio also focuses on narrative writing. Children are immersed in and are guided through discussions about the craft of memoir writing. Children use the authors and texts from the Reading Studio as mentors for their memoir writing in the Writing Studio.

December: Interdependence

"Interdependence" is an integrated language arts and science unit investigating connections within ecosystems. Theme-related questions are, "How are living being connected, and how do we affect change on one another?"

Writing in the Writing Studio
In the Writing Studio, children investigate the practices, process, and craft of informative poetry related to ecosystems.

Discipline Learning That Supports the Writing Studio
In the Reading Studio, children read informative poetry and investigate the author's craft of informative poetry. In science, children participate in experiments, watch videos, and read texts to build their knowledge of ecosystems as a means to research a topic to write informative poetry during Writing Studio.

January: Author Study

"Author Study" is an integrated language arts unit where children investigate and inquire about a select author. A theme-related question is, "How can an author study change my writing practice, process, and craft?"

Writing in the Writing Studio
In the Writing Studio, children experiment with writing under the influence of a mentor author incorporating the author's practices or processes or craft in their own writing. Broadcasting final work is a speaking and audience-response project addressing CCSS in Speaking and Listening.

Discipline Learning That Supports the Writing Studio
In the Reading Studio, children read books by varied authors and identify an author they find interesting. Children read like writers, identifying practices, processes, and craft of a single author to use as a mentor during Writing Studio. Literature discussion groups are specifically directed toward meeting CCSS Speaking and Listening Standards.

February and March: Investigations

The "Investigations" unit integrates language arts, social studies, science, and mathematics. Children read, write, and formally present on an investigation of their choice. Science and social studies blocks are combined with Reading and Writing Studios. A theme-related question is, "How do investigations change society?"

Writing in the Writing Studio/Writing in the Disciplines

In the Writing Studio, children learn to write like scientists by writing questions, hypotheses, experiment steps, results, and discussion about their social studies/science investigation.

Discipline Learning That Supports the Writing Studio

In the Reading Studio, children read and discuss scientific texts: experiments and science fair tri-folds. During science and social studies, children create and enact experiments to serve as the content for their writing. Children orally present experiments working toward CCSS Speaking and Listening Standards.

April: Our Community Through Time

"Our Community Through Time" is an integrated language arts and social studies unit investigating the historical changes within the community. A theme-related question is, "How has our community changed over time?"

Writing in the Writing Studio

In the Writing Studio, children learn the practices, processes, and craft of historical fiction short stories, picture books, and photo essays.

Discipline Learning That Supports the Writing Studio

In the Reading Studio, children read and discuss historical fiction text. During social studies, children listen to guest speakers, attend field trips, read texts, and watch videos about the historical changes in their community. Children use the content of their learning in social studies as inspiration for their historical fiction stories in Writing Studio.

May: Decision Making

"Decision Making" is an integrated language arts, social studies and science unit investigating interactions of people and objects. Theme-related question: How does decision-making change depending upon context?

Writing in the Writing Studio/Writing in Social Studies and Science

In the Writing Studio, children build on their knowledge of opinion writing to draft, revise, edit, and publish opinion essays and/or graphic novels on a topic of their choice.

Discipline Learning That Supports the Writing Studio

In social studies, children learn about decision making related to the economy and government. In science, children learn about cause and effect of forces and interactions. The information learned during social studies and science is what drives the content of children's opinion essays and/or graphic novels in the Writing Studio.

June: Life Cycle and Choice Reading and Writing

"Life Cycle" is an integrated language arts and science unit exploring the role of inheritance and variation of traits within the life cycle. A theme related-question is, "How do life cycles change?"

The choice reading and writing unit provides children time to expand their reading and writing identities through free choice of reading texts and writing modes and genres. A theme-related question is, "How have I changed as a reader and writer this year?"

Writing in the Writing Studio

Children are provided time to expand their writing identities through writing in any mode and genre of their choice.

Writing in the Disciplines

During science, children write about life cycles of insects and animals through creating diagrams with captions.

Discipline Learning That Supports the Writing Studio

During the Reading Studio children are provided opportunity to read in a variety of genres as they expand their reading identities. The Reading Studio supports the work of the Writing Studio through mini-lessons on "Reading like a Writer" and finding mentor authors.

 Pause to consider more deeply the yearlong curriculum map described earlier. How does the curriculum position children? Teachers? What kinds of opportunities and possibilities are embedded in the curriculum map? What might be the arguments for and against integrated teaching and learning? Discuss your responses with colleagues.

The Grade 3 team's yearlong writing curriculum map is a place to start as you think about designing curriculum for your future class. Yearlong writing curriculum maps will differ from grade to grade depending on children's skills, interests, and previous writing experiences as well as the length of the school day and the standards to which you are teaching. Next we will describe ways to adapt writing curriculum for early grades.

Adapting Writing Instruction for Early Grades

There are some important aspects to remember when planning yearlong writing curriculum for the early grades: kindergarten through Grade 2. First, it is vital to allow young writers choice in what mode and genre as well as topics. This will support children in developing their identities as writers (Graves, 1993). The teacher may focus his or her mini-lessons on a specific mode and genre of writing but allow children to decide if they want to try the writing practices, process, and craft their teacher modeled during writing mini-lessons, writing conferences, and guided writing groups. Know that young children, like all writers, write to make meaning of their world. The difference is that the world of young children is small and revolves around personal experiences and living in the moment. Immerse the classroom world of children in varied and rich text of all kinds; create shared experiences to facilitate interactive writing.

Adapting writing curriculum to include a stronger focus on illustrating is a means to develop stamina of young writers. Ray (2010) notes that "when young children make books, teachers may value the time children spend illustrating as much as they value the time children spend writing, not because they privilege one over the other, but simply because they value children *spending time*" (p. 33). Allowing for more time and focus on illustrating is also a benefit for English learners (Fu, 2003). Illustrating allows the young writer to tell a story even when he or she doesn't have the oral or written language to write or a letter–sound correspondence to express their ideas.

James Britton (1970) famously remarked, "Writing floats on the sea of talk" (p. 164). Key to young writers' development is providing them with ample opportunities to talk with others so they can develop their oral and written language. "Children discover things to write about by talking—and writing (and listening to the writing of others) elicits more stories" (Newkirk & Kittle, 2013, p. 101).

Often, time is a factor for all grades, but especially in half-day kindergarten classrooms. It is essential in this situation to integrate writing throughout the day in order to provide children with the necessary time to develop as writers. There are many simple integration strategies: children can write on their individual whiteboard as the teacher models writing the title of a poster about the life cycle of a frog; children can participate in an interactive writing lesson, sharing the pen with the teacher, to record the labels on a classroom jobs chart; children can write their favorite character with a sentence to support their opinion in their reading log after silent reading or guided reading; children can write lists . . . about everything!

Now let's take a look at a "Life Cycle" integrated language arts and science unit and imagine how it might be adapted for a kindergarten classroom.

Illustration: Kindergarten Integrated "Life Cycle" Unit

The "Life Cycle" unit integrates language arts and science to investigate the life cycle of frogs.

Writing in the Writing Studio

During Writing Studio children write about their field trip to the local pond and draw illustrations of the life cycle of frogs, labeling each stage. They write informational books about frogs. If there is no access to a pond, bring the pond to children by setting up an appropriate indoor tank. Plans for the Writing Studio include the teacher talking about his or her ideas, sketching pictures, and modeling writing. Specifically, the teacher models hearing sounds in words, using spaces, capital letters to begin a sentence, and end of sentence punctuation. Children are provided time to talk with a neighbor about their ideas for writing before they head to independent writing. Children share their writing with their table groups by talking about their ideas, illustrations, and/or words.

Writing in the Disciplines

During science children rotate through stations throughout the unit. One station includes an opportunity for children to observe tadpoles in an aquarium. While observing the tadpoles, children are encouraged to draw and write observations in their science notebooks, noting how the frogs change throughout their life cycle.

While reading texts (books, chants, poems) during Reading Studio the teacher uses interactive writing (sharing the pen with children) to write down facts they are learning about frogs on a class chart.

Discipline Learning That Supports the Writing Studio

During the science stations, children are learning about frogs and their life cycle to provide language and concepts to write about during Writing Studio. During read-aloud and shared reading, the teacher and children are reading books and poems and singing chants about frogs. These texts provide additional language and concepts for children to write about in Writing Studio. Play supports learning as children pretend to be frogs and use the language from the disciplines in their play.

"Design Curriculum? I Am Given Curriculum!"

Many school districts adopt writing curriculum. The curriculum comes packaged in bright colors, often with several spiral-bound binders and boxes and boxes of "resources." Where to begin in evaluating and making teaching choices? How does a teacher incorporate this sea of curriculum into the Writing Studio?

 The companion website includes criteria for evaluating writing curriculum and for adapting writing curriculum for the specific interests, strengths, and needs of writers in your Writing Studio. We encourage you to take a look!

The Curriculum Map as a Living Document

A yearlong curriculum map is a blueprint for the year. Once the school year has begun and the beginning-of-the-year assessments are completed, the curriculum map will be adjusted for whole-class and individual needs. Chapter 4 describes beginning-of-the-year assessments and provides examples of how to analyze and use these assessments. Chapter 5 describes general assessments of the Writing Studio; these, too, will result in adapting writing curriculum as you analyze the data generated through their intentional use. Key to knowing when and how to adapt curriculum is to keep the focus on writers and their interests, strengths, and needs. Children as writers drive writing instruction and if you have organized teaching and learning in such a way that you can hear them, you will know when and how to make adjustments.

Other "Bumps in the Night" and Reasons for Curriculum Adaptation

Let's be honest. Starting a unit is the easy part. Bad weather cancels school some days; children are absent; new children transfer into the classroom; tragedy strikes—the school maintenance crew replaces playground equipment right outside your classroom window. Additionally, a writer or a group of writers does not finish the writing. You find you simply lack the luster for the letter-writing unit this year. There are pieces of writing started and abandoned in October only to be picked up and completed in April. Sometimes, pieces of writing stay buried in a Daily Writing Folder. Remind yourself that teaching and learning, as writing, is a process. Each "bump in the night" is an opportunity: frame it as such. Whatever decision you make in adapting curriculum, it is both/and, not either/or. Embrace the unexpected: neither our lives nor our curriculum is a predetermined script. *Possibilities abound.*

Problematizing Practice

The goals of Problematizing Practice are to deconstruct assumptions and beliefs and to consider multiple responses and implications of teaching decisions. It is best to do this in the company of colleagues and your instructor:

1. Read the scenario.
2. Quickly write down assumptions about the scenario. *Study your assumptions.*

3. Discuss and problematize assumptions with others and your instructor.
4. Discuss and write possible responses to the scenario.
5. Discuss the possible consequences (intended and unintended) of each response.

Scenario

Rosa has not completed her memoir—and she doesn't want to finish a memoir. In truth, she has not been interested in writing a memoir since the writing unit started. It is not that Rosa is a contrary child or a hesitant or below-grade-level writer. Memoirs are just not this Grade 4 child's "thing." Rosa's Cumulative Writing Folder shows steady growth in writing practice, process, and craft. Her Daily Folder demonstrates that she is willing to take risks. In the last unit on opinion writing, Rosa used innovative storytelling to illustrate how families should be more thoughtful before purchasing guinea pigs as pets. But her memoir? Not even. She has a very rough draft that is going nowhere fast.

Should you require that Rosa complete the memoir in order to "pass" or move on to the next writing unit?

References

Britton, J. (1970). *Language and learning.* Coral Gables, FL: University of Miami Press.

Fu, D. (2003). *An island of English: Teaching ESL in Chinatown.* Portsmouth, NH: Heinemann.

Graves, D. H. (1993). Children can write authentically if we help them. *Primary Voices K-6, 1*(1), 2–6.

National Council for the Social Studies. (2013). *The College, Career, and Civic Life (C3) framework for social studies state standards: Guidance for enhancing the rigor of K-12 civics, economics, geography, and history.* Silver Spring, MD: Author.

National Governors Association (NGA) Center for Best Practices & Council of Chief State School Officers (CCSSO). (2010a). Common Core State Standards for English language arts and literacy in history/social studies, science, and technical subjects. Washington, DC: Authors.

National Governors Association (NGA) Center for Best Practices & Council of Chief State School Officers (CCSSO). (2010b). *Common core standards for English language arts & literacy in history/social studies, science, and technical subjects. Appendix A: Research supporting key elements of the standards and glossary of terms.* Washington DC: Author.

Newkirk, T., & Kittle, P. (Eds.). (2013). *Children want to write: Donald Graves and the revolution in children's writing.* Portsmouth, NH: Heinemann.

NGSS Lead States. (2013). *Next generation science standards: For states, by states.* Retrieved from http://www.nextgenscience.org/

Ray, K. W. (2010). *In pictures and in words: Teaching the qualities of good writing through illustration study.* Portsmouth, NH: Heienmann.

Shanahan, T., & Shanahan, C. (2008). Teaching disciplinary literacy to adolescents: Rethinking content-area literacy. *Harvard Educational Review, 78*(1), 40–59.

Chapter Eleven
Planning and Living an Integrated Language Arts Writing Unit

It is early March, and Ms. J has noticed her fifth graders love to read magazines—National Geographic Kids, Sports Illustrated for Kids, BMXplus!, anything they can get their hands on from the school library. Even Zane, who hasn't read much all year, seems to consume any magazine with a video game review!

During this same time, Ms. J's school district's transition to the CCSS has altered the talk in literacy in-service meetings to terms like text types—opinion, narrative, and informative reading and writing. "Text types." Ms. J smiles to herself. "The latest term for mode, the meaning work of writing." She wonders aloud to her colleagues, "Just how motivational is it to say to children, 'Today we are going to write informative text?' How can that possibly inspire writers?"

A colleague commented, "The children in my class rarely even say, 'I would like to write more fiction,' let alone something like informative text. They say something more specific, like 'I want to write sci-fi' or 'I am going to write a story like Suzanne Collins.'"

"Genre." Ms. J nods in reply. "It is all about genre."

This is what got her thinking even more about the writers in her class and their love of magazine articles . . . why not introduce the varied genres of magazines? Why not weave a district mandate with children's interest?

True, Ms. J's curriculum map for April did not include magazine writing, but this is an opportunity too good to miss. Besides, already on the curriculum map is the plan to end the year with all the Grade 5 writers in the elementary school producing a magazine on "space" for an integrated science and language arts unit. A choice magazine unit will position writers perfectly for this grand finale!

Truthfully, Ms. J has never taught a writing unit on magazine articles. She knows it will be messy, it will take time to plan and yet it will give her energy as a teacher to try something new and teach a genre she and children enjoy as readers. She imagines the faces of children when she proposes reading and writing magazines articles. She can almost hear Zane saying, "I get to read these video reviews for real?"

"Yes," she thinks to herself, "this is going to be good."

———————————

Ms. J is not going to take a commercially published magazine article unit of study off the shelf of her school's curriculum library. Nor does she have a list of lesson plans with predetermined lesson objectives that will be delivered in a scripted, artificial way devoid of any contextual knowledge of her specific class and individual writers. Rather, Ms. J knows the interests and abilities of the children in her class based on the ongoing data she collects; she knows the fifth-grade standards and the required standardized exams Grade 5 children must take and pass. This, along with her identity as a teacher of writing, knowledge of writing as a socially situated act, understanding of children's development as writers, and her experience as a writer, provides solid footing for her to develop and design her own unit of study. This is the ultimate work of the bricoleur, the deliberate piecing together curriculum to move children closer toward writer independence.

In this final chapter of *Becoming a Teacher of Writing in Elementary Classrooms*, we travel along with Ms. J through the decisions of planning and living an integrated language arts unit, providing ways of thinking, and a learning frame for possibilities. In doing so, we will apply, and ask you to apply, critical concepts of the Writing Studio presented throughout this book.

Framing Decisions

When we discuss unit planning, we use the term *framing decisions*. These are planning decisions that work to frame the unit. Framing decisions include connecting interests and abilities of writers with standards and the desired unit outcome; analyzing the genre to clarify the unit; determining specific writing practices, process, and craft writers will need to learn; and deciding how much choice writers will have in the unit.

Framing Decisions: Connect the Interest and Abilities of Writers With Standards

In the opening scenario, Ms. J illustrates the critical framing step of connecting the interests and abilities of writers with required standards and benchmarks they must meet. As described in Chapter 2, read standards as possibility. Know the difference between mode and genre and use this knowledge to make this critical connection.

Consider the writing abilities of children in your writing studio. We begin teaching based upon analysis of assessments that give us clear direction about writers' development, their strengths, and their needs. We take children wherever they are in this broad continuum and we begin our teaching at these multiple points. (Review Chapter 1.)

Ms. J has 26 writers in her Writing Studio. Of these 26, four read slightly below grade level. Four are English learners, and of these, one is still receiving English language services. The others have just recently exited the English language development program and continue to require additional English-language scaffolding. Three of these English learners are first-language Spanish speakers; the fourth is a first-language Somalia speaker. Ms. J's school has a "pull-in" model, meaning all English learners stay in her class during language arts and receive additional services with a specialist who collaborates with Ms. J in her classroom. In addition, Ms. J has one child on a 504 plan diagnosed with ADHD; Jeff has difficulty focusing. Sara and Molly are above grade level in reading and writing and need to be challenged appropriately. The remaining children fall loosely into the expected continuum of writing abilities for Grade 5, depending on the day and the writing moment.

In addition to collecting data and documenting reading and writing development, Ms. J has been observing and noting how these Grade 5 children are growing and maturing. Now, in March, they are preadolescents, longing for independence. They also have such varied interests—Minecraft, llamas (yes, llamas!), swimming, origami, cooking, skateboarding. This is further evidence of why the magazine writing unit is a good fit: magazine reading is so "adult-like," so many topics are possibilities, and article writing can be differentiated for various reading and writing abilities.

 Pause now and think about the children in Ms. J's class. Recall what you have learned about the Writing Studio. How is the structure of the Writing Studio uniquely positioned to support learning for all children in Ms. J's class? How will Ms. J manage the learning given the diversity represented in her classroom?

Framing Decisions: Genre Immersion

If a teacher has never taught a unit before, how does he or she get started? Begin planning by immersing yourself in the genre, as appropriate for the grade level you are teaching. This is exactly what you will have the writers in your Writing Studio do. Read authentic texts. Read to inquire about writer's craft. Read with a dynamic-learning frame of discovery. Make use of school and public library services, frequent used-books stores, and find useful online sellers of used print: collect texts of all kinds for possible use in teaching integrated language arts.

Ms. J, for example, heads to the library to find high-interest magazines for children. The magazines must be written well, with engaging photographs. A quick flip through the magazines quickly informs her which titles are too commercial filled with advertisements disguised as articles. She isn't interested in reading magazines created for school use, printed on cheap paper, four pages in length with embedded multiple-choice comprehension questions. Ms. J checks out a large stack of magazines that based on her knowledge of the children in her classroom, she is confident will capture their interests: *New Moon*, *National Geographic for Kids*, *Odyssey*, *Muse*, *Ranger Rick*, and *Ask*, to name a few.

Ms. J studies these magazines, searching for genres unique to magazine writing, discovering specific writing craft embedded within the genres. Table 11.1 Magazine Article Genre, Purpose, and Craft details the results of Ms. J's inquiry. In this table, Ms. J has named the genre of articles most prevalent in the magazines she has read and notes the specific writer's craft a journalist would use in writing such an article. This will provide the foundation for writing unit goals and objectives, lesson planning, and assessment.

Framing Decisions: Writing Practices, Process, and Craft

After immersing yourself in the genre, the teacher of writing can analyze what specific writing practices, process, and craft will be necessary to teach. In making this teaching decision, we keep in mind the interests and abilities of writers in our classes.

 Review the results of Ms. J's inquiry into magazine genres once again. From her list and based upon the interests and abilities in her class, what writing practices, process, and craft might she need to teach? You may find it useful to review Chapter 6, "The Writing Studio Goes *Live*," to recall the kinds of practices, process, and craft that are taught in the Writing Studio.

TABLE 11.1 Magazine Article Genre, Purpose, and Craft

Magazine Article Genre	Magazine Article Purpose	Magazine Article Craft
Top 5/Top 10	Tell you the best places or products (e.g., vacation spots, video games, books).	Written as a numbered list sometimes with accompanying short paragraphs for each item. Photographs of some or all of the items.
Review	Positive and/or negative aspects about an item (e.g., video games, books, places).	One or more items are reviewed. Facts and/or opinions provided for the item reviewed. Photograph of the item is included.
How To Make/ How To Do	Teach you how to make something (e.g., a craft, recipe) or how to do something (e.g., play a game, spy on your friends).	Step-by-step list of instructions often with accompanying photographs or graphics. Sometimes includes a simple introduction or conclusion.
All About	Inform the reader about a topic. (e.g., animal, region of the world, music)	One or more paragraphs about the topic. Often includes an introduction and conclusion.
Advice	Give the reader advice on a submitted question.	Written on topics of interest to children about questions they are concerned with. Often includes the question written in by a reader with a response from the advice columnist.
Debate	Provide two sides or perspectives on an issue.	Written by one or two writers offering different perspectives on an issue relevant to children, sometimes labeled yes/no or pro/con.

Framing Decision: Planning for Writing Practices

Ask of the unit you are planning, "What writing practices are associated with this particular genre? What is the practice of professional authors? How does this relate to the writers in my grade level?" Recall that in Chapter 5, we defined writing practice as the writing life of the writer. The daily habit of writing, of finding ideas, using writing as thinking, seeking information, and organizing and prioritizing writing tasks (CCSS Writing Anchor Standards 8 & 10).

 Apply this to the magazine article writing unit. What will Ms. J need to consider in scaffolding the writing practice of the Grade 5 writers? Recall that Ms. J is teaching this unit in March, so she can build on the writing practices children have been developing throughout the year. Draft a list of possible writing practices you think Ms. J will need to teach. Then compare your list to the one that Ms. J develops in the following discussion.

Ms. J determines that for her magazine writing unit, she will focus on the following writing practices:

- Read magazines as a writer to discover writing ideas
- Read as a writer to learn the writing craft of magazine-article genres
- Use time wisely—avoid rushing through the writing to design
- Learn basic article design layout as required by genre

Framing Decision: Planning for Writing Process

Ask of the unit you are planning, "What writing processes are associated with this particular genre? Given the specific writing practices writers in your Studio have and are developing, where should the focus be for this unit?" Recall that in Chapter 5, we defined writing process as the "stops and starts and cycles of writing," the use of revision, asking for and giving feedback, editing and choosing how a final piece is published and broadcasted (CCSS Writing Anchor Standards 5 & 6).

 Apply this to the magazine-article writing unit. What writing processes do you imagine Ms. J should most support in the magazine-article writing unit? There are multiple possibilities; we teach across the year and choose to focus on specific areas within each unit. Make a list of possibilities. Compare your thinking to Ms. J's, which follows.

Ms. J determines that for her magazine writing unit, she will focus on the writing process shown in Table 11.2.

TABLE 11.2 Focus on Writing Process: Ms. J's Magazine Writing Unit

Writing Process	Rationale
Selecting a complementary topic and genre	*The unit is a perfect time to practice this writing decision. Example: if a writer wants to write about llamas, does she choose an "All About" genre to describe llamas; and "Advice column" in response to an imagined and specific reader's question, or perhaps she specifically wants to list the steps for sheering a llama?*
Drafting under the influence of a mentor magazine article	*A mentor article can guide writers in structure and style. A mentor article is an authentic "template," and because this is a new kind of writing, it will support all writers' abilities.*
Revising for specific magazine writing craft	*Again, because this is a new unit, writers will benefit from a specific craft checklist to guide their revisions.*
Editing with precision Broadcasting on class website	*Editing for magazine articles must be precise: the audience is the entire subscription base! Final articles will be broadcast on the class website, simulating magazine publishing. This is an authentic reason to edit well.*

Framing Decision: Planning for Writing Craft

Ask of the unit you are planning, "What writing craft is associated with this particular genre? How does this relate to the writers in my grade level?" Recall that in Chapter 5, we noted, "writing craft encompasses the wide variety of modes, voice, style, word choice, organization, conventions, use of sentencing, creative twists and turns that capture the reader's attention" (CCSS Writing Anchor Standards 1, 2, 3, 4, 7, & 9).

 How will Ms. J determine the specific writing craft to focus on during this magazine writing unit? There are many options, more than she can adequately teach in one unit. Consider Ms. J's Grade 5 writers and the magazine genre and brainstorm possibilities. Compare your thinking with that of Ms. J's by analyzing Table 11.3.

Ms. J determines that for her magazine writing unit, she will focus on the writing practices shown in Table 11.3.

TABLE 11.3 Focus on Writing Craft: Ms. J's Magazine Writing Unit

Writing Craft	Ms. J's Thinking
Organizational nuances of the genre	*Most magazine articles all have a beginning, a middle, and an end. This unit will reinforce previous learning in this area. However, the beginning, middle, and end look different in an advice column versus a "how-to-do" piece. The unit will provide an opportunity for writers to examine and practice nuanced beginning, middle, and endings.*
Specialized vocabulary	*Because design is important to magazine writing, I will introduce specialized vocabulary used in journalism: layout, white space, teaser, pull quote, and justification. I will introduce this vocabulary during this unit to build a foundation for our upcoming integrated language arts and science unit. During this last unit, writers will actually be designing a magazine and will put these terms to use. For this unit, I want them to begin hearing the words in the context of our magazine discussions.*
Genre design as it relates to the writing; writing as it relates to genre design	*Writing is adapted and supported by headings, subheadings, and use of pictures and illustration. How text wraps around images is important to the meaning of the piece.*

Framing Decision: How Much Writer Choice Will the Unit Include?

There is one more teaching decision you must make before further focusing the writing unit you are designing. How much choice will writers have in choosing a topic and/or genre? Here are some possibilities: writers may have choice of a topic, but not a genre. Or writers may choose the genre and the topic. Or a topic may be narrowed and parameters more limited if it is integrated into a discipline area. In making this decision, review the data: What will develop writer independence? What previous units have been taught? Is it important to be consistent or to mix things up? What will promote synergy and learning in the Writing Studio?

Ms. J, for example, could choose any of the following for her magazine-article writing unit:

- All writers will write how-to articles (same genre), about a topic of their choice.
- Writers may choose any magazine genre and topic.
- Writers may choose any magazine genre and topic based upon an inquiry of narrowed possibilities.
- Writers may choose a genre for a themed magazine *Our Community*. However, all topics will be generated from predetermined categories about the community: people, business, recreation, and history.

How much choice writers will have influences the unit goal and individual writing goals. It also influences management of the unit. For example, if Ms. J chooses the first option, all writers writing how-to articles, her planning and teaching will be more streamlined. Allowing choice, on the other hand, will allow writers to practice specific kinds of writing decisions, exercise the independence their preadolescent selves long for, and play toward their many interests. Ms. J notes that according to her curriculum map, the last unit of the school year is an integrated language arts and science unit; the entire Grade 5 teaching team plans for writers to produce a magazine on space systems. Having experts in various genres of magazine writing prior to this unit would be advantageous. For these reasons, she chooses the third option: writers may choose any magazine genre and topic based on an inquiry of narrowed possibilities.

Focusing Decisions

When planning a writing unit, framing decisions guide us as teachers in developing a framework for describing the unit we want to teach. Literally, these decisions "frame" our thinking. Focusing narrows the unit into teachable actions through a succession of decisions: drafting final assessment to reflect unit goal; creating a unit outline; considering and planning for integration, differentiation, and individual writer goals; and drafting weekly plans.

Focusing Decision: The Unit Goal

Once you have immersed yourself in the genre you choose to teach, have considered the writing practices, process, and craft on which you will focus based on the strengths, needs, and interests of writers in your Studio (including standards they must reach), and determined the structure of the writing unit, you are reading to imagine the end of the unit and the writing accomplishment you desire for each writer. Now is the time to compose a unit goal. Think of a unit goal as a vision statement. It ought to serve as a kind of guiding light when you begin the more detailed work of planning weekly mini-lessons. There are usually multiple possibilities for a unit goal. As with all composing, draft; let the goal sit; revise; play with the wording, being mindful of the nuance of words; talk it over with colleagues; and write again. A goal-statement as vision statement ought to be carefully crafted.

 Give it a try! Based on the writers in Ms. J's class, her genre immersion chart; her identified writing practices, process, and craft; and the choice structure of the unit, draft possible unit goal for the magazine unit. Compare the goal you draft with Ms. J's final unit goal that follows.

Ms. J, after multiple attempts, tentatively writes the following goal statement:

Writers will apply their knowledge of writing practices, process, and craft of magazine articles to write an article in a genre and topic of their choice.

Focusing Decision: Final Assessment

How will you know if writers have met the unit goal? What possible criteria and tool will you use for this purpose? Any assessment criteria are aligned with the unit goal and the specific writing practices, process, and craft that the specific unit supports. Recall in Chapter 5 our discussion of assessment practices. *Meaningful assessments serve and promote learning they do not get in the way of learning.* Assessments ought to not only inform the teacher and the writer *if* they met a unit goal but also *how* they met the goal in order to be useful to future instruction.

In Chapter 5 we described writing assessments that frame writing instruction and learning throughout the Writing Studio. We discussed the role of individual writing goals and the Cumulative Writing Folder and Writer Self-Assessment and suggested that final pieces of writing from any writing unit are a possible entry into the Cumulative Writing Folder. When designing unit-specific assessments, keep in mind how the unit assessment will support individualized learning goals and provide evidence of writer development toward those goals. Plan for Writer Self-Assessment and how the assessment tool will contribute to the database of the Cumulative Writing Folder.

Ms. J designed a magazine article assessment tool that serves as a checklist for writers as they write and gives writers a clear picture of the end goal of the writing unit. It also acts as a tool for writer self-assessment and teacher assessment (see Figure 11.1).

Figure 11.1 Magazine Article Assessment

Student Self-Assessment Checklist	Student Self-Assessment Narrative	Teacher Assessment Narrative
Ideas and content ☐ Main ideas are interesting and fit article topic and genre. ☐ Supporting details support the main ideas and fit the article topic and genre.	I am proud of the way my main ideas and supporting details are written because. . . .	
Organization ☐ Article flows smoothly for the reader and aligns with genre. ☐ Introduction makes the reader want to keep reading. ☐ Conclusion wraps up the article for the reader.	My magazine article is organized because . . .	
Word choice ☐ Interesting words related to the topic	The most interesting words I used were . . .	
Edited with precision for conventions ☐ Spelling ☐ Punctuation ☐ Capitalization ☐ Grammar (Does it sound right?)	Review your individual goals for writing conventions. How does your magazine article show that you are working toward your goals?	
	One (or more) writing craft I tried is . . .	What I notice you did as a writer that I haven't seen you do before . . .
	When I write a magazine article for the Space unit, I might try . . .	When you write a magazine article for the Space unit, I wonder if . . .

 Study Ms. J's Magazine Article Assessment tool. What can you notice and name about this tool? How will it work? What does it do? Review Ms. J's analysis of magazine genres (Table 11.1); her thinking work about writing practices, process, and craft; and her unit goal: How will her Magazine Article Assessment tool serve writers and Ms. J?

Focusing Decision: How Much Time Should Be Allotted to the Unit?

Having determined the unit goal and final assessment, you have a vision for the end of the unit. You can imagine the writers in your Writing Studio accomplishing specific writing practices, processes, and craft. A final decision to be made before outlining the unit is to determine the amount of time you will allot to the writing unit and how it may integrate with other disciplines. Make this decision by considering writer's strengths, needs, and standards; language arts curriculum map; and other discipline planning (see Chapter 10). Also consider the amount of time daily allotted to the Writing Studio. Ms. J allots 70 minutes a day for this purpose.

Ms. J had not planned to teach a unit on magazine writing but based on the school district's new focus on "informative writing" and the interests of writers in her Writing Studio, she adapted her curriculum map. The original plan was a 5-week unit on report writing. She decides to maintain the 5-week report-writing time slot but convert it to the magazine writing unit.

Focusing Decision: The Unit Outline

Once you have made decisions regarding the writing practices, process, and craft you will teach through the writing unit; composed the writing goal or vision statement; and determined the length of time available to devote to your unit, you are ready to begin a unit outline. You do this based on your experience as a writer and as a teacher of writing, on your understanding of the writers in your class, on the required standards and individualized writing goals toward which writers are working, and by applying the knowledge of the genre you are teaching. This, too, like all writing that is thinking, is a process of "starts and stops and cycles." Use a calendar format and plan out weekly goals that serve as a scaffold toward moving writers toward the end goal. Keep in mind the varied levels of writers' development (see Chapter 1). What is realistic for the writers of your Writing Studio? Don't just act on hunches; review data from your Teaching, Conferencing & Planning Notebook (see Chapter 5) or if it is the beginning of the year, review these related assessments (see Chapter 4). If necessary, revise the unit goal and vision, and related assessment tools. At all times, focus on the writers in your Writing Studio and their writing strengths and needs.

Focusing Decision: Consider Integration

Reading and writing clearly complement one another, so as you begin to plan your writing unit, pause and consider how specific instruction in reading might support the writing you are going to ask your writers to compose. How might integration deepen language arts instruction (see Chapter 10)?

In reviewing Ms. J's unit planning thus far, it is clear that writers first need to be readers of magazine genres in order to become writers of this genre. It makes sense, then, for the writing unit to be introduced during the Reading Studio. This is a typical pattern of integrated language arts planning: immersion in the genre, followed by writing (review Chapter 6). This means that a new genre is often introduced in the Reading Studio while writers are still completing a different genre of writing in the Writing Studio. Then, the focus of the new genre moves into the Writing Studio, even as the Reading Studio begins to focus on other genres or reading skills. This continuous cycle supports the complementary nature of reading and writing.

Ms. J uses this cycle in planning for her magazine unit. Children as readers begin reading magazines and exploring the genres of magazines in the Reading Studio while completing a memoir writing unit in the Writing Studio. By Week 3, magazine genre is the focus of both the Reading and the Writing Studio. However, in Week 4, the Reading Studio takes up science reading in preparation for the next integrated unit, and children as writers focus on applying their knowledge from the Reading Studio to writing their own magazine articles. See Table 11.4 for Ms. J's Magazine Article 5-Week Unit Plan on the next page.

 Review Ms. J's Magazine-Article 5-Week Unit Plan in Table 11.4. What do you notice and name about this outline? How does it inform your future integrated language arts planning? Review Chapter 5 and the critical assessments of the Writing Studio (Status of the Class or My Writing World; Daily Writing Folder; and the Teaching, Conferencing & Planning Notebook): How do you envision these assessment tools being used in Ms. J's outline?

TABLE 11.4 Ms. J's Magazine-Article 5-Week Unit Plan

Week	Unit Goal: Writers will apply their knowledge of writing practices, process, and craft of magazine articles to write an article in a genre and topic of their choice.	
	Reading Studio	**Writing Studio**
1	*Goal:* Immerse children in reading magazine articles. *Mini-lessons* • Determining important information. *Guided reading:* Self-selected groups by children's interest in magazine article topic. Focus on determining important information.	*Goal:* Revise memoir writing.
2	*Goal:* Continued exploration of magazine articles. *Mini-lessons* • Model reading articles and identifying the different genres of magazine articles. • Model reading magazine articles and filling out the Magazine Article Genres Chart. *Guided reading:* Self-selected groups by children's interest in magazine genre. Focus on noticing and naming writing genre, purpose and craft of magazine articles.	*Goal:* Edit and broadcast memoirs.
3	*Goal:* Continued exploration and search for a mentor article. *Mini-lessons* • Add information to the Magazine Article Genres Chart. • Model finding a mentor magazine article that will connect with topic. *Guided reading:* Groups determined by common reading strategy children need. Focus will vary based on each group's need.	*Goal:* Identify a topic and genre; and draft under the influence of a mentor article. *Mini-lessons* • Model brainstorming a list of topics for magazine articles. • Model selecting a topic. • Model selecting a genre well suited for topic. • Introduce the Magazine Assessment. • Model planning the presentation/layout of the article using mentor article and selected journalist vocabulary. • Model writing multiple introductions. *Guided writing:* Groups determined by common needs and progress towards mini-lesson goals.
4	*Goal:* Immerse children in Space unit texts.	*Goal:* Draft and revise under the influence of a mentor article. *Mini-lessons* • Model how to research to find more information on topic. • Model writing main ideas that are interesting and fit topic and genre. • Model writing supporting details to support my main ideas that fit my topic and genre. • Model organizing main ideas and details to flow smoothly for readers and align with genre. • Model writing multiple conclusion options. *Guided writing:* Groups determined by magazine genre writers selected.

Week	Unit Goal: Writers will apply their knowledge of writing practices, process, and craft of magazine articles to write an article in a genre and topic of their choice.	
	Reading Studio	**Writing Studio**
5	*Goal:* Continued exploration of Space texts.	*Goal:* Revise, edit, publish and broadcast magazine articles. *Mini-lessons* • Model having a conference with yourself. • Model having a peer conference. • Model editing with precision for conventions (spelling, punctuation, capitalization, grammar). • Model creating a published copy of article. • Model self-assessing article. *Guided writing:* Groups determined by common needs and progress towards mini-lesson.

Focusing Decisions: Planning for Differentiation

Having outlined the integrated unit, pause now and anticipate how you may need to differentiate the unit for specific learning strengths and needs for some children. Consider English learners: what specific strengths and needs do they have? And remember in considering this question that there are many stages of English language development, so tailor the instruction toward the specific needs of the English learners in your class. Do you have children with writing disabilities on IEPs or on 504 educational plans? What are these children's strengths and needs? Do you have children who are talented and gifted? Again what are their strengths and needs? Anticipate and plan how you will differentiate for instruction. Collaborate with specialists in your school in doing so.

 Review the description of the children in Ms. J's class found at the beginning of this chapter. Make a list of questions reflecting additional information you would need to know in order to differentiate the magazine writing unit for them.

Ms. J anticipates the needs of specific children in her classroom by adding to her unit outline some specific strategies for each child:

Antonio, Julian, Maribel, Early Intermediate English Learners. First Language: Spanish

- Provide Spanish-language magazines if requested by children.
- Request assistance from English language development specialist to facilitated guided writing as needed.
- Keep open the option for children to write in Spanish or English or a combination of both.
- Analyze writing for any patterns of miscues that may represent a need for specific language instruction.

Azir, Beginning English Learner. First Language: Somali

- Difficult to find children's magazines in Somali. Phone mother to see about possible texts.
- Use structured template for genre writing and teach specific vocabulary to support English learning.
- Use buddy reading.
- Ask English language specialist to conduct teacher–student reading and writing conferences.

Jeff, 504 Plan, ADHD

- Jeff loves reading magazines articles! His love of the genre will help him focus.
- Jeff's parent recently suggested the option of an exercise ball as a chair for Jeff. He will be trying this out during the Reading Studio.

Molly and Sara/Talented and Gifted Writers

- Allow a wider parameter of genre choice.
- Suggest girls write individually and then collaborate on a second article, using a different genre or design.

Focusing Decision: Individualizing Writer's Goals

In the Writing Studio, every writer is really on his or her own individual learning plan. This is made possible since every child has his/her individualized writing goals (see Chapter 5). However, as discussed in Chapter 5, while some children required specialized differentiation, most of the writers in any given classroom will have similar writing goals based on their writing development (see Chapter 2). These more general goals can be adjusted based on individual writer's strengths and needs. Whenever you are beginning a new unit and ending another, it is a good time to revisit individual writer goals and revise as needed.

This is best illustrated with a review of Ms. J's Magazine Article Writing Assessment and a closer look at one writer's individual goals. First, review Ms. J's Magazine Writing Assessment and notice how she designed the checklist/assessment items so they can be individualized for each writer. All writers have the same focused unit goals: ideas and content, organization, word choice, and editing with precision. Most all writers have versions of these goals as their individual goals. For example, Alejandra's individual writing goal sheet includes the following four writing goals:

- I will revise my writing by developing my ideas with additional details and supporting ideas.
- I will take writing risks by exploring different ways to conclude my writing.
- I will double-check the spelling of words that are plural.
- I will learn different ways to format my writing, including attention to headings and subheadings, which will make my writing easier for the reader to understand.

At the end of the magazine-article writing unit, Alejandra and Ms. J will be able to revisit these goals with new data specific to magazine writing. For example, if Alejandra chooses to write a how-to article, she will need to focus on several main points and supporting details. Alejandra has a pattern of losing writing stamina toward the end of a piece. Ms. J plans to teach writers different strategies for writing article conclusions during the magazine-article writing unit. Alejandra will have ample opportunity and time to work toward her second goal. In this unit, Ms. J plans for all writers to focus their editing skills on conventions, to make sure their work is ready for a wide audience. Alejandra is learning the different rules for making words plural; there should be evidence in her final writing that perhaps she has even mastered this goal and is ready for a new spelling focus. Finally, Alejandra has been experimenting with headings and subheadings as meaningful signposts for readers of her work; this also is helping her better organize her writing. All the magazine genres have specific kinds of headings and subheadings and have additional design considerations that will provide opportunity to show mastery of this writing goal.

Focusing Decisions: Weekly Planning

Once you have outlined the unit, you are ready to design weekly lesson plans. These are outlines and possibilities, not directives. Using your unit outline, break the weeks into smaller units and plan according to the predicable schedule of the Studio: mini-lesson, independent reading/writing, guided small-group instruction, and sharing. (Review Chapter 7, 8, and 9) It is possible after drafting weekly plans, you may discover you cannot teach as much as you thought possible when you initially outlined the unit and designed the final assessment. If this occurs, return to both and adjust as necessary. This may result in revising the unit goal as well.

Ms. J's Magazine Article Unit Weekly Plans are detailed in Tables 11.5, 11.6, 11.7, 11.8, and 11.9.

 Study Ms. J's weekly lesson plans. How do they focus on writers' interests, strengths, and needs? How do they align with the unit goal? How do they support the CCSS? What else can you notice and name about her weekly plans?

The Studio *Live* Decisions

Once you are living the unit plan you have developed, you will make a series of decisions based on data you collected in the Reading and Writing Studios. These are decisions made *live, in action,* while teaching. You will be living the rhythm of the studio: the teacher collects data via the Status of the Class/My Writing World and teacher–student writing conferences (review Chapters 5 and 7); the teacher analyzes the data; based on the data, the teacher adjusts and individualizes instructions.

TABLE 11.5 Ms. J's Magazine Article Unit Week 1 Plans

Reading Studio

Week 1 Goal: Immerse children in reading magazine articles.

Read aloud mini-lesson focus: Determining important information

Guided reading groups determined by children's interest in topic:

1. Kayla, Julia, Kylar, Rebekah, Sara, and Manuel: "2 Million Hairs and More: How to Make an Animated Movie" (Hutter, 2013), How To article
2. Adam, Ian, Tyler, and Jennifer: "Certified Helmet Buyer's Guide" (BMXphus!, 2013), Review article
3. Alejandra, Antonio, Chris, David, and Kylar: "Activity to discover" (D'Alto, 2013), All About article
4. Jeff, Julian, Noah, Molly, and Isaac: "6 Surprising Animal Singers" (Hulick, 2013), Top 6 article
5. Azir, James, Jason, Zane, and Maribel: "Music & Emotion: Why Do Sad Songs Make Us Cry?" (Millar, 2013), All About article

Guided reading focus: Determining important information

Mon	Read aloud: "Soda Leads to Lisps" (Muse, 2014e), all-about article
	Guided reading groups: 1 & 2
	Reading conferences: Adam & Jeff
Tues	Read aloud: "Muse Mail" (Muse, 2014d), opinion article
	Guided reading groups: 3 & 4
	Reading conferences: Noah & Maribel
Wed	Read aloud: "DIY CSI Lifting Prints" (*Muse*, 2014c) & "DIY CSI Ink Chromatography" (*Muse*, 2014b), how-to articles
	Guided reading groups: 1 & 5
	Reading conferences: Zane & Antonio
Thurs	Read aloud: "DIY CSI Shoe Prints" " (Mooney, 2014), how-to article
	Guided reading groups: 2 & 3
	Reading conferences: Manual & Julian
Fri	Read aloud: "Ancient Bird Had Two Tails" (*Muse*, 2014a), all-about article
	Guided reading groups: 4 & 5
	Reading conferences: Jennifer & Kobin

TABLE 11.6 Ms. J's Magazine Article Unit Week Two Plans

Reading Studio	

Week 2 Goal: Continued exploration of magazine articles.

Read aloud mini-lesson focus: Magazine Article Genre Chart

Guided reading groups determined by children's interest in magazine genre, one group based on students' interest in reading a magazine article in Spanish.

1. **How To (Spanish):** Adam, Manuel, Julian, Maribel, Zane, "Brazaletes de amistad" (Santos, 2012)
2. **How To:** Antonio, Noah, Molly, Sara, Kayla, Tyler, "How to Make an Egghead" (Hess & Hess, 2013)
3. **Review:** Azir, Alejandra, David, Greg, Jason, Kobin, "Check it Out" (Unan, 2013)
4. **Debate:** Jeff, Jennifer, Julia, Kristopher, Rebekah, "The Sports Goal: Just for Kicks or in it to Win?" (Chin & Throckmorton, 2007)
5. **All About:** Chris, Ian, Isaac, James, "Meet an Illustrator: Sophie Blackall" (*New Moon*, 2013b)

Guided reading focus: Noticing and naming writing genre, purpose and craft of magazine article

Mon	Read aloud: "Defend Yourself 8 Simple Ways" (Belvis, 2013), how-to article Guided reading group: 1 Reading conferences: Azir, Alejandra, Chris, and Jeff
Tues	Read aloud: "Girl of the Year: Malala Yousafzai" (*New Moon*, 2013a), how-to article Guided reading group: 2 Reading conferences: David, Greg, Ian, and Jeff
Wed	Read aloud: "Cool Inventions" (Boyer, 2012), top 3 article Guided reading group: 3 Reading conferences: Isaac, James, Jason, and Jeff
Thurs	Read aloud: "The Cell Phone Sell: Distraction or Satisfaction? (Serrano & Leach, 2007), debate article Guided reading group: 4 Reading conferences: Julia, Kayla, Kyler, and Jeff
Fri	Read aloud mini-lesson: "Top 5 Open Water Moments in 2013" (Cummins, 2013), top 5 article Guided reading group: 5 Reading conferences: Molly, Rebekah, Sara, Tyler, and Jeff

TABLE 11.7 Ms. J's Magazine Article Unit Week 3 Plans

Reading Studio	

Week 3 Goal: Continued exploration and search for a mentor article.

Read aloud mini-lesson focus: Magazine Article Genre Chart

Guided reading groups determined by strategy need.

1. Read a challenging article in Spanish: Adam, Maribel, Zane, "El reino animal: el oso hormiguero una especie solitaria" (Alpizar, 2012)
2. Identify writer's craft in article: Jeff, Chris, David, Kayla, "Wake Up" (Schardt, 2014)
3. Determine important information: Manuel & Julian, "Ocean Oddball" (Kranking, 2014)

Guided reading focus: Noticing and naming writing genre, purpose, and craft of magazine article. Select a mentor article.

Mon	Read aloud: "To GMO or Not to GMO? Genetically Engineered Food Has Strong Advocates and Harsh Critics" (Erdosh & Lusted, 2014), debate article Reading conferences: Antonio, David, Isaac, Manuel, Julia, Tyler

Tues	Read aloud: "To GMO or Not to GMO? Genetically Engineered Food Has Strong Advocates and Harsh Critics" (Erdosh & Lusted, 2014)
	Reading conferences: Zane, Rebekah, Noah, Kobin, James, Alejandra
Wed	Read aloud: "Calories 101: Eating for Size, Eating for Health: Sumo Wrestlers Are Made, Not Born" (Cox, 2014), all-about article
	Reading conferences: Azir, Chris, Jeff, Julian, Kayla, Maribel
Thurs	Read aloud: "Calories 101: Eating for Size, Eating for Health: Sumo Wrestlers Are Made, Not Born" (Cox, 2014)
	Guided reading group: 1
	Reading conferences: Aaron, Gavin, Ian, Sara
Fri	Read aloud: Top 5: "Top 5 Tricks of the Month" (Hodgson, 2003)
	Guided reading groups: 2 & 3
	Reading conferences: Kristopher & Jason

Writing Studio

Week 3 Goal: Identify a topic and genre; and draft under the influence of a mentor article.

Guided writing focus: Determined by common needs within genre groups and progress toward daily writing mini-lesson goals. Analyze data from Status of the Class, Teaching, Conferencing & Planning Notebook to form groups.

Teacher–student writing conference focus: Individual needs and progress toward daily writing mini-lesson goals.

Mon	Writing mini-lesson: Model brainstorming a list of topics for magazine articles.
	Guided writing group: Focus: Creating a list of possible topics
	Writing conferences:
	Sharing: Possible topics writers are exploring.
Tues	Writing mini-lesson: Model selecting a topic from my brainstormed list.
	Guided writing group: Focus: Selecting a topic and magazine genre
	Writing conferences:
	Sharing: Genre/topic connections.
Wed	Writing mini-lesson: Model selecting a genre well suited for my topic.
	Guided writing group: Focus: Selecting a genre well suited for topic
	Writing conferences:
	Sharing: Genre/topic connections.
Thurs	Writing mini-lesson: Introduce the Magazine Article Assessment and model using my mentor article as a guide to plan the layout/presentation of my article.
	Guided writing group 1: Focus: Plan layout/presentation on paper
	Guided writing group 2: Focus: Plan layout/presentation with ShowMe
	Writing conferences:
	Sharing: Select writers based upon writing conferences.
Fri	Writing mini-lesson: Model writing multiple introductions to my article. Use mentor texts that use different craft for introductions (e.g., question, dialogue, description).
	Guided writing groups: Meet with children in genre groups Focus: Introductions in genre
	Sharing: Select writers based upon writing conferences.

TABLE 11.8 Ms. J's Magazine Article Unit Week 4 Plans

Writing Studio

Week 4 Goal: Draft and revise under the influence of a mentor article.

Guided writing groups determined by the genre children selected:

Advice: Julia

How-To Do: Alejandra, Antonio, Zane

How-To Make: Jeff, Kayla, Maribel

Top 3/5/10: Adam, Greg, Isaac, Kobin, Kristopher, Tyler

All About: Chris, David, James, Jennifer, Rebekah

Review: Ian, Jason, Julian, Noah

Debate: Sara, Molly

Guided writing focus: Common needs within genre groups or progress toward daily writing mini-lesson goals.
Writing conference focus: Individual needs or progress toward daily writing mini-lesson goals.

Mon	Writing mini-lesson: Model how to research to find more information on my topic, "Top 5 Family Hikes at Zion National Park." Read and take notes from three sources: • Sunset magazine article, "Heavenly Hiking," (Law, 2002), • Lonely Planet guidebook on Zion National Park (Benson, Dunford, & McCarthy, 2011) • Travel journal about the hikes my family took at Zion National Park Guided writing groups: All About, Top 3/5/10, Review Writing conferences: Ian, Jeff, Kyler Sharing: How and why writers made information choices
Tues	Writing mini-lesson: Model writing my article so my main ideas are interesting and fit my topic and genre. Guided writing groups: How To Do, How To Make, Debate Writing conferences: Julia, Molly, Rebekah, Sara Sharing: Select writers based upon writing conferences.
Wed	Writing mini-lesson: Model writing supporting details to support my main ideas that fit my topic and genre. Guided writing group: Writing conferences: Sharing: How and why writers chose supporting details
Thurs	Writing mini-lesson: Model organizing my main ideas and details so my article flows smoothly for readers and align with my genre. Guided writing group: Writing conferences: Sharing: How writers figured out a writing problem
Fri	Writing mini-lesson: Model writing multiple introductions to my article. Use mentor texts that use different craft for introductions (e.g., summarize most important information, ask a question, evoke a feeling, give a command) Guided writing group: Review article (Julian & Noah) Writing conferences: Sharing: Creative introductions.

TABLE 11.9 Ms. J's Magazine Article Unit Week 5 Plans

Writing Studio

Week 5 Goal: Revise, edit, publish, and broadcast magazine articles.

Guided writing focus: Common needs within genre groups, progress toward daily writing mini-lesson goals.

Writing conference focus: Individual needs, progress toward daily writing mini-lesson goals.

Mon	Writing mini-lesson: Model having a conference with myself
	Guided writing group 1: Julia, Kristopher, Molly, Sara, Focus: Feedback from Ms. J
	Writing conferences:
	Sharing: Strategies writers used for having a self-conference
Tues	Writing mini-lesson: Model having a peer conference
	Guided writing group:
	Writing conferences:
	Sharing: What writers learned from a peer conference or new strategies for making peer conference more effective
Wed	Writing mini-lesson: Model editing with precision for conventions
	Guided writing group:
	Writing conferences:
	Sharing: Editing challenges and how writers overcame them
Thurs	Writing mini-lesson: Model making design choices for final publication
	Guided writing group:
	Writing conferences:
	Sharing: Cool design choices
Fri	Writing mini-lesson: Model self-assessing my article
	Guided writing group:
	Writing conferences:
	Sharing: Writers share what they did as writers in the magazine writing unit that they hadn't done before
Contingency Plan	Writers may need extra time to publish their work. If needed, merge Reading and Writing Studio on last day.
	Not all writers will finish at the same time. Options for early finishers:
	Volunteer as a peer editing coach
	Volunteer as a computer coach for design or uploading work to web
	Independently or collaboratively read magazine articles of choice

To gain a sense of the rhythm of the Writing Studio and the kinds of decisions made during the teaching of a writing unit, read and analyze Ms. J's reflective analysis written at the end of Week 3 of the magazine writing unit:

Ms. J's Week 3 Reflective Analysis

Writing Mini-Lessons

After two weeks of immersing themselves in reading magazine articles, the class is excited that they are FINALLY going to be able to write their very own magazine articles. The mini-lessons were kept short on Monday, Tuesday, and Wednesday, which allowed me to have more time for guided writing groups and writing conferences. Sara, Molly, Ian, and Kobin could hardly contain themselves as I modeled brainstorming my list of topics to write about; they wanted to get started on their own lists immediately! Thursday's mini-lesson took longer than I planned. I shared the Magazine Article Assessment so the children clearly see the writing goals for their magazine article. I also modeled drafting my article's layout/presentation using my mentor article while deliberately using some of the vocabulary of journalists: white space, justification, and pull quote. During partner discussion, it was evident children had a clear sense of how to plan the layout/presentation of their article. It would have been a more efficient use of time during Friday's mini-lesson if I had read the three mentor articles showing different ways magazine-article authors write introductions during Reading Studio.

Guided Writing

Meeting in guided writing groups by common needs related to the daily writing mini-lesson goals worked well this week. Monday, Julian, Maribel, Greg, and Jeff all asked during the Status of the Class for help brainstorming a list of interesting topics to write magazine articles about. We spent a few minutes orally brainstorming ideas and thumbing through some magazines for ideas. Once writers had some ideas they began writing their lists furiously.

Tuesday I facilitated a guided writing group with Azir, Noah, Antonio, and Adam to help them select an interesting topic from their brainstormed list. It was a lively discussion with children's voices layering over each other's as they tried to convince one another which topics they found most interesting. It was encouraging to hear Azir actively engaged in the conversation with his emerging English.

Wednesday, I had the children that weren't sure what genre they wanted to use in writing their magazine article stay in the carpet area after the mini-lesson. Together we spent a few minutes discussing genre options for Antonio. This helped the group as a whole have a better understanding of the thinking behind determining which genre to select and that several genres can work for a single topic. For example, Antonio's idea about kickball could be a how-to article on learning to play kickball or an all-about article discussing the origins of the game and versions of the game. He could write a Review article about the best and worst parts about playing kickball or even a debate article, writing from two perspectives of why children should be allowed or not be allowed to play kickball at school. I framed these choices as "writer decisions." By the end of Writing Studio on Wednesday, everyone had a topic to write about and a genre that aligned with his or her topic—whew!

Thursday, I facilitated two guided writing groups. One group was for children wanting help planning their article's layout/presentation on paper. The other group was for children whom wanted a quick tutorial on how to use the iPad ShowMe application (Learnbat Inc., 2013) to plan their layout/presentation. Luckily, Sara had used the application previously and was able to help her peers when I transitioned to a writing conference.

Friday, I asked writers to sit at tables by genre. I was able to meet with five of the seven genre groups (All About, Top 3/5/10, How To Do, How To Make, and Review) for short, guided writing conversations about how the leads of their genre mentor texts. These genre-based discussions helped writers discover a variety of possible lead options.

After reading through the writers' Daily Writing Folder after school on Friday, I noted six children (Ian, Jeff, Kristopher, Molly, Rebekah, and Sara) didn't have any introductions written. They were all still working on various layout/presentation ideas on their iPads. I will need to check in with these writers early next week to make sure they have some possible introductions written and are progressing in writing their magazine articles.

Writing Conferences

I conducted writing conferences on Monday, Tuesday, Wednesday, and Thursday. I checked in briefly with Jeff on Tuesday, Wednesday, and Thursday to see if the strategies we were trying out (standing when needed and sitting on a yoga ball) were helping him stay on task. He said he really liked being able to sit on the yoga ball and write in the back carpet area where it is quieter. We are making progress! On Wednesday, Julia requested a writing conference because she was ready to start writing her Advice column and wanted permission to talk with a few children in the class to "write in" with issues at school for her to respond to in her column. I met with Azir on Thursday after his guided writing group to provide him with a how-to-make article template to guide his layout planning, because his mentor text was too difficult given his English-language abilities.

Sharing

Monday I had Maribel and Julian share their brainstormed list with the class. They rarely volunteer to share, and I knew they both had generated a solid list of topics during our guided writing group. On Tuesday and Wednesday after a quick Status of the Class at the end of independent and collaborative writing time, all the children shared their topic and genre. On Thursday, Sara and Molly volunteered to share how they were collaborating to design the layout/presentation for their debate article on whether we should keep animals in zoos. Friday, I asked the children in the all-about genre to share their introductions: Chris, David, James, Jennifer, and Rebekah.

 What can you notice and name about Ms. J's reflective analysis? If you were Ms. J, what decisions would you make about the next instructional week of the magazine unit? Would you adjust or adapt any mini-lesson plans? (Review Table 11.9 Magazine Unit Week 5 Plans.) What guided writing and teacher–student conferencing plans might you make?

Designing and living a writing unit specifically created for the writers in your Writing Studio can be one of the most satisfying aspects of teaching. There is no set guide to planning and teaching writing, but the guiding principles of unit planning and teaching described in *Becoming a Teacher of Writing in Elementary Classrooms* can be adjusted and adapted to support the learning of diverse children in many contexts and introduce them to all that writing can do for them.

Throughout this book, we have attempted to illustrate the Writing Studio as a place where practicing writers engage in meaningful process, learning and sharing writing craft, in an act of writing our lives into existence (again). Natalie Goldberg (1986) says it best: "Writers live twice" (p. 48). We live life, and then we write our life. Writing as a deeply beautiful and human endeavor is the possibility to write life in whatever way we choose to story it through the many modes and genres of living. As teachers of writing, we have the incredible opportunity to open up this writer's life to children.

In the introduction of this book, we expressed our desire that this book act as evocation as you apply what you have learned to your own Writing Studio, even as you continue in living and writing your own story of becoming-teacher of writing:

May you never arrive,
may you know joy in the practice,
gratefulness in the process,
wonder in craft,
and generosity in sharing.

References

Alpizar, M. (20012). El reino animal: El oso hormiguero una especie solitaria [Animal kingdom: The anteater a solidary species]. *Iguana, 7*(5), 14–15.

Belvis, K. (2013). Defend yourself 8 simple ways. *New Moon, 20*(4), 8–9.

Benson, S., Dunford, L., & McCarthy, C. (2011). *Zion & Bryce Canyon National Parks.* Oakland, CA: Lonely Planet.

BMXplus! (2013, April). Certified helmet buyer's guide: Our safest helmet guide yet. *BMXplus!,* 28–32.

Boyer, C. (2012). Cool inventions. *National Geographic Kids, 425,* 6.

Chin, M., & Throckmorton, A. (2007). Debates! The sports goal: Just for kicks or in it to win? *New Moon, 15*(1), 22.

Cox, M. B. (2014). Calories 101: Eating for size, eating for health: sumo wrestlers are made, not born. *Odyssey, 23*(3), 20.

Cummins, J. (2013). Top 5 open water moments in 2013. *Swimming World, 54*(11), 9–10.

D'Alto, N. (2013). Activity to discover. *Odyssey, 22*(7), 42–46.

Erdosh, G., & Lusted, M. (2014). To GMO or not to GMO? Genetically engineered food has strong advocates and harsh critics. *Odyssey, 23*(2), 15.

Goldberg, N. (1986). *Writing down the bones: Freeing the writer within.* Boston, MA: Shambhala.

Hess, L., & Hess, M. (2013). How to make an egghead. *Hopscotch, 25*(1), 42–43.

Hodgson, D. J. (2003). Top 5 Tricks of the Month. *Electronic Gaming Monthly,* (166), 144.

Hulick, K. (2013). 6 surprising animal singers. *Odyssey, 22*(7), 32–35.

Hutter, C. (2013). 2 million hairs and more: How to make an animated movie. *Appleseeds, 16*(3), 10–13.

Kranking, K. (2014). Ocean oddball. *Ranger Rick, 43*(2), 16–19.

Law, S. (2002). Heavenly hiking. *Sunset, 208*(4), 40.

Learnbat Inc. (2013, October 15). ShowMe interactive whiteboard application 4.2.2 [Mobile applicaton]. New York, NY.

Millar, A. (2013). Music & emotion: Why do sad songs make us cry? *Odyssey, 22*(7), 14–17.

Mooney, C. (2014). DIY CSI: Shoe prints. *Muse, 18*(1), 32.

Muse. (2014a). Ancient bird had two tails. *Muse, 18*(1), 10.

Muse. (2014b). DIY CSI: Ink chromatography. *Muse, 18*(1), 35.

Muse. (2014c). DIY CSI: Lifting prints. *Muse, 18*(1), 31.

Muse. (2014d). Muse mail. *Muse, 18*(1), 36.

Muse. (2014e). Soda leads to lisps. *Muse, 18*(1), 5.

New Moon. (2013a). Girl of the year: Malala yousafzai. *New Moon, 20*(4), 33.

New Moon. (2013b). Meet an illustrator: Sophie Blackall. *New Moon, 20*(4), 29.

Santos, L. (2012). Manualidades: Brazaletes de amistad [Crafts: Friendship bracelets]. *Iguana, 7*(5), 26.

Schardt, H. (2014). Wake up. *Ranger Rick, 43*(2), 24–29.

Serrano, S., & Leach, T. (2007). Debate! The cell phone sell: Distraction or satisfaction? *New Moon, 15*(1), 23.

Unan, S. (2013). Check it out. *New Moon, 20*(4), 28–29.

Appendices

Appendix A
Maddie, Kindergarten Writing Sample

Figure A.1 Maddie, Kindergarten Writing Sample, Page 1

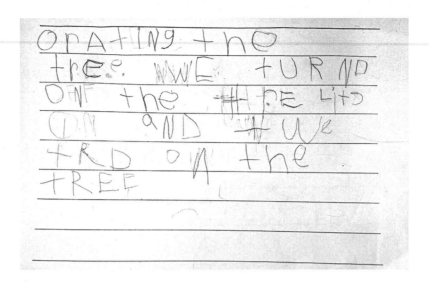

Figure A.2 Maddie, Kindergarten Writing Sample, Page 2

My brother was drinking eggnog and I was decorating the tree. We turned on the tree lights and we turned on the tree.

Appendix B
Morgan, Grade 3 Writing Sample

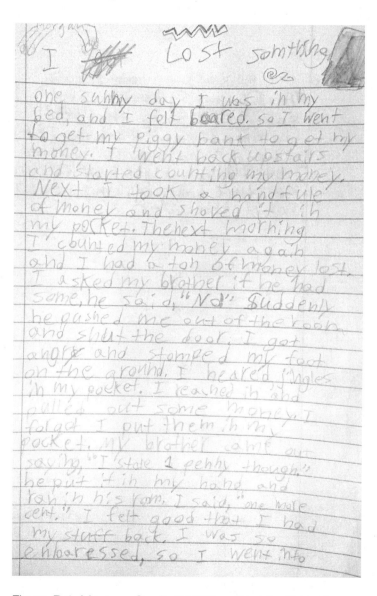

Figure B.1 Morgan, Grade 3 Writing Sample, Page 1

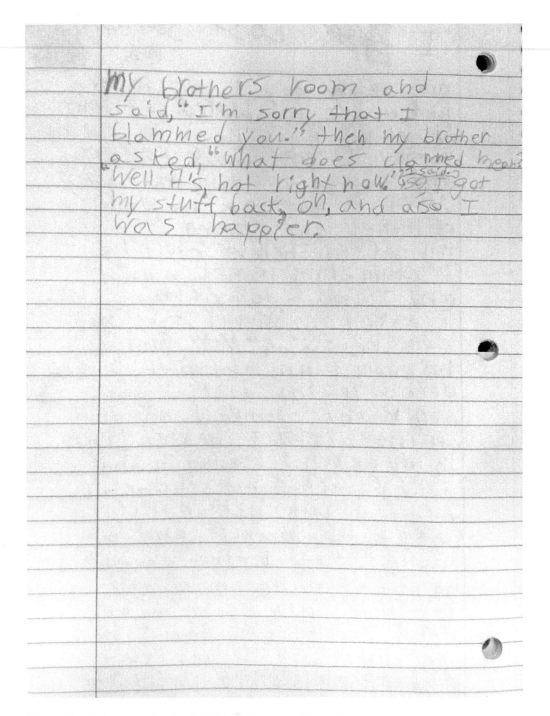

my brothers room and said, "I'm sorry that I blammed you." then my brother asked, "what does clammed mean?" "well it's hot right now" so I got my stuff back, oh, and also I was happier.

Figure B.2 Morgan, Grade 3 Writing Sample, Page 2

Appendix C
Carolina, Grade 3 Writing Sample

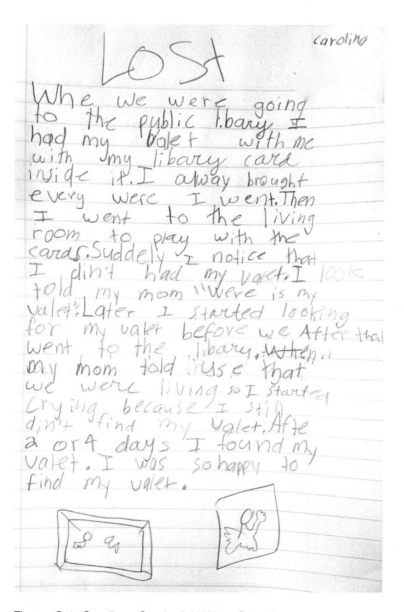

Figure C.1 Carolina, Grade 3 Writing Sample

Appendix D
Nickolas, Grade 5 Writing Sample

Figure D.1 Nickolas, Grade 5 Writing Sample

Appendix E
Sebas' Story "Middle East Revenge"

Middle East Revenge

MONDAY   SEPT 16TH   2001

ANDREW PETTISON ACE PLATOON SERGEANT 501st AIRBORN

We were just stunned when we heard of the plane crashing in the Twin Towers and the president just declared war on Iraq and sending us out tomorrow. Boy am I glad we get to show not to mess with us again! We get ready to move out in about six weeks. It's so busy here at the base, everybody keeps coming and going. We plan to move out with our drill sergeant and hit the air in about two weeks.

THURSDAY   DEC 15TH   2001

We were being shot at, half our planes gone, and the drill sergeant says the chant, "WHO DO THE LADIES LOVE THE MOST?" he says, and we all reply, "AIRBORNE!", drill sergeant continues, "WHO DOES THE ARMY TRUST THE MOST?", "AIRBORNE!", "WHO DOES THE TALIBAN FEAR THE MOST?", "AIRBORNE! YEAH!" And we all jump from the plane and pulled our chutes and laid down covering fire for our planes to get out of there.

FRIDAY   DEC 16TH   2001

We are in our "STRYKER" and had about zero combat ever since we got here. There's a rumor going around that we scared the Taliban so much, their afraid of fighting us cause they know they would lose. Well, nothing exciting happened to us today.

SUNDAY   DEC 18TH   2001

Everybody was nervous and I was a little homesick and nervous. Then they had their RPG ready and aiming right at us. BOOOOOM!!!! They took our escort jeep out and we unloaded all our ammunition on them. There must've been at least fifty or sixty of them, but we just kept on shooting at anything that moves. My squad silenced probably about two or three RPG nests and our convoy lost one Stryker and two jeeps. They retreated after about twenty minutes of return fire.

MONDAY   FEB 1ST   2002

Well after what happened last month, I'm scared to take any more lives. But when I get this feeling I remember my dad, killed in action in Afghanistan during Operation Desert Storm. This makes me mad and want to take REVENGE and destroy their makeshift empire here and liberate all the helpless little souls and bring peace and order to their home so they can once again look up and smile. Today we took a convoy to look for IED's and see if we can chase the Taliban out of the city. We were looking but not hard enough and my jeep was blown sky high and landed right on its back. We were able to walk away safely and we were unharmed, with the exception of our gunner. He got a minor concussion and broke both his legs. Other than that he's fine.

TUESDAY   FEB 2ND   2002

Today we were ordered back to the Main Base and I was so happy and relieved, I literally jumped out of the tank and ran to the chopper that came to pick us up. It felt so good to get back to where it's mostly safe and lots of men and women who had also been ordered back, I was finally not alone and I felt so alive. We all went back to our barracks and felt safe and we all fell asleep fast.

WEDNESDAY   FEB 3RD   2002

We woke up to the sound of alarms blaring all around and we all suddenly got up and dressed as fast as we could, went to the armory and grab our guns and we ran outside to people shouting orders and I asked one of the drill sergeant and they said "We're under attack!" All we did was stand motionless and saw the huge mass of Taliban soldiers charging the base. We stared shooting and we took down the first wave, but they kept coming, wave after wave, but then we heard it, "budabuddabudda." The sound of the chopper mini-gun was warming, relieving even. The Taliban men were falling over each other as if they were all tripping down a mountain.

THURSDAY   FEB 4TH   2002

The fighting lasted about 23 hours and they eventually gave up, so we celebrated with champagne and a nice bath to get the smell of blood and dirt from my body and after, I would head back to the barracks. We were going to try tank exercises and some free firing a couple of shells.

MONDAY   FEB 30TH   2002

We were going to the Black Hawk that would take us back to Kabul. The staff sergeant assigned us city patrol (which by the way is so boring) and head out at 0600 hours. We were going to take the south entrance and the other half took the north entrance. It was market day for the rest of Kabul's inhabitants, it was crowded like sardines. We couldn't move, it was like one big mall but outside. Our convoy was stuck so we set out on foot and when we got to the market, all the merchants started to look at us suspiciously and also the civilians. Than the merchants started to close up their caravans, and I felt a shearing pain in my shoulder and all the windows opened and started to open fire on us. We all took cover and returned fire but they didn't run. The jeep explodes right behind me and kills Jek and Brock. Then we were ordered back to base and we basically ran. But when we got back to base, nothing could have prepared us for what lay ahead.

FRIDAY   MARCH 20TH   2002

The base was no more alive than Latin itself. NO SURVIVORS . . .

THURSDAY   MARCH 26TH   2002

We were picked at base alpha and we were granted free flight back home, so this is the last you'll hear from me for a while. We're boarding now and the rest of the platoon is splitting up for a while. So until we're shipped out again goodbye.

Appendix F
Teaching Event with *March: Book One*

Today as we continue our study of *reading like writers*, we will read a book titled *March: Book One* written by John Lewis and Andrew Aydin and illustrated by Nate Powell (2013). As I read *March: Book One* I'm going to think aloud as I notice what the authors and illustrator are doing and why it works and how we might want to use them as mentors for our own writing. I want to notice the author's craft and how that ties in to what *kind of writing* it is, also called *genre*, and what the purpose or meaning work the authors are trying to convey, also called *mode*. . . .

Now that I've read aloud the first four pages, I'm going to start thinking aloud for you. In the first few pages, the authors use dialogue to tell the story of the march over the Edmund Pettus Bridge. I see that the state trooper's speech bubbles are outlined in jagged lines and the text is in all caps to give the reader the sense that the state trooper is yelling through a bullhorn while John Lewis and Hosea Williams' speech bubbles are circular in shape with a much smaller font and lower case letters. The size of the speech bubbles and the font symbolize the imbalance of power between the peaceful protestors and the state troopers. As I turn the page, I notice it is filled with violence against the peaceful demonstrators in both the illustrations and the use of onomatopoeia such as: "*Whap*" and "*Oof*," "*Krak*," and "*Thud*." The authors' use of vivid language shows how effective they are with word choice to create a mood or a feeling for the reader. I'm also noticing how the story is organized through comic panels that describe the event chronologically. What I am noticing in the first nine pages, is the *mode* of the text, the purpose of the text, appears to both tell a story through dialogue and inform the reader about a historical civil rights event in the United States. I am predicting that the book's genre is literary nonfiction story.

Let's read a couple of more pages. . . . Wow, that was surprising to see the title page on pages 10 and 11. I like the way the illustrator, Nate Powell, used such a large font for the word *march* and how he drew the sun rising on the Washington Mall. It is such an interesting perspective how he makes me, as the reader feel like I am sitting on top of the Lincoln Memorial. I'm wondering why he did this? How does Powell want to position me as a reader?

As I turn the page again I'm noticing that when the authors want to change the setting or time period in the story, they use narrator boxes, like the one on page 12 that says, "Washington D.C. January 20, 2009." It is like a road sign for me as a reader that the setting has changed.

Let's continue reading. . . . Okay, I want to think aloud about what I am noticing on page 38 when the authors are telling about John Lewis' road trip to his Uncle Otis to New York in 1951. When I read,

There would be no restaurants for us to stop at until we were well out of the south, so we carried our restaurant right in the car with us. Stopping for gas and bathroom breaks took careful planning. Uncle Otis had made this trip before, and he knew which places along the way offered 'colored' bathrooms—and which were safer to just pass on by. (p. 38)

I started getting a lump in my throat. I thought back to road trips I have taken with my family and how I could always stop and use the restroom whenever I needed one and I thought about all the interesting places I have stopped to eat with my family and how John Lewis and many other people of color didn't get this same opportunity. This is the meaning work of mode, when the authors write in a way that makes me as a reader connect to the story. It makes me think maybe the authors wrote this book with the purpose to persuade me to not only empathize with people who have suffered injustice and inequality but also to persuade me to think about my actions and what I can do to change my own perspectives and societal perspectives.

Let's continue reading. . . .

Ok, now that I have finished *March: Book One* I'm going to change my original *genre* prediction from *literary nonfiction* to *biography*. I know it is a biography because it is the kind of writing that tells about the life of an important historical figure, John Lewis from his early life as a child in Alabama up until a key moment in U.S. civil rights history in 1965 when John Lewis was the coleader of the Student Nonviolent Coordinating Committee (SNCC). I also would revise my thinking about the book's *mode*. I believe that the author's purpose was not only *to tell a story* and *to inform* me about an important historical figure but that it was also written *to persuade* me as a reader and citizen to stand for justice and equality for all people like John Lewis did in his early life.

So as writers we can learn a lot from the authors and illustrator of *March: Book One*. If we want to write a biography about an important person in history, we could use Lewis and Aydin as mentors. We might think about the person we want to write about and determine the most important moments in his or her life like Lewis and Aydin did with John Lewis' life. Then, we may want to select just one of the moments and start imagining the dialogue that would have taken place at that moment. Lewis and Aydin used dialogue throughout *March: Book One* to make the key moments in John Lewis's life come alive for the reader. In addition, we may want to think about adding narrator boxes as road signs in our book to help the reader know when a setting or time changes, like Lewis and Aydin did when they used flash-forwards and flashbacks throughout John Lewis' life.

Appendix G
Daniel's Data Set

Daniel's Survey

1. What is hard about writing? *It is hard to write a lot.*
2. What kind of writer are you? *A slow writer.*
3. What is your favorite piece of writing you wrote? *I don't know what it's called. It was about Christmas. I wrote it last year.*
4. Where do you get your ideas for writing? *Sometimes books.*
5. Are you working on a piece of writing? If yes, what is it about? *Yes, It is about Halloween.*
6. Where do you like to write? *In my desk. Sometimes I write at home.*
7. What makes someone a good writer? *They write a lot.*

Daniel's Parent Survey

1. ¿Escribe su estudiante en casa? (Does your child write/draw at home?) Si sí, ¿qué escribe? (If so, what does he/she write/draw?) *Sí. Dibuja y pinta. Yes. (Draws and colors.)*
2. ¿Qué se ha dado cuento de su estudiante como escritor? (What have you noticed about your child as a writer?) *Buen escritor. (Good writer.)*
3. ¿Cuáles son sus metas o esperanzas para su estudiante como escritor este año? (What are your goals/ hopes for your child as a writer this year?) *Espero que sea major que otro año. (I hope he is better than last year.)*
4. Otros comentarios. (Additional comments or questions.) *Ojalá sea el major. (I hope he will be the best that he can.)*

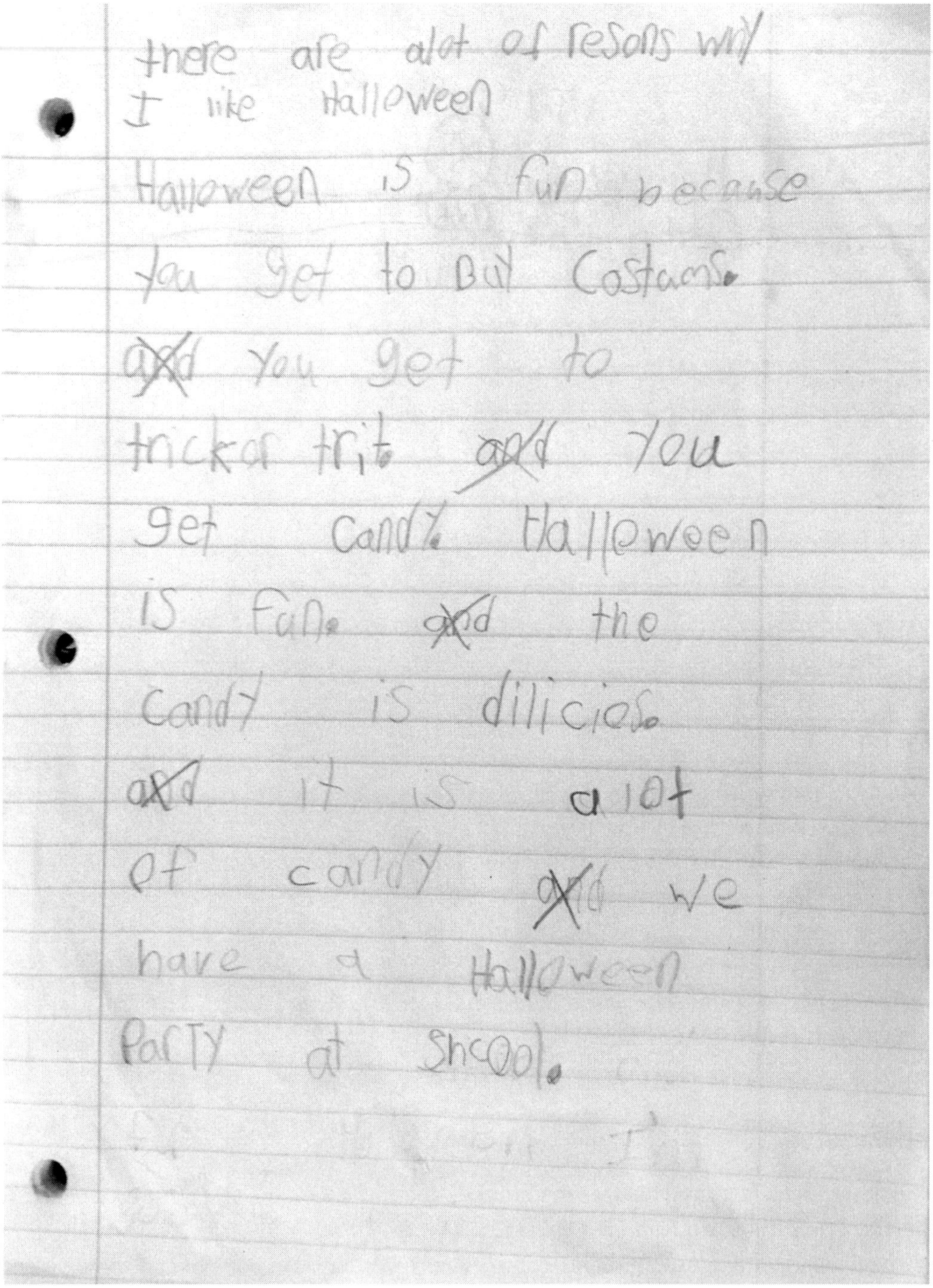

there are alot of resons why
I like Halloween

Halloween is fun because
you get to buy Costams
and you get to
trick or trit and you
get candy. Halloween
is fun. and the
candy is dilicies.
and it is a lot
of candy and we
have a Halloween
Party at shcool.

Figure G.1 Daniel's Writing Sample

Appendix H
Marc's Data Set

Marc's Survey

1. What is easy about writing? *Thinking of stories. The topic sentence, how to make it funny.*
2. What is hard about writing? *It is hard for me in writing to keep thinking about more and more to make my story longer.*
3. What kind of writer are you? *A fiction writer.*
4. What is your favorite piece of writing you wrote? *Super donut. I wrote part 1 last year and I am working on part 2 this year. It is about this donut and he is called Super Donut. And there is a bad guy called Darth Banana because he is a banana.*
5. Where do you get your ideas for writing? *Super donut from the video game my grandma has "Hot Donut." You are a super donut and you get passed levels. Sometimes I get them from seeing stuff.*
6. Where do you like to write? *At school. I write in my Parent-Teacher-Student journal at home. Usually I just want to hang out.*
7. What makes someone a good writer? *With topic sentence, facts, details and a conclusion.*
8. Anything else I should know about you as a writer? *Nothing.*

Marc's Parent Survey

1. Does your child write/draw at home? If so, what does he/she write/draw? *Yes, fictional short stories.*
2. What have you noticed about your child as a writer? *He enjoys it. He can describe step-by-step instructions well.*
3. What are your goals/hopes for your child as a writer this year? *To expand on his ideas.*

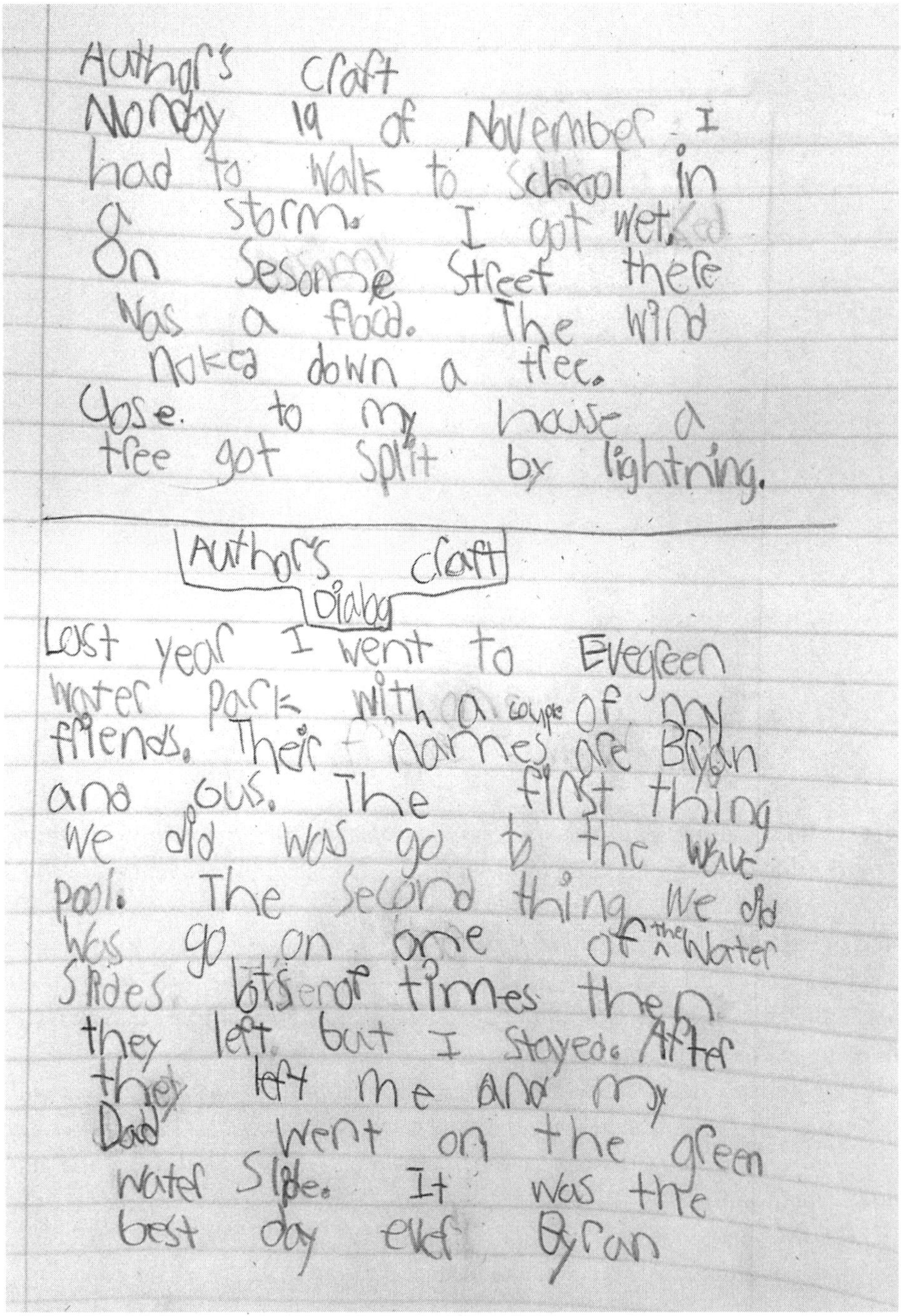

Author's Craft

Monday 19 of November. I had to walk to school in a storm. I got wet. On Sesonse Street there was a flood. The wind noked down a tree. Close to my house a tree got split by lightning.

Author's Craft
Diary

Last year I went to Evegreen water park with a couple of my friends. Their names are Bryan and Gus. The first thing we did was go to the wave pool. The second thing we did was go on one of the water slides. bts for times then they left but I stayed. After they left me and my Dad went on the green water slide. It was the best day ever. Bryan

Figure H.1 Marc's Writing Sample 1

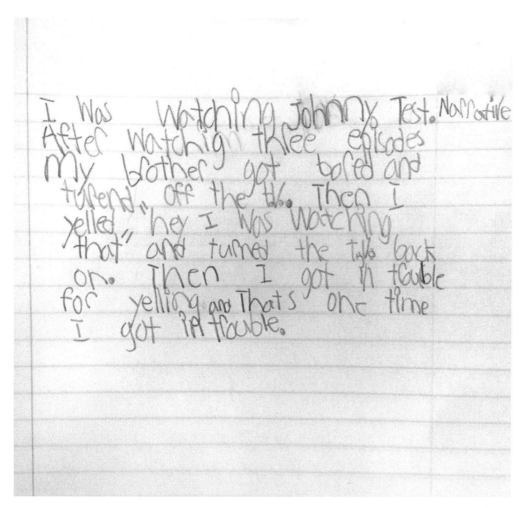

I was watching Johnny Test. Narrative After watching three episodes my brother got bored and turend off the tv. Then I yelled, "hey I was watching that" and turned the tv back on. Then I got in trouble for yelling and Thats one time I got in trouble.

Figure H.2 Marc's Writing Sample 2

Appendix I
Marisol's Data Set

Marisol's Survey

1. What is easy about writing? *Freewrites to write whatever we want. Doing a topic sentence.*
2. What is hard about writing? *Something like having ten sentences. Sometimes my teacher says to write ten sentences and sometimes it's hard to write ten sentences.*
3. What kind of writer are you? *Fairy-tale writing.*
4. What is your favorite piece of writing you wrote? *Fairyland. I wrote it last year. It was about a girl with lots of friends and another girl that didn't have lots of friends. I invented it.*
5. Where do you get your ideas for writing? *I watch Sleeping Beauty and I think about writing about fairies because there is a problem and a solution.*
6. Are you working on a piece of writing? If yes, what is it about? *Yes, it is called Smart Princess. It is about a princess that is the smartest girl in her class. There is another girl that is pretty and she is mad because she thought that everyone wanted to be pretty.*
7. Where do you like to write? *Here at school in my desk.*
8. What makes someone a good writer? *A good writer has a beginning, middle and end. They have a problem and a solution.*

Marisol's Parent Survey

1. ¿Escribe su estudiante en casa? (Does your child write/draw at home?) Si sí, ¿qué escribe? (If so, what does he/she write/draw?) *Ella escribe todos los días su journal trabajo de escuela más aparte, escribe los libros traídos de la biblioteca o de los que hay en casa con el propósito de mejorar su letra. (She writes in her school journal everyday. In addition, she writes the books she brings from the library or the ones at home with the intention of improving her writing.)*

2. ¿Qué se ha dado cuento de su estudiante como escritor? (What have you noticed about your child as a writer?) *Ella tiene buena imaginación, le gusta mucho escribir historias, narra sucesos de la escuela, tiene buena memoria, siempre trata de hacer un buen trabajo. (She has good imagination, likes to write stories a lot, narrates happenings of the school, has a good memory, always tries to do a good job.)*

3. ¿Cuáles son sus metas o esperanzas para su estudiante como escritor este año? (What are your goals/ hopes for your child as a writer this year?) *Que logre alcanzar sus metas, mejore su escritura y aprenda más día con día. (That she is able to achieve her goals, improve her writing and learn more every day.)*

4. Otros comentarios. (Additional comments or questions.) *Trata de ser la mejor cada día mantiene buena amistad con sus compañeros y maestros. ha maestro le pone notas con buenos comentarios que le dan mucha alegría y la animan mucho. (Try to be the best every day maintain good friendships with fellow students and teachers. When her teacher writes her notes with good comments it makes her really happy and motivates her.)*

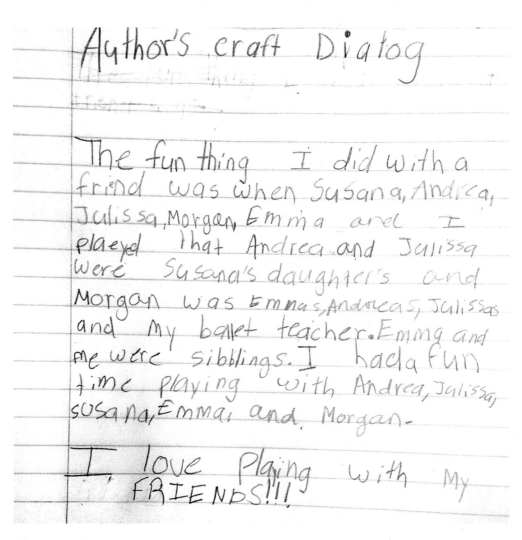

Figure I.1 Marisol's Writing Sample

Appendix J
Harper's Data Set

Harper's Survey

1. What is easy about writing? *Because sometimes you think of a story and you can make up your own stories.*
2. What is hard about writing? *You have to learn how to write—you have to learn all the letters and the sounds they make, like sh and ph and capitals and vowels.*
3. What kind of writer are you? *I usually write fairy tales. Sometimes I write real stories.*
4. What is your favorite piece of writing you wrote? *My mom told me to write something for her scrapbook. I wrote about my first day of second grade.*
5. Where do you get your ideas for writing? *Sometimes I get my ideas from a flashback or if it's a fairy tale I think about it.*
6. Are you working on a piece of writing? If yes, what is it about? *Yes, it is called Special Gift. It is about a horse who had a baby who was a unicorn and she gets a gift.*
7. Where do you like to write? *In a quiet room so I can think easier if it's loud I can't.*
8. What makes someone a good writer? *You don't just write on the computer. You have to have some details and ideas. If you write Once upon a time and then start writing about a new thing then that should be a new book.*
9. Anything else I should know about you as a writer? *I like to write because you get to write about your own story and its fun.*

Harper's Parent Survey

1. Does your child write/draw at home? If so, what does he/she write/draw? *Harper likes to write make believe stories usually about princesses or animals. She spends a lot of time writing or typing these stories up in her room. She loves to draw lots of pictures. She usually draws animals.*

2. What have you noticed about your child as a writer? *I love her imagination! She uses writing and drawing as her quiet down time in her room. It seems like something that she enjoys because it is not something we have had to force or prompt her to do*

3. What are your goals/hopes for your child as a writer this year? *Well, I would love her to continue working on her handwriting and develop skills at more precise sentences that structure her points better. I want her to continue enjoying her time writing and feel comfortable putting down on paper what she is imagining in her head.*

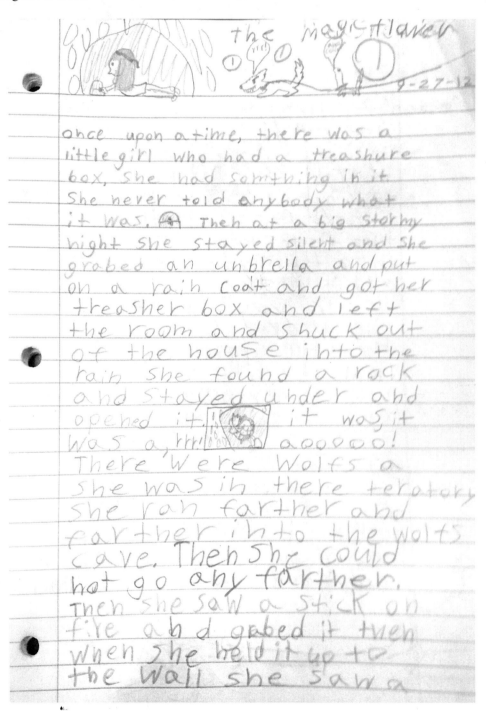

the magic flaver
7-27-12

once upon a time, there was a little girl who had a treashure box, she had somthing in it. She never told anybody what it was. Then at a big stormy night she stayed silent and she grabed an unbrella and put on a rain coat and got her treasher box and left the room and shuck out of the house into the rain she found a rock and stayed under and opened it. it was, it was a, rrrr aooooo! There were wolfs a she was in there teratory she ran farther and farther into the wolfs cave. Then she could not go any farther. Then she saw a stick on fire and grabed it then when she held it up to the wall she saw a

Figure J.1 Harper's Writing Sample, Page 1

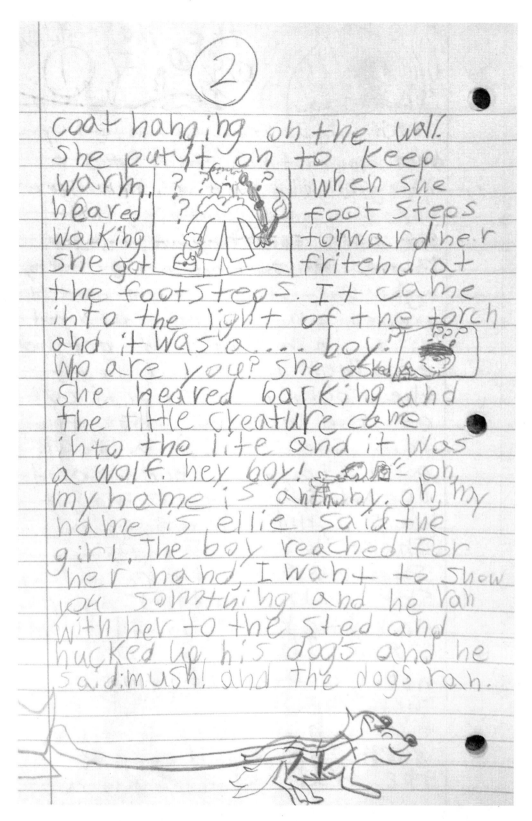

coat hanging on the wall.
She put it on to keep
warm, when she
heared foot steps
walking toward her
she got fritend at
the footsteps. It came
into the light of the torch
and it was a..... boy!
Who are you? she asked
she heared barking and
the little creature came
into the lite and it was
a wolf. hey boy! oh,
my name is anthony. oh, my
name is ellie said the
girl. The boy reached for
her hand. I want to show
you something and he ran
with her to the sled and
hucked up his dogs and he
said:mush! and the dogs ran.

Figure J.2 Harper's Writing Sample, Page 2

he said woow! The dogs
stoped. There was a dog with
a flower in is moath
how what you find boll
here, fetch! he threw the
flower and the dog saw
one of the petties come
of and the wind blew it
on the girls hand.
it glowed and she turn
into a wolf baby. She
ran in circles
and saw a rat and went
it to jumping position and
got her claws out she said.
what am I doing?
she mada big jump
and missed. she also
wonderd were her
tresher box was
she remembered the same
flower was in there she
ran to the flower but when
she got ther the flower
got blown up into the air
and she could not reach it

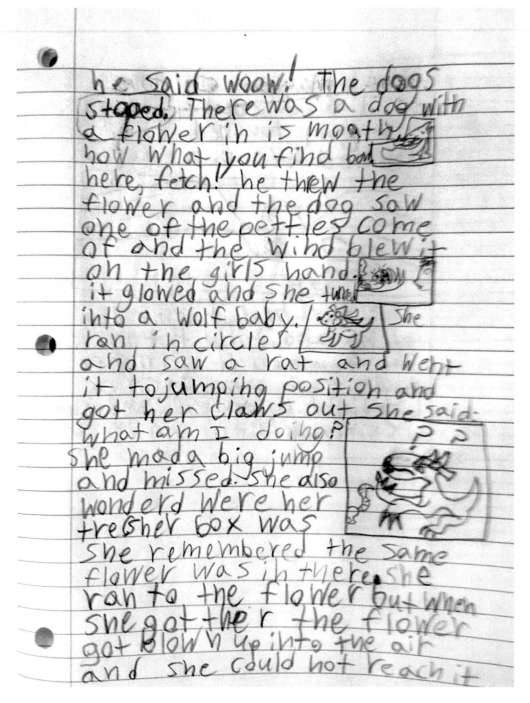

Figure J.3 Harper's Writing Sample, Page 3

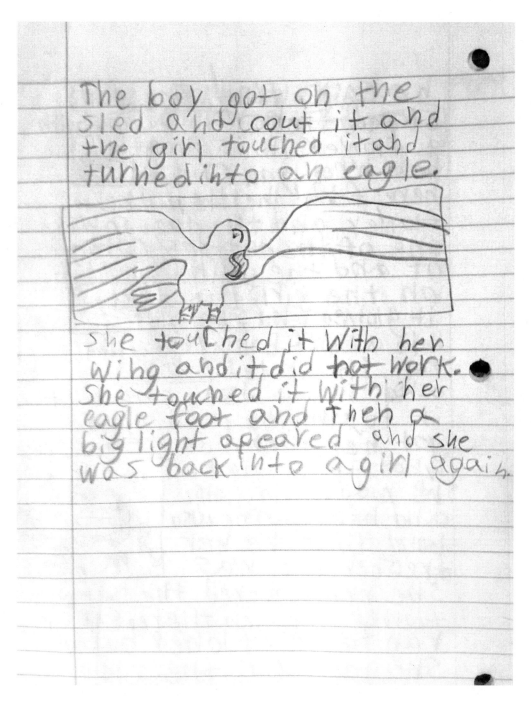

The boy got on the sled and cout it and the girl touched it and turned into an eagle.

she touched it with her wing and it did not work. She touched it with her eagle foot and then a big light apeared and she was back into a girl again.

Figure J.4 Harper's Writing Sample, Page 4

Appendix K
Peyton's Data Set

Peyton's Survey

1. What is easy about writing? *If you have an idea then you can write it down. It doesn't have to be perfect, it's just your idea.*
2. What is hard about writing? *Sometimes spelling for some kids. Sometimes getting an idea, for some kids. For me, spelling most of the time and just getting up with an idea.*
3. What kind of writer are you? *I like to write fictional stories.*
4. What is your favorite piece of writing you wrote? *There is this one story called Bob and Ginger and something like that. It was really long. It was kind of like Jack and Jill at the same time Hansel and Gretel. It was like fairytales mixed together. I wrote it in 3rd grade.*
5. Where do you get your ideas for writing? *I write a lot about plays because I am in plays.*
6. Where do you like to write? *I like to type and write so mostly at my house.*
7. What makes someone a good writer? *I think they are inspiration.*

Peyton's Parent Survey

1. Does your child write/draw at home? If so, what does he/she write/draw? *She draws more than she writes. She draws mainly landscape things. She writes for homework not "just because."*
2. What have you noticed about your child as a writer? *She writes very fast, just to get it done. I get the feeling that she does not enjoy writing very much.*
3. What are your goals/hopes for your child as a writer this year? *Have her slow down, sound out her words and put more description into her writing.*

The Ship Wreck

One day a girl named Lily and her family went on a boat ride. It was so much fun! There were water slides and yummy smoothies. But on the second day there was a big crash! Her family was ok but Lily was nowhere to be found.

The day after the crash she found herself on an island "What is this place?" Her first thought was to gather food and water and to build a warm fire and shelter. Before dinner Lily went on a walk. Lily found another girl that was 3 years younger than her. The other girl had dinner with her.

They had many adventures on the island like swinging from branches and walking through creepy forest and things like that. They soon got used to the island.

The next day they both worked on a boat so they can sail away and find land. When they were working on the boat the other girl saw something. "What is that?" "It is a boat!" So the girls flagged it down. It turned out that the people in the boat were the other girl's family. They came to take her home.

They asked Lily if she wanted to come too. She said, "Yes but will you please help me find my family?" The other girls parents said, "Yes."

They were off looking for her family. They did not find them the first day. But on the second day they found Lily's family. "I had missed you so much!" said Lily. "Me, too!"

They lived together happily and they never went on a ship ride again.   The End

Figure K.1 Peyton's Writing Sample

Appendix L
Sample Parent Survey Letter

Dear Families,

We are enjoying great beginnings in the Writing Studio of Room 23 here at Greenwill Elementary School! Here is a list of some of the possible writing topics children generated this first week of school:

- Super Heroes Rules
- The Smart Princess and Her New Wand
- All about Retrievers
- Why Fishing is the Best
- How to Make a Bracelet

Ask your child about their writing ideas from this week!

I am enjoying getting to know each writer in the classroom. Will you help me get to know your child as a writer? On the backside of this letter is a short survey. Please complete and return to me in your child's homework folder. I will use your response to individualize writing instruction for your child.

Here is a home writing tip for the week: Find real reasons to write with your child. How about composing a note or an e-mail to a family member and friend this week? Look for more tips in our monthly newsletter. The children and I will be writing the newsletter together this next week!

Thank you!
Ms. J

Appendix M
Mr. Mackie's Status of the Class

TABLE M.1 Mr. Mackie's Status of the Class

Status of the Class—Grade 5—Mr. Mackie Week: February 10 Focus: Science/Nonfiction						
Students	M	Tu	W	Th	F	Notes
Conner	Research	Research	Research	Research	Org. Chart	
Marcos	Graphic Org	Graphic Org	Research/Francis	Request TC	Draft 1 Web	Collaborating Francis; Combine Rajesh, Weston, Xavier/Guided WR/Web
Lilly	Request TC	Letter Poem D1	PC/Suelita	Research	Letter Poem D2	Find other mentor text Guided WR: Suelita
Alannah	Research	Research	Graphic Org	PC/Joaquim	Storyboard D1	Guided WR/Ada, Yolanda, Hallie, Carmelita: inquiry science exploratory text
Esteban	Research/Austin	Research/Austin	Research/Austin	Storyboard D1	Storyboard D2	Collaborating Austin
Jade	Graphic Org	Letter Ed/D1	Letter Ed/D1	PC/Kara	Letter Ed/D2	Earnest! On track!
Caesar	Request TC	Research/Complete Chart	Request TC	Complete illustrations	D1 Poster	Staying focused Ck w/ELD teacher
Colin	TC – focus	Research/Complete Chart	Research/Complete Chart	Complete Chart	D1 Poster	On track! Detailed drawings —
Ada	Research	Research	Storyboard D1	Storyboard D2	D1 Chapter Bk	Guided WR: Alannah, Yolanda, Hallie, Carmelita
Gabby	PC/Maddie	Storyboard Maddie/D1	Storyboard Maddie/D1	Request TC	SB/Maddie/D2	Ck: checking for purpose
Xavier	Web D1/Weston	Web D1/Weston	PC/Rajesh	Request TC	Web D2/Weston & Rajesh	Rajesh now collaborating: Ck sources
Francis	Research	Graphic Org	Research/Francis Now collaborating with Marcos	D1 Game	D1 Game	Using good model
Yolanda	Research	Research	Storyboard D1	D1 Chapter Bk	D1 Chapter Bk	Guided WR: Ada, Alannah, Hallie, Carmelita

Status of the Class—Grade 5—Mr. Mackie Week: February 10 Focus: Science/Nonfiction

Students	M	Tu	W	Th	F	Notes
Conner	Research	Research	Research	Research	Org. Chart	
Rajesh	Research	Research	Peer Conference/ Weston & Xavier	Request TC	Web D2/Weston & Xavier	Joined Weston/Rajesh Guided WR: Web
Hallie	Research/Bella	Research/Bella	Graphic Org/Bella	D1 Storyboard	D1 Storyboard	1st collaborative project; Guided WR: Alannah, Ada, Yolanda, Carmelita
Carmelita	Research	Research	Storyboard D1	Storyboard D2	D1 Chapter Bk	Guided WR: Alannah, Ada, Yolanda
Suelita	Research	Ballad D1	PC/Lilly	Ballad D2	TC Requested	Guided WR: Lilly
Enzo	Research/ Joaquin, T.J.	Research/Joaquin, T. J.	TC Request	D1 Storyboard Joaquin, T. J.	D1 Storyboard Joaquin, T. J.	Should move to D2—checking for purpose
Joaquin	Research/ Enzo, T.J.	Research/ Enzo, T. J.	TC Request	D1 Storyboard Enzo, T. J.	D1 Storyboard Enzo, T. J.	Should move to D2—checking for purpose
Kara	TC—focus	Write 5 sentences	Find 5 pictures	Find 5 pictures	Match sentences with pictures.	Start new piece? Ck with SPED
T.J.	Research/Joaquin, Enzo	Research/Joaquin, Enzo	TC Request	D1 Storyboard Joaquin, Enzo	D1 Storyboard Joaquin, Enzo	Should move to D2—checking for purpose
Bella	Research/Hallie	Research/Hallie	Graphic Org/Hallie	D1 Storyboard	D1 Storyboard	1st collaborative project; Should move to D2—on track
Weston	Web D1/Xavier	Web D2/Xavier	PC/Rajesh	Request TC	Web D2/Xavier & Rajesh	Rajesh now collaborating Guided WR: Web
Maddie	PC/Gabby	Storyboard/Gabby D1	Storyboard/Gabby D1	Request TC	Storyboard Gabby D2	Collaborating Gabby—Guided WR: checking for purpose
Austin	Research/Esteban	Research/Esteban	Research/Esteban	Storyboard D1	Storyboard D2	Collaborating Esteban—Guided WR: checking for purpose

PC: Peer Conference

TC: Teacher–student Conference

SB: Storyboard

D1 or D2: Draft 1 or Draft 2

Appendix N
Emme's Writing Sample

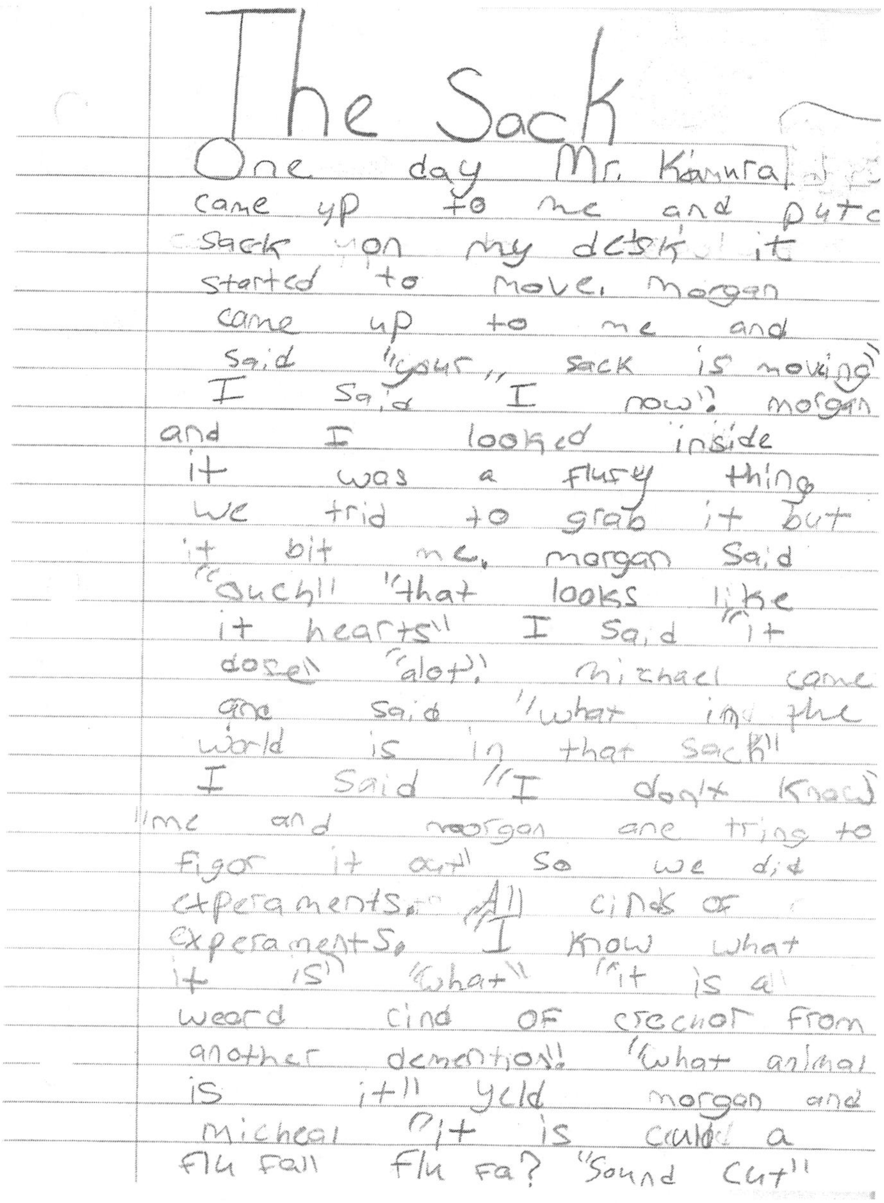

The Sack

One day Mr. Kamura
came up to me and put a
sack on my desk. it
started to move, morgan
came up to me and
said "your sack is moving"
I said "I now". morgan
and I looked inside
it was a flury thing
we trid to grab it but
it bit me. morgan said
"ouch! "that looks like
it hearts" I said "it
does" "alot". michael came
and said "what in the
world is in that sack"
I said "I don't know"
"me and morgan are tring to
figor it out" so we did
experaments, All cinds of
experaments. I know what
it is" "what" "it is a
weard cind of crechor from
another demention" "what animal
is it" yeld morgan and
micheal "it is called a
flu fall flu fa? "Sound cut"

Figure N.1 Emme's Writing Sample, Page 1

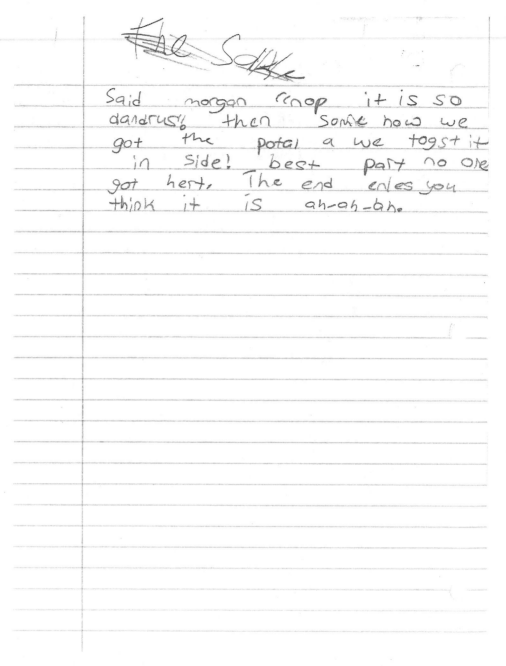

Said morgan cnop it is so
dandrus; then some how we
got the potal a we togst it
in side! best part no one
got hert, The end enles you
think it is ah-oh-oh.

Figure N.2 Emme's Writing Sample, Page 2

Appendix O
Resource Books for Developing Writing Practices, Process, and Craft

Anderson, J. (2005). *Mechanically inclined: Building grammar, usage, and style into writer's workshop.* Portland, ME: Stenhouse.

Anderson, J. (2007). *Everyday editing: Inviting students to develop skill and craft in writer's workshop.* Portland, ME: Stenhouse.

Atwell, N. (2002). *Lessons that change writers.* Portsmouth, NH: firsthand.

Bomer, K. (2005). *Teaching memoir to sharpen insight, shape meaning—and triumph over tests.* Portsmouth, NH: Heinemann.

Bomer, R., & Bomer, K. (2001). *For a better world: Reading and writing for social action.* Portsmouth, NH: Heinemann.

Fletcher, R. (2010). *Pyrotechnics on the page: Playful craft that sparks writing.* Portland, ME: Stenhouse.

Fletcher, R. (2011). *Mentor author, mentor texts: Short texts, craft notes, and practical classroom uses.* Portsmouth, NH: Heinemann.

Fletcher, R. (2013). *What a writer needs* (2nd ed.). Portsmouth, NH: Heinemann.

Fletcher, R., & Portalupi, J. (2007). *Craft lessons: Teaching writing K-8.* Portland, ME: Stenhouse.

Heard, G. (1999). *Awakening the heart: Exploring poetry in elementary and middle school.* Portsmouth, NH: Heinemann.

Heard, G. (2002). *The revision toolbox: Teaching techniques that work.* Portsmouth, NH: Heinemann.

Heard, G. (2013). *Finding the heart of nonfiction: Teaching 7 essential craft tools with mentor texts.* Portsmouth, NH: Heinemann.

Horn, M., & Giacobbe, M. (2007). *Talking, drawing, writing: Lessons for our youngest writers.* Portland, ME: Stenhouse.

Laman, T. T. (2013). *From ideas to words: Writing strategies for English language learners.* Portsmouth, NH: Heinemann.

Laminack, L., & Wadsworth, R. (2013). *The writing teacher's troubleshooting guide.* Portsmouth, NH: Heinemann.

Portalupi, J., & Fletcher, R. (2001). *Nonfiction craft lessons: Teaching information writing K-8.* Portland, ME: Stenhouse.

Ray, K. W. (2006). *Study driven: A framework for planning units of study in the writing workshop.* Portsmouth, NH: Heinemann.

Ray, K. W. (2010). *In pictures and in words: Teaching the qualities of good writing through illustration study.* Portsmouth, NH: Heinemann.

Routman, R. (2000). *Kids' poems: Teaching first graders to love writing poetry.* New York, NY: Sholastic.

Routman, R. (2000). *Kids' poems: Teaching second graders to love writing poetry.* New York, NY: Scholastic.

Routman, R. (2000). *Kids' poems: Teaching third and fourth graders to love writing poetry.* New York, NY: Scholastic.

Glossary

Common Core State Standards Common Core State Standards (CCSS) are a set of national standards defining what students K–12 ought to learn in English Language Arts & Literacy in History/Social Studies, Science, and Technical Subjects and Mathematics. The CCSS are sponsored by the Council of Chief State Standards Officers and the National Governors Association. The English Language Arts & Literacy in History/Social Studies, Science, and Technical Subjects were coauthored by David Coleman and Susan Pimentel. As of March 2014, 45 states have adopted the CCSS. While not a federal government initiative, by adopting the CCSS, states were eligible to opt out of certain provisions of No Child Left Behind and are able to qualify for additional federal dollars.

English learner A person whose first language is a language other than English and who may be any place along a broad continuum of English language development.

Genre A specific category of a literary composition identifiable by a common set of characteristics, such as realism, formula fiction, fantasy, traditional tales, poetry, informational books, and biography.

Guided writing Guided writing is small-group-focused instruction based on writers' interests and needs. Like individual writing conferences, guided writing is a teaching and learning structure that meets writers where they are and moves them towards independence by providing "just right" instruction and feedback.

Independent and collaborative writing time The largest chunk of time in the Writing Studio during which children write either individually or collaboratively.

Integrated language arts Integrated language arts refer to reading, writing, listening, and speaking.

Mini-lesson Teacher-directed lesson focusing on one or two objectives based on ongoing classroom assessment and overall unit goals. The mini-lesson begins the Writing Studio.

Mode A literary term describing the meaning work of writing. According to Ray (2006), "modes describes the meaning work that a piece of writing is doing at any given place in the text" (p. 57).

Peer conference Two writers seeking feedback from one another for the purpose of improving their writing.

Peer-response groups An established group of writers who meet regularly or throughout a given writing unit to seek feedback about their writing with the express purpose of improving writing.

Sharing The Writing Studio concludes with sharing and celebrating the work that has and is being accomplished by writers.

Status of the Class A term is borrowed from Nancie Atwell (1998). This routine is completed at the beginning of the class, during which the teacher calls the name of each writer and the writer declares his or her writing goal for writing that day. The purpose is to focus writers.

Teacher–student writing conference A teacher sits one-on-one with a writer, listening and observing to determine the kind of writing support, instruction, and feedback necessary.

Writing traits Writer's craft or how a writer develops his/her work through such areas as ideas, word choice, and the organization of the writing.

References

Atwell, N. (1998). *In the middle: New understandings about writing, reading and learning* (2nd ed.). Portsmouth, NH: Heinemann.

Ray, K. W. (2006). *Study driven: A framework for planning units of study in the writing workshop.* Portsmouth, NH: Heinemann.

Index

Education Northwest 6+1* writing trait rubrics 72, 99–100, 101

English learners 15, 25–6, 30, 253; differentiation 48, 120, 123–4, 126, 128, 147, 154, 160, 187, 201; illustrated 85, 192, 201; *see also* curriculum design; editing; guided writing; teacher-student writing conference; writing process, teaching editing strategies

fixed-performance frame 130; *see also* Johnston, P.
Fletcher, R. 12, 164, 251
focusing decisions 197–9, 201–3; final assessment 197–8; individualizing writer's goals 202; integrating content areas 199; length of unit 198; planning for differentiation 199, 201–2; unit goal 197; unit outline 199; weekly planning 202–3
framing decisions 192–7; connect the interest and abilities of writers with standards 192; genre immersion 193; planning for writing practices 194; planning for writing process 195; planning for writing craft 196–7; writer choice 196

genre 23–4, 26, 253; genre in Grade 3 integrated units 182–6; genre in Grade 5 integrated units 193, 197, 199; genre in kindergarten 14; illustrated 225–6
Graves, D. 6, 13, 35–6, 43, 46, 48, 148, 158, 167, 186
guided writing 36–7, 43–4, 133, 134, 146, 152, 253; determining who and when 82, 152–4; discussion questions 116; English learners 123–4; mentor texts 124; planning guided writing group lessons 154; planning guided writing lesson illustrated Grade 5 86–7, 118, 142, 154–5

Heard, G. 8, 139, 251
heart map 8; *see also* Heard, G.

identity 5, 13, 43, 63, 64, 75, 92, 114–15, 167, 177; identity illustrated 13, 21–2, 65, 66, 69, 71, 74, 89–90, 95, 151, 192
informative writing 26–7, 50, 84, 93, 95, 126–7, 154–5
integrated language arts units: definition 253; Grade 3 unit, Songbirds: Threatened! 141–2; Grade 3 yearlong integrated units 181–6; Grade 5 magazine article unit 191–209; kindergarten integrated "life cycle" unit 187–8

Johnston, P. 16, 18. 114–15

Lamott, A. 9, 110, 122, 124
Lenz Taguchi, H. 11, 12
literary devices 119, 128

mentor text: choosing mentor texts 134–5; definition 124; illustrated 79, 113–14, 121, 125, 126–7, 135; mentor text inquiry lesson 154–5

metacognition 96, 116–17, 147, 151, 159; illustrated 10, 60, 111; practice 10, 60, 110, 176
mini-lesson: choosing mentor texts 134–5; definition 36, 133, 253; demonstration mini-lesson kindergarten illustrated 135–7; Grade 3 illustrated 38–40; Grade 5 illustrated 40–2; inquiry mini-lesson Grade 3 illustrated 137–9; interactive mini-lesson Grade 5 illustrated 139–40; kindergarten illustrated 37–8; managing 134; planning mini-lessons illustrated, Grade 5 141–2
mode 22–4, 26–7, 225–6, 253
Mooney, M. 133, 146, 158
Murray, D. 13
My Writing World 52–3, 82–4, 85, 163, 207

narrative writing 26; illustrated 71, 184

observations 69–71, 85, 118
opinion writing 26, 127–8; illustrated 101, 142, 183, 185, 189
organization and routines 36–7, 117–18, 170

parent surveys 67–9; sample parent survey letter 243
peer conference 160–2, 253
peer response groups 163, 253
Pinnell, G., and Fountas, I. 14, 15, 16, 48, 49, 92
problematizing practice 18, 33, 53, 77–8, 102–3, 142–3, 156, 170–1, 188–9
publishing *see* broadcasting

Range of Writing 27, 32, 94
Ray, K. W. 13, 22, 23, 24, 26, 46, 148, 186, 252, 253
Research to Build and Present Knowledge 27, 32, 94
revision *see* writing process
routines *see* organization and routines
rubrics 72, 96, 97, 98–9; *see also* Education Northwest 6+1* writing trait rubrics

sharing and celebrating 163–4, 254
standards: C3 Framework for Social Studies Standards 180; New Generation Science Standards 180; *see also* Common Core State Standards for English Language Arts and Literacy in History/Social Studies, Science, and Technical Subjects (CCSS)
Status of the Class 36, 53, 82, 83, 102, 122, 149, 163, 254; illustrated Grade 5 41, 84–5, 142, 245–7; illustrated kindergarten 37; illustrated Ms J 208, 209
student writing sample 82, 98–101; informing instruction 153
student writing sample, Grade 3: Carolina 217; Daniel 227; Emme 249; Marc 229; Marisol 233; Morgan 215
student writing sample, Grade 5: Alonso 78; Nickolas 219; Peyton 241; Sebas "Middle East Revenge" 221
student writing sample, kindergarten: Maddie 213
supplies 44–52

teacher-student writing conference 146–9, 254; area 43; determining who needs a conference 99, 149; English learners 147, 149; structure 148; teach expectations 147; teacher-student writing conference illustrated 149–52; *see also* Calkins, L.; Graves, D.

Teaching, Conferencing & Planning Notebook: definition 82, 85; early grades 88; illustrated Grade 1 88–90; illustrated Grade 5 86–8, 141, 142; informing instruction 96, 149, 152, 153, 199

Teaching Event with *March: Book One* 225–6

technology: applications 15–16, 47, 48, 73, 124, 160, 164–5, 166, 176; collaboration and technology 160; tablet 64, 83, 86, 96, 175

text types and purposes 26, 32, 84, 93

to, with, by 133; *see also* Mooney, M.

trait rubrics *see* Education Northwest 6+1˙ writing trait rubrics

traits *see* writing traits

unit planning *see* curriculum design

wall charts 45, 49, 50, 51

writer self-assessment: definition 82, 96–8, 102, 197; grades K–2 questions 96; grades 3–5 questions 97; illustrated Grade 3 97

writer survey 63–5

writing assessment *see* Cumulative Writing Folder; Daily Writing Folder; My Writing World; observations; parent surveys; Status of the Class; Teaching, Conferencing & Planning Notebook; student writing sample; writer self-assessment

writing craft 102, 124–8; assessment 102; general writing strategies 128; informative writing strategies 126–7; magazine article craft 194; narrative writing strategies 124–6; opinion writing strategies 127–8

writing mini-lesson *see* mini-lesson

writing practices 116–18; assessment 102

writing process 102, 118–24; assessment 102; finding a topic strategies 118–19; teach about drafting 119–20; teaching editing strategies 122–4; teaching revision 120–2

writing sample *see* student writing sample

writing schedules *see* curriculum design, writing all day long

writing strategies *see* writing craft; writing practices; writing process

Writing Studio challenges 168–9

writing traits 28–32, 198, 254; assessment 82, 100, 198; *see also* Education Northwest 6+1˙ writing trait rubrics

yearlong themes *see* curriculum design, yearlong themes